The Lies of the Artists

The Lies of the Artists
Essays on Italian Art, 1450–1750

Ingrid D. Rowland

THE MIT PRESS
Cambridge, Massachusetts . London, England

To the memory of Bob Silvers
Con istudio, diligenza, et amorevole fatica
With dedication, diligence, and loving labor
—Giorgio Vasari

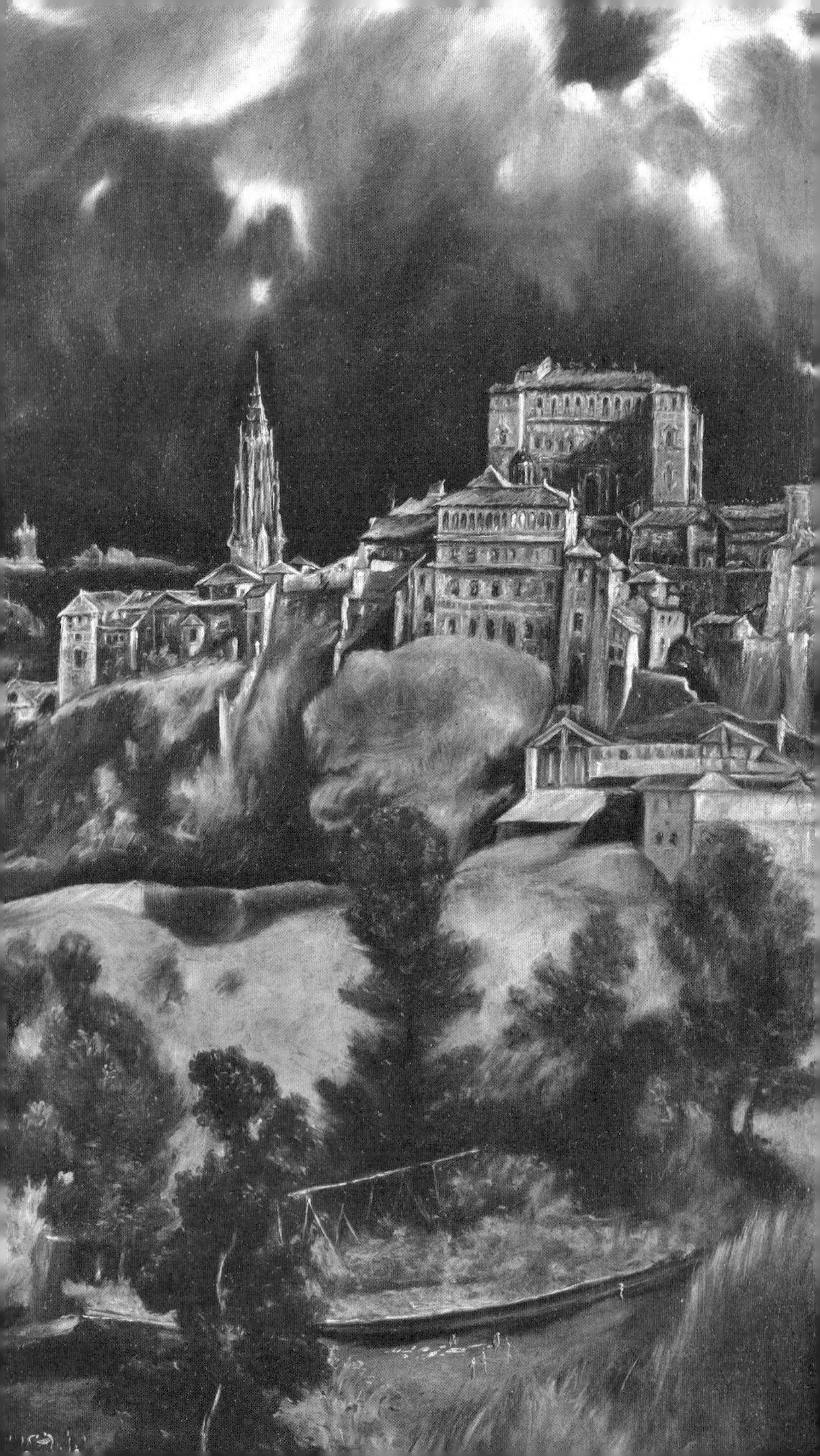

Introduction: The Lies of the Artists

One early spring some 2,700 years ago, a Greek shepherd pastured his lambs on a lonely mountain slope. Suddenly, he heard the sound of women: nine of them, in the middle of the wilderness, singing and dancing and telling marvelous tales. Disdainfully, they finally addressed some winged words toward the ragged, solitary wanderer:

> You rough country shepherds, poor wretches, mere bellies,
> We know how to tell many lies that seem true
> But we also know, when we wish, how to sing the truth.[1]

And then, abruptly, they relented: "they plucked me a branch of luxuriant laurel, a marvel, and breathed a divine voice into me, so I could recount what has been and what will be," and the highland shepherd Hesiod began to sing with authority about the origin of the gods, forever mindful of his ambiguous gift from the nine daughters of Zeus, the Muses, who tell the truth, and many lies besides.

Four centuries later, Aristotle would insist that the purpose of the human arts was to imitate Nature, but his teacher Plato knew better: art found its own unpredictable way whenever a spark of divinity ignited the soul, inspiring it to make something new. Plato's personal art of dialogue found its way through fictional conversations and myths he created himself, not for the joy of telling "lies that seem true"—though the conversations between Socrates and Plato's brothers in the *Republic* or the banter of the participants in his *Symposium* sound like real gatherings, and his tale of Atlantis quickly spread out of control—but rather to convey a more exalted version of truth. "The person who created Atlantis can make it go away again," Aristotle is said to have declared while Plato was still alive, vainly hoping that readers of Plato's *Timaeus*

El Greco (Domenikos Theotokopoulos), *View of Toledo*, c. 1597–1599, detail. Metropolitan Museum of Art, New York, USA/Bridgeman Images.

and *Critias* would realize that Atlantis was a cautionary version of Athens rather than a real city lost beneath the waves.[2]

The Roman architect Vitruvius, a reader of both Plato and Aristotle (as well as Cicero, Vergil, and many other writers) composed *Ten Books on Architecture* for the Emperor Augustus in which he provided a host of ways to make an irregular building look regular, reveling in all the ways that optical illusions could create an artificially improved perception of reality. And then, with perfectly human inconsistency, he railed against painters who perch statues on the tendrils of plants or show fish-tailed goats flying through the air. His description of the basilica he claims to have built in the city of Fanum Fortunae (today's Fano) inspired Michelangelo's design for St. Peter's Basilica, but its traces have yet to be found. Vitruvius, for all his insistence that good art and architecture should imitate nature, only confirmed that art and nature are as shifty as the Muses who dance between them.

The early modern artists examined in the following essays (fourteen Italians and a Greek who spent time in Italy) took these ancient writers as guides for what they regarded as a thrilling rebirth of art in their own era, a Renaissance vividly detailed by the artist and biographer Giorgio Vasari in his *Lives of the Most Excellent Painters, Sculptors and Architects* (in which he regarded women as equally talented participants). All fifteen would almost certainly agree in principle with Aristotle and Vitruvius that their job was to imitate nature. Michelangelo Merisi da Caravaggio proclaimed the ancient creed explicitly. During an interrogation by the Roman police in 1603, he described the qualities of a good painter after having posted scurrilous poems identifying his contemporary Giovanni Baglioni as a bad one:

> To me, that expression "a worthy man" means he knows
> how to work well, that is, he knows how to do his job well;
> so a worthy painter is one who knows how to paint well and
> imitate natural things well.[3]

Fifty years earlier, however, Vasari's *Lives of the Artists* had already demoted the imitation of nature to a first step, although an essential one, in the creation of true art: in the preface to the third section of his collective biography (discussed in chapter 15), he insists that his own contemporaries have learned (following an ancient anecdote about the painter Zeuxis, who painted the goddess Aphrodite by combining the best features of several beautiful human models) to create a synthesis of what was best in nature, and ultimately to surpass it. The fifth-century mosaicists who created the image of Christ the Savior in the apse of the Roman basilica of St. John Lateran were apparently treated to an epiphany by Jesus himself to ensure the likeness of their image to its holy subject, and Saint Luke was said to have earned the same kind of celestial intervention when he painted an icon of the Virgin Mary, but early modern artists could only portray transcendent beings and transcendent phenomena by extrapolating their visions from the concrete reality of the materials they worked with and the things they saw. Caravaggio drew criticism by using a Roman prostitute to model for the Virgin Mary, but every painter of Madonnas could only draw from human examples, or some other work of human hands, and hope that inspiration would provide an additional flash of holiness. Inevitably, their work became fiction.

El Greco's *View of Toledo* shifts the location of the city's buildings to streamline its profile against a phantasmagoric cloudscape that is clearly painted from life (just as Rome's clouds really are identical to those baroque piles that send forth bursts of winged babies), and he uses the same incredible clouds of La Mancha to imagine the structure of Heaven. As a map of Toledo, the *View of Toledo* misleads, telling a factual lie to emphasize the city's dramatic, charged setting between earth and sky, a place where heaven can come to earth, or, as in El Greco's *Laocoön*, set against a background of Toledo's skyline, a classical hero can relive his agonizing death beneath the gates of Troy.

Caravaggio's *Calling of Saint Matthew* shows the future saint sitting among a group of tax collectors in a dingy tavern, when Jesus and Saint Peter suddenly enter the space. "Follow me," Jesus says, extending a hand to—whom? One colorfully clad youth bows his head; an elderly colleague stares through his spectacles at a pile of coins. Matthew, in his wine-dark velvet hat, points to his own chest as if to say "Who, me?," but underneath the table where they sit his legs have already answered the call long before the message has reached his brain. We can see Matthew's legs because Caravaggio has omitted one leg of the table. In the real world, it would crash to the ground. In the world Caravaggio has created, we barely notice: we are too absorbed in the dilemma of an ordinary man whose mind lags behind his heart.

Such are the lies of the artists: windows onto other varieties of truth.

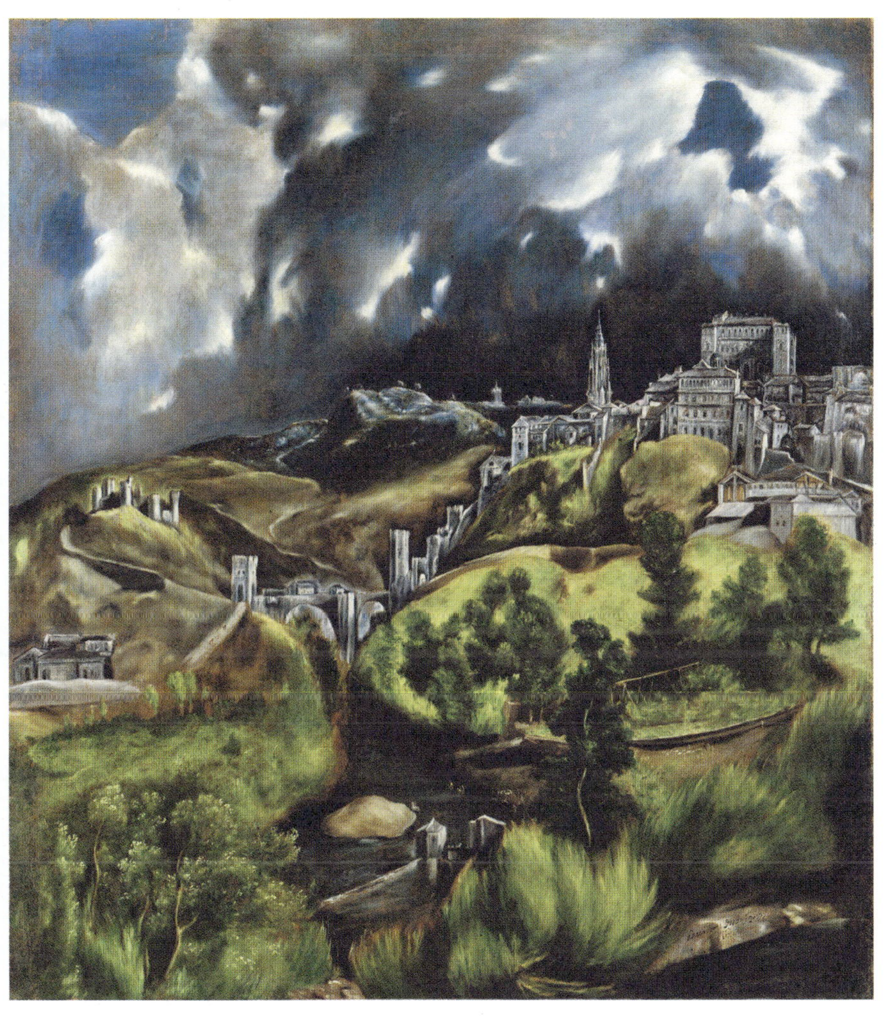

El Greco (Domenikos Theotokopoulos), *View of Toledo*, c. 1597–1599. Metropolitan Museum of Art, New York, USA/Bridgeman Images.

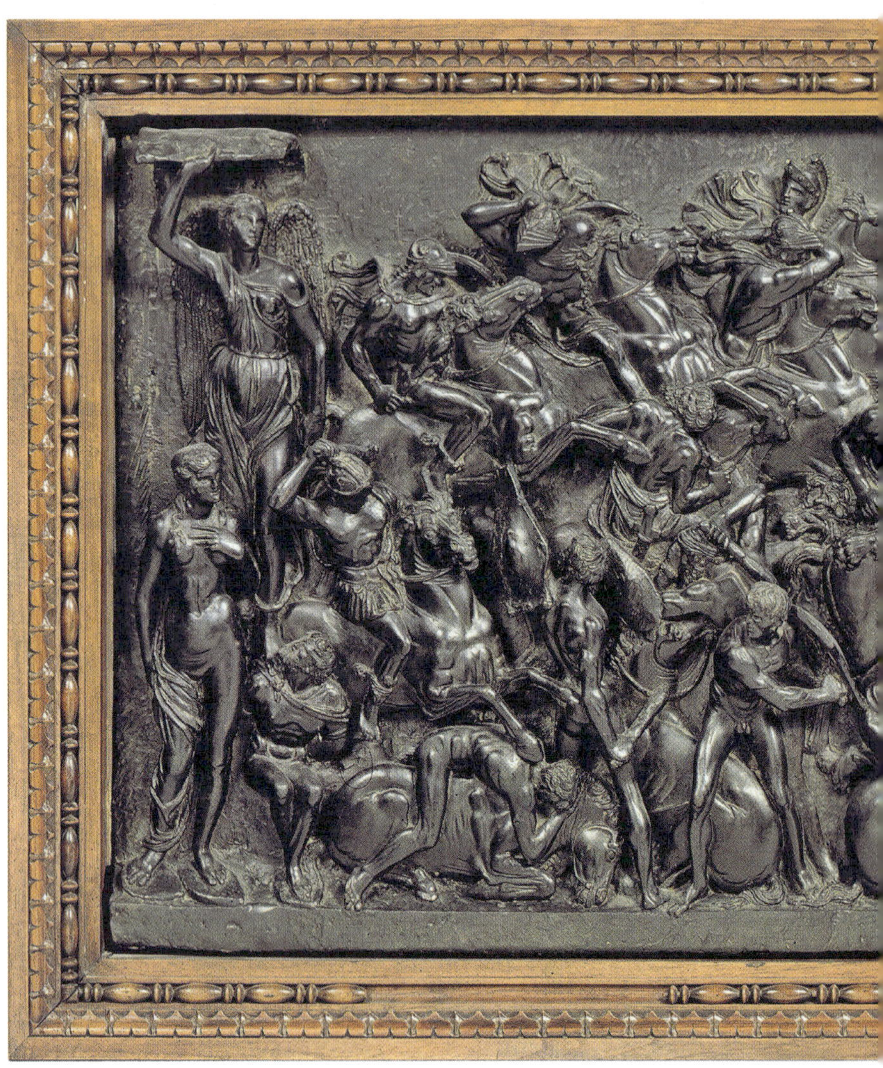

Bertoldo di Giovanni, *Battle between Romans and Barbarians*, after 1478. Museo Nazionale del Bargello, Florence, Italy/Bridgeman Images.

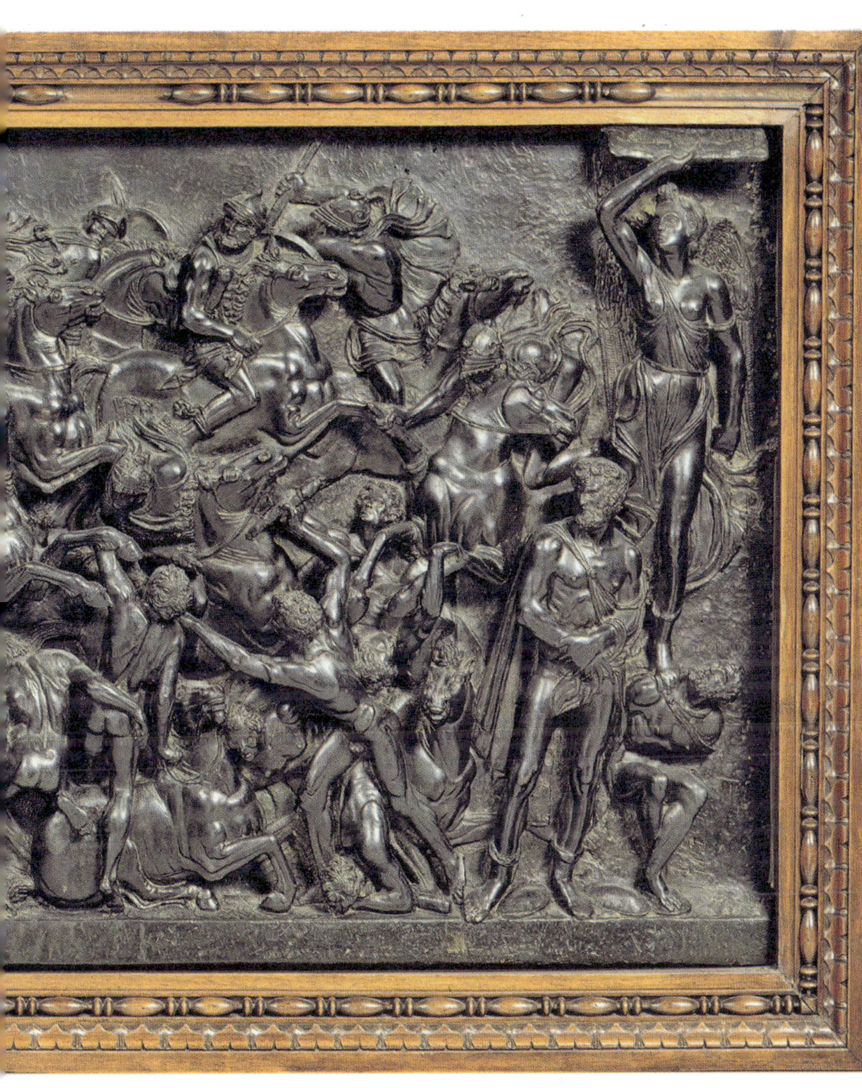

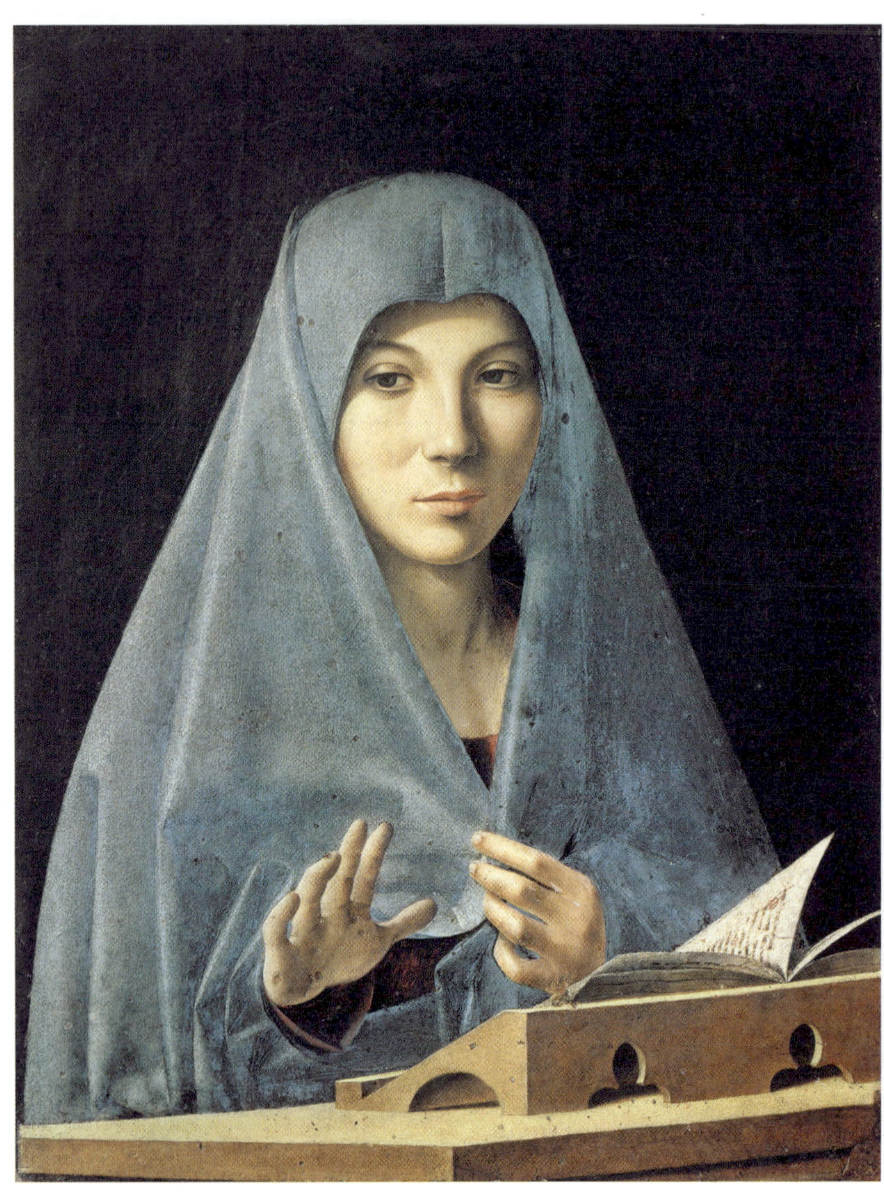

Antonello da Messina, *The Virgin Annunciate*, 1474–1475. Galleria Regionale della Sicilia, Palermo, Italy/Bridgeman Images.

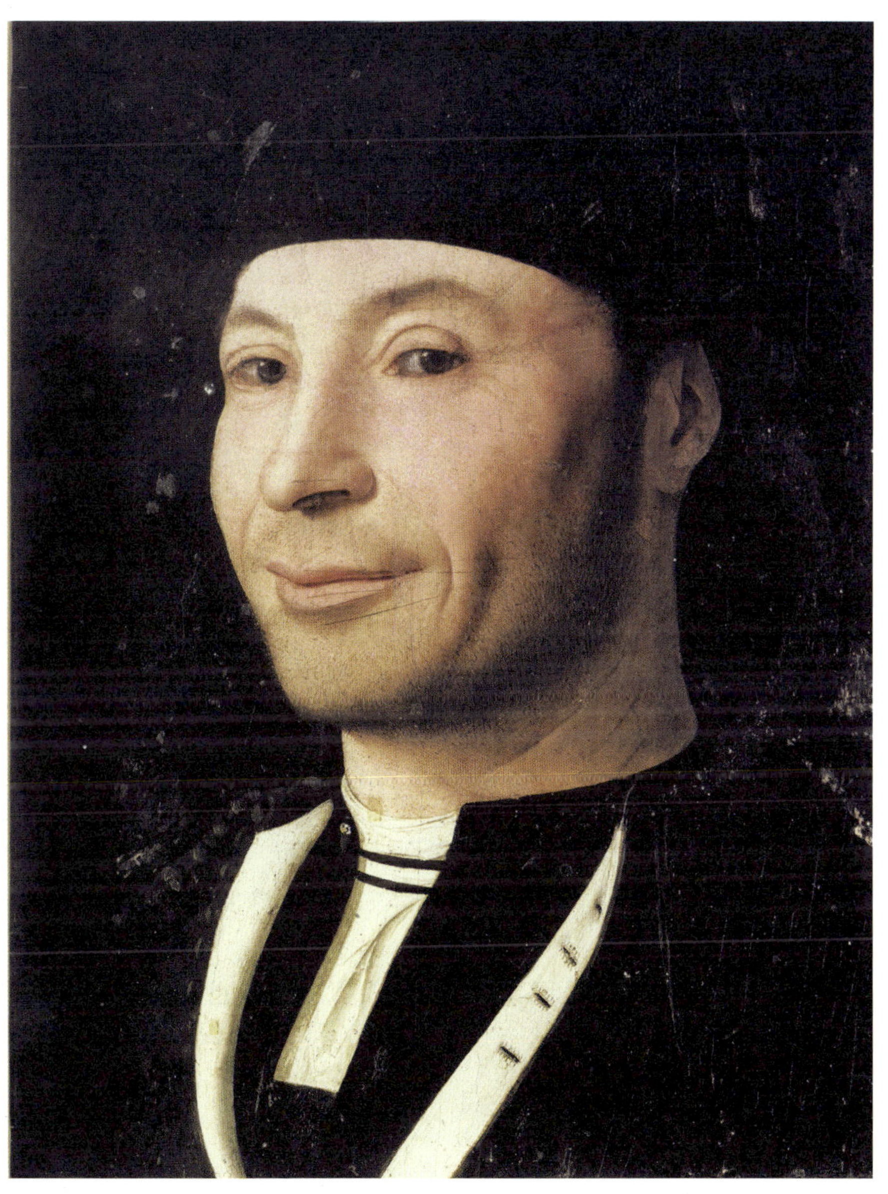

Antonello da Messina, *Portrait of an Unknown Man*, c. 1475–1476. Museo Mandralisca, Cefalù, Italy/Bridgeman Images.

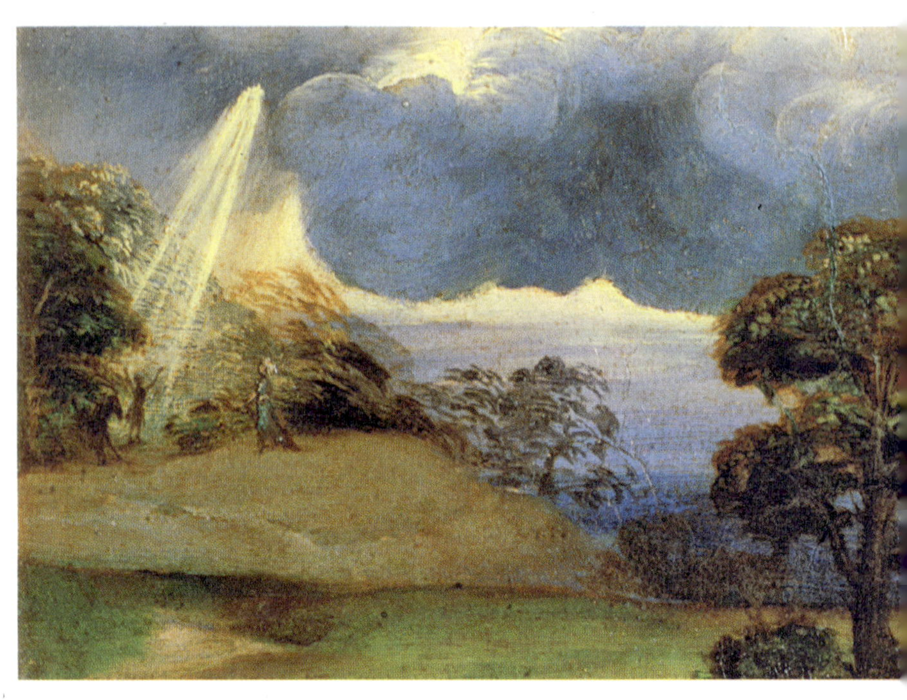

Raphael, *The Vision of Ezekiel*, c. 1518, detail. Galleria Palatina, Florence, Italy/Bridgeman Images.

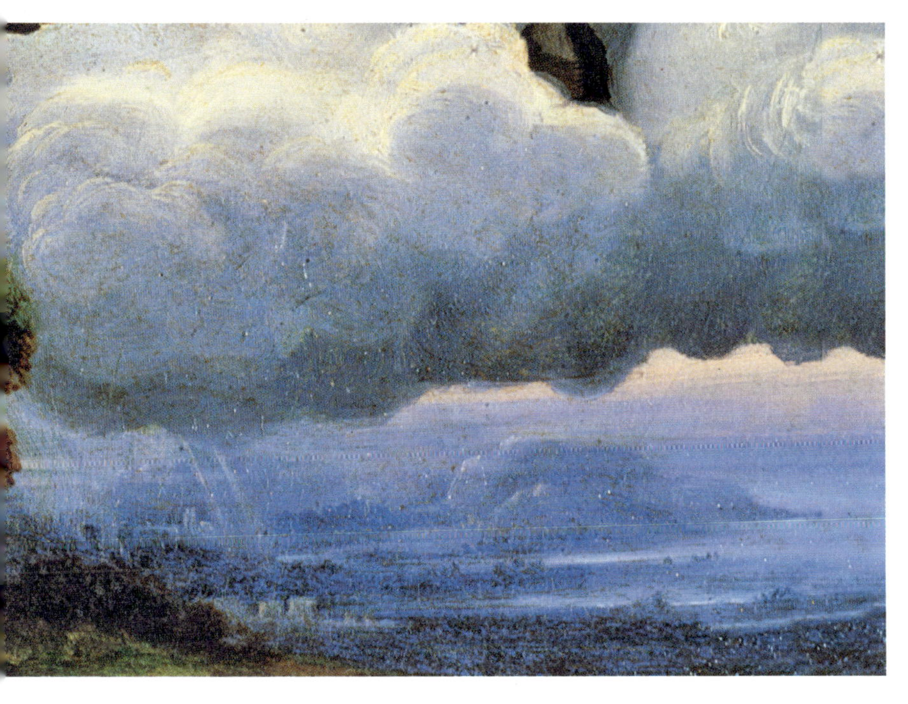

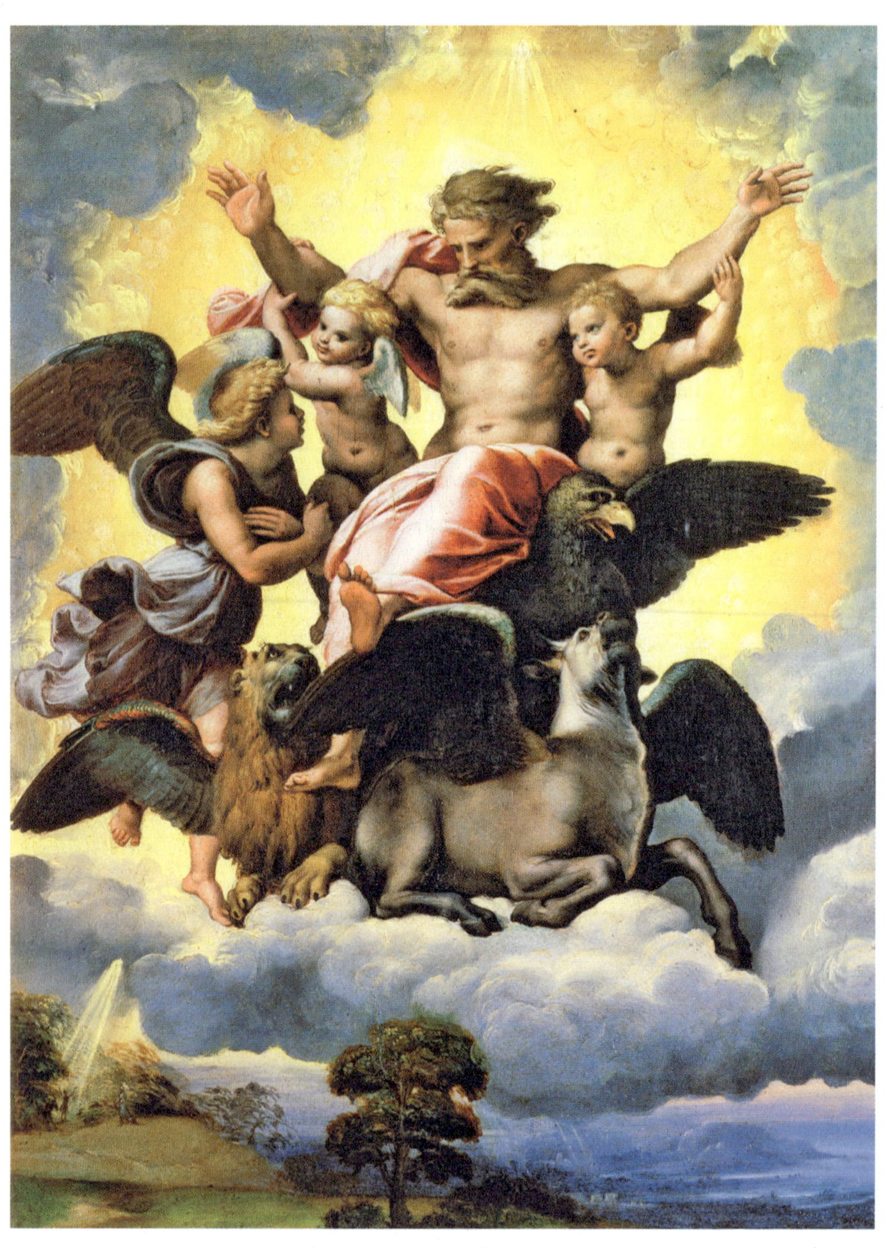

Raphael, *The Vision of Ezekiel*, c. 1518. Galleria Palatina, Florence, Italy/Bridgeman Images.

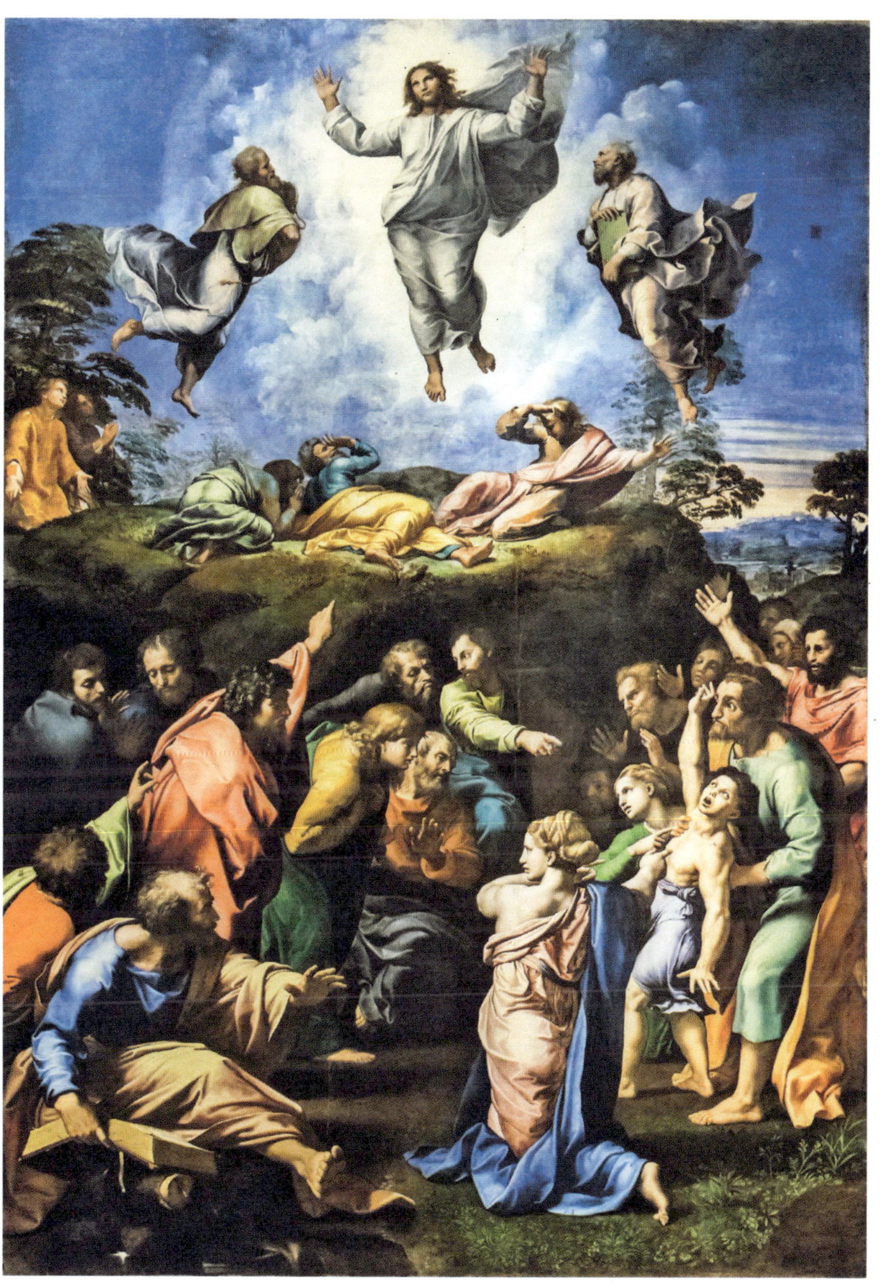

Raphael, *The Transfiguration*, 1520. Vatican Museums and Galleries, Vatican City. Photo © Stefano Baldini/Bridgeman Images.

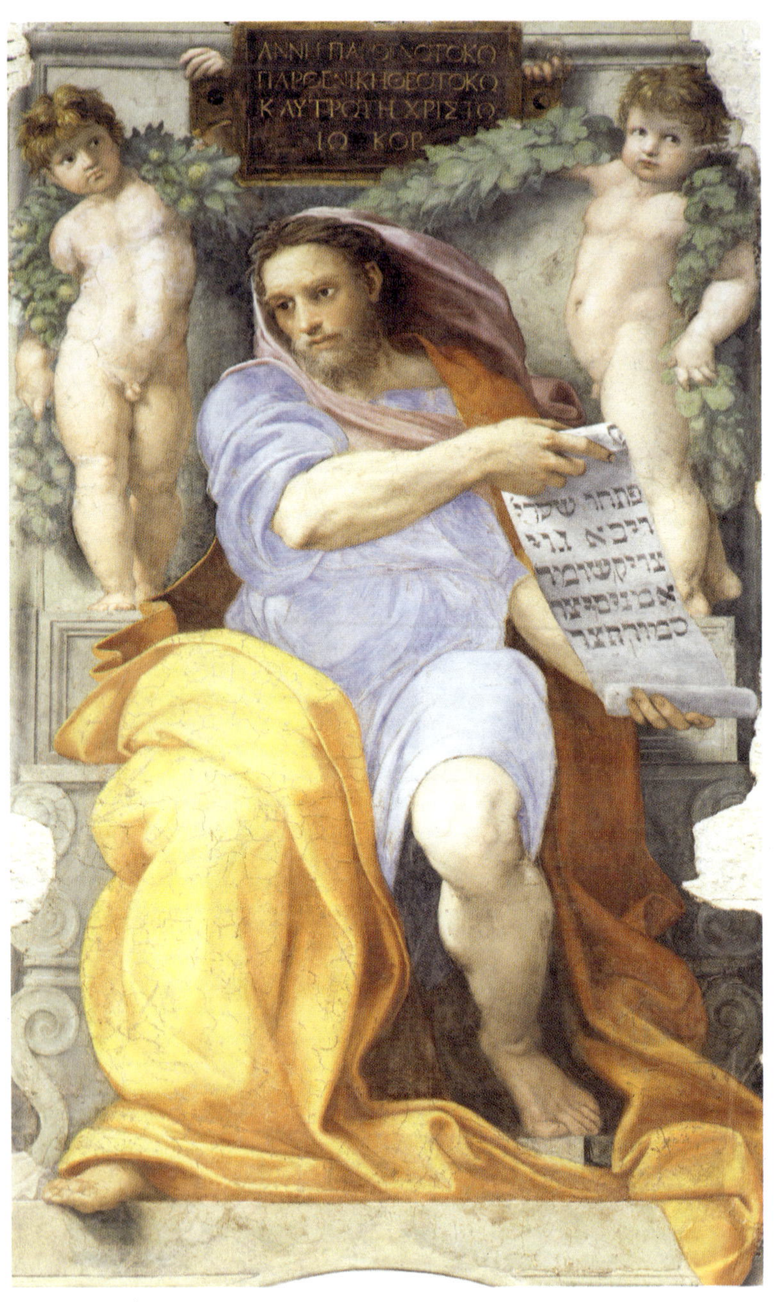

Raphael, *The Prophet Isaiah*, 1512. Basilica di Sant'Agostino, Rome, Italy/Bridgeman Images.

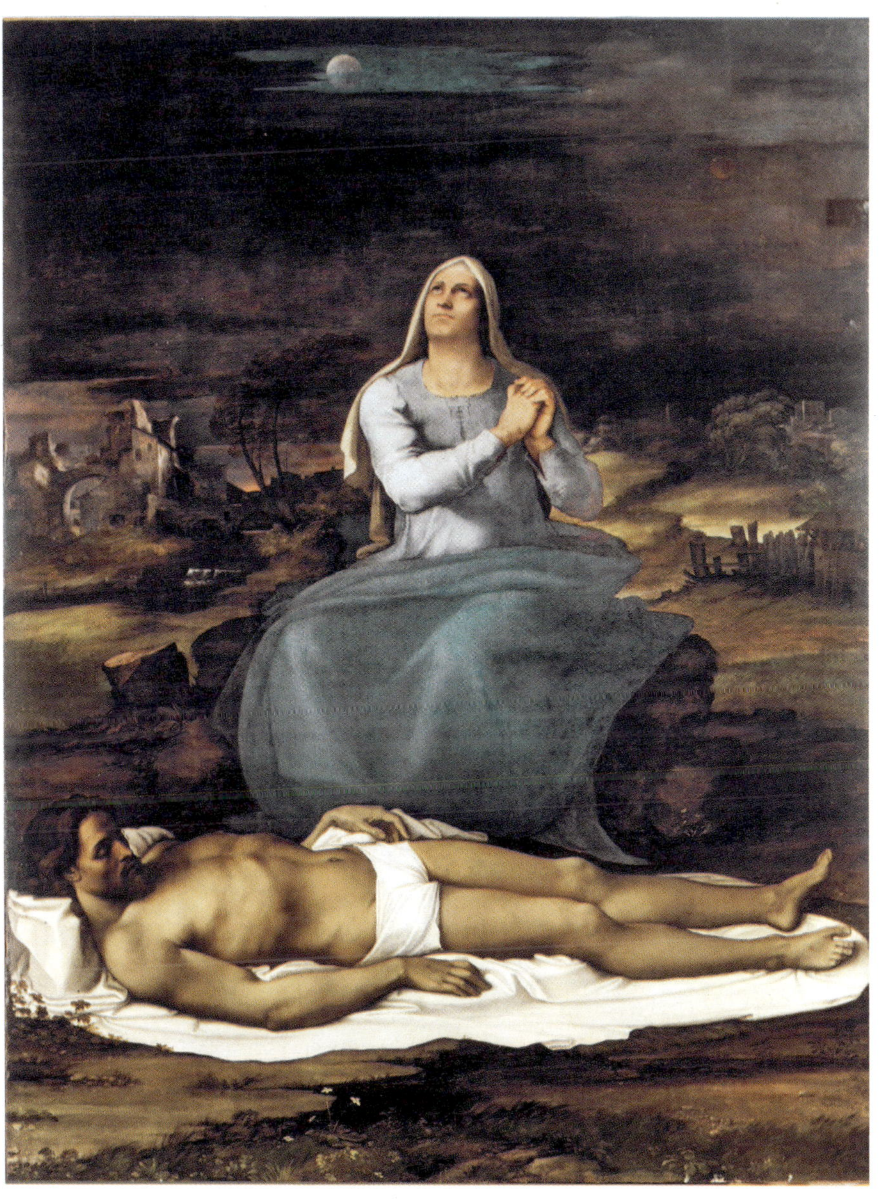

Sebastiano Luciani, called Sebastiano del Piombo, *Pietà*, c. 1515 Oil on wooden panel. Museo Civico, Viterbo, Italy. Luisa Ricciarini/Bridgeman Images.

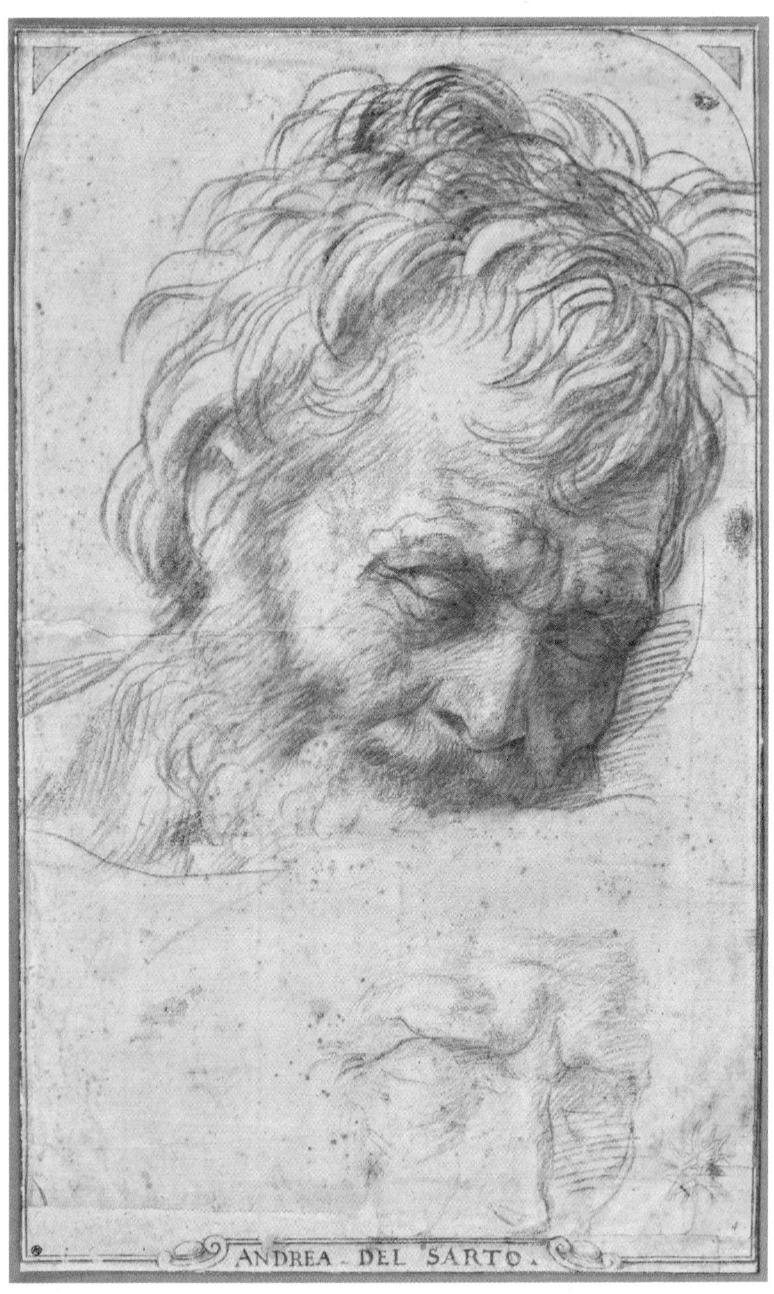

Andrea del Sarto, *Study for the Head of Saint Joseph* (recto), circa 1526–1527. Red and black chalks. J. Paul Getty Museum, Los Angeles, USA. Penta Springs Limited/Alamy Stock Photo.

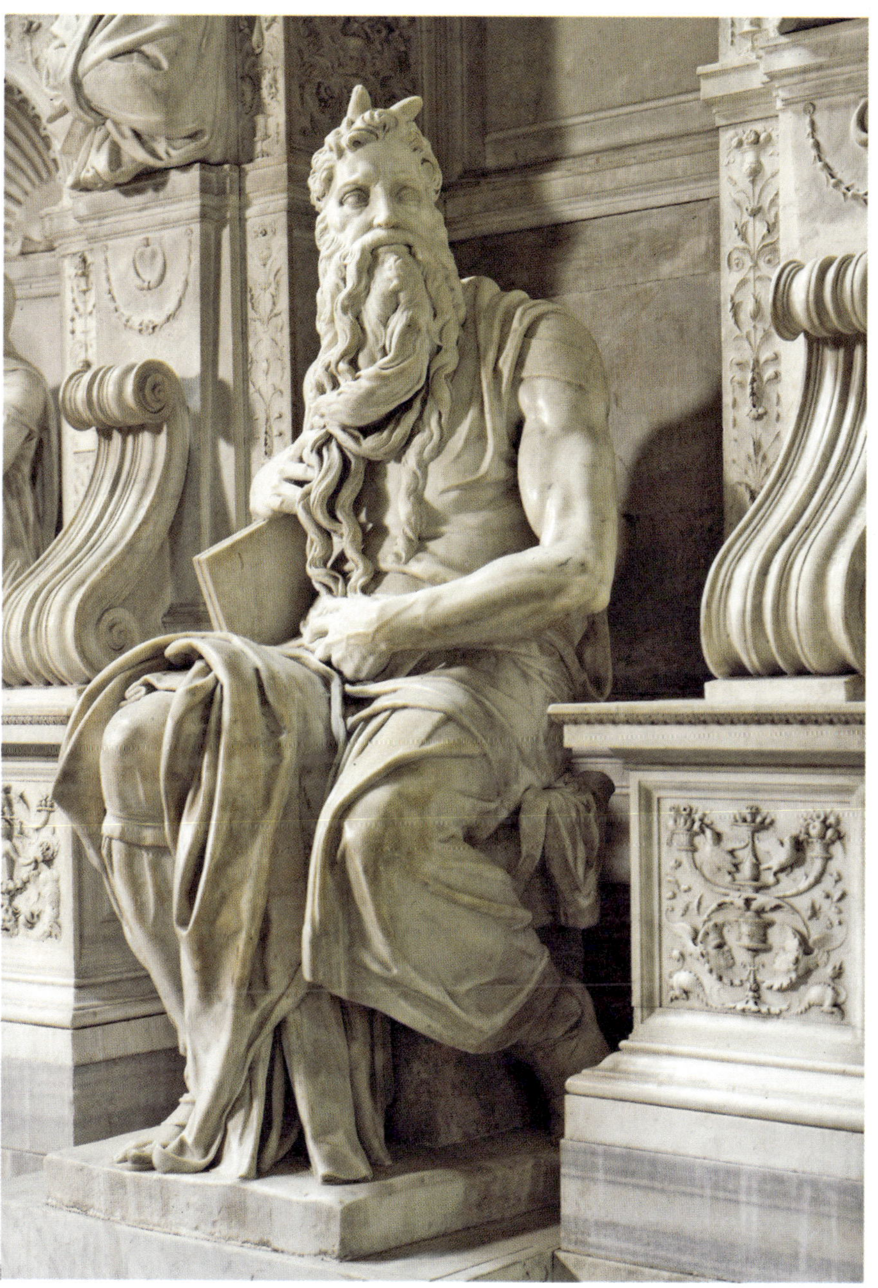

Michelangelo, *Moses*, 1513–1515. Tomb of Pope Julius II, San Pietro in Vincoli, Rome, Italy. Luisa Ricciarini/Bridgeman Images.

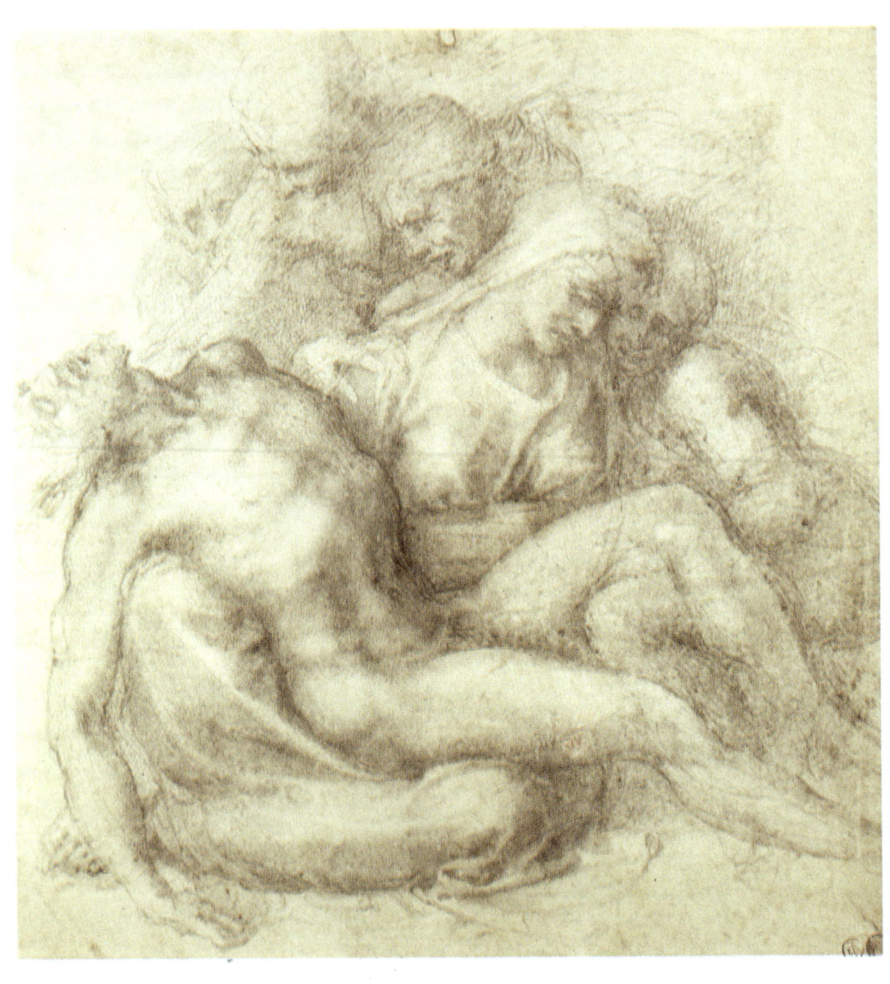

Michelangelo, *Figure Study for the Lamentation over the Dead Christ*, 1530–1535. British Museum, London, UK/Bridgeman Images.

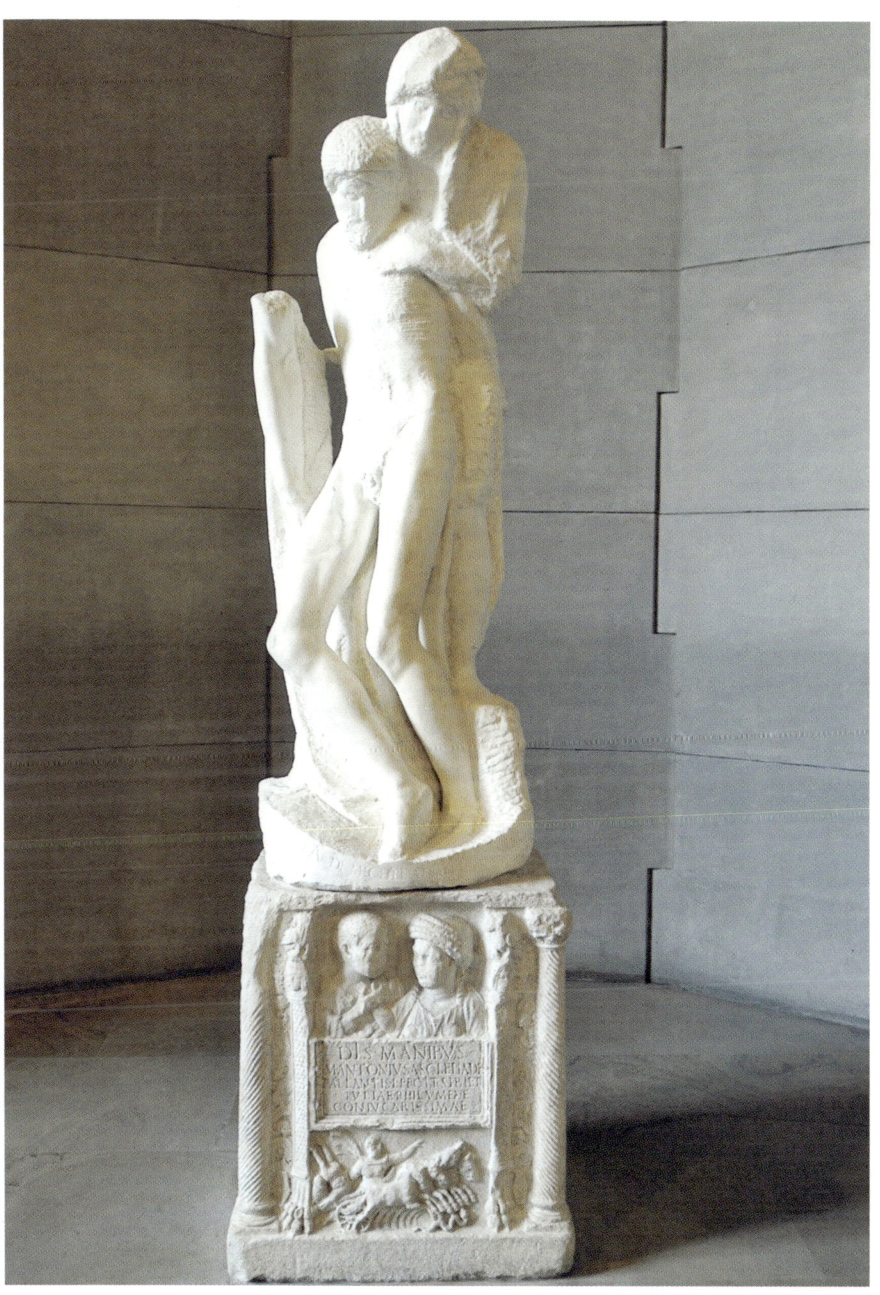

Michelangelo, *Rondanini Pietà*, 1564 Musei del Castello Sforzesco, Milan, Italy. 2010Stockvs/
Alamy Stock Photo.

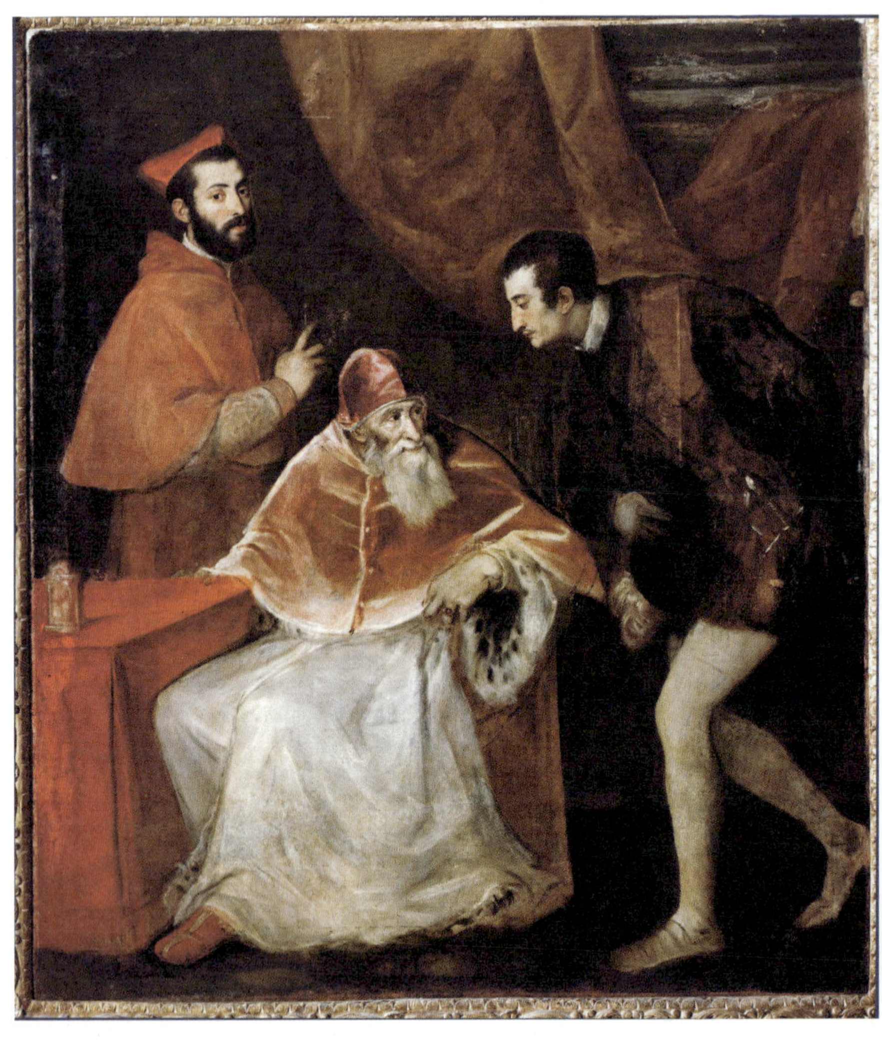

Titian, *Pope Paul III and His Grandsons Alessandro and Ottavio Farnese*, 1546. Museo di Capodimonte, Naples, Italy. Luisa Ricciarini/Bridgeman Images.

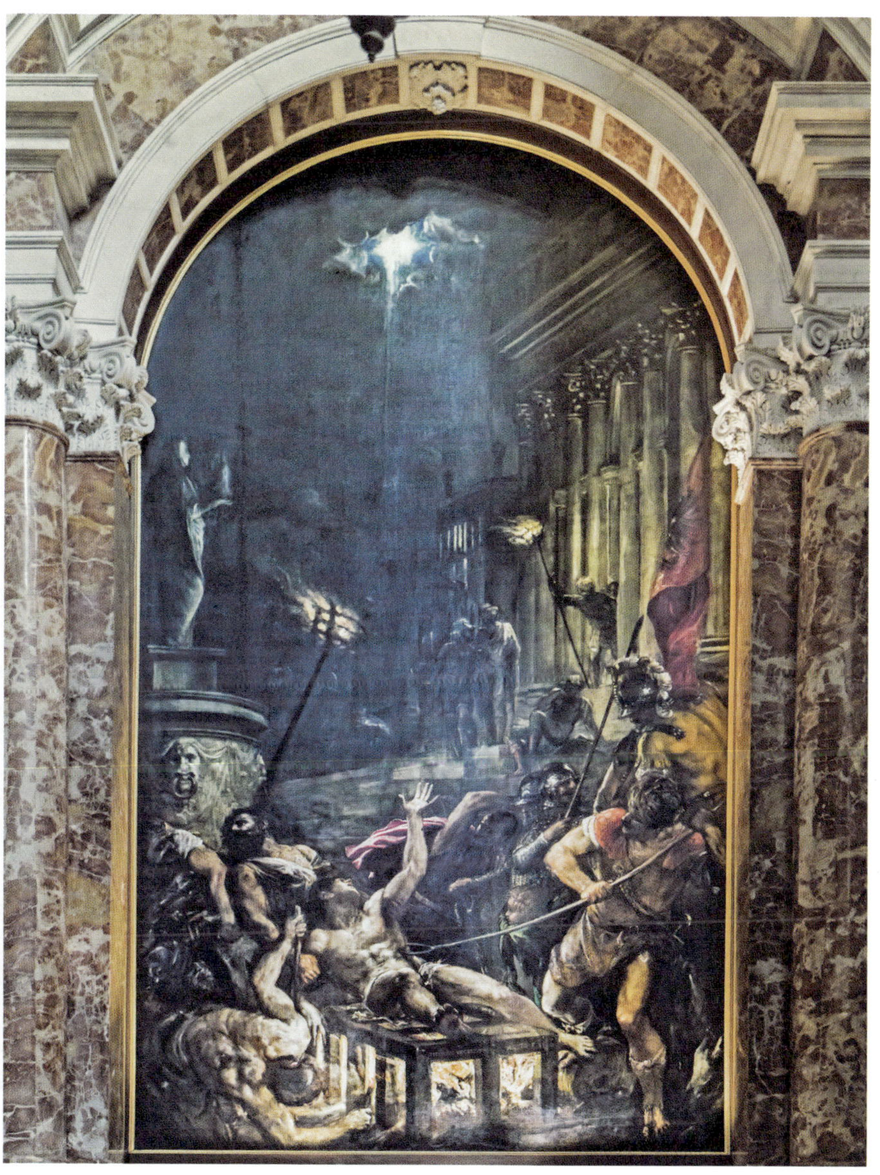

Titian, *Martyrdom of Saint Lawrence*, circa 1560. Santa Maria Assunta dei Gesuiti, Venice, Italy. Didier Descouens, Wikimedia Commons.

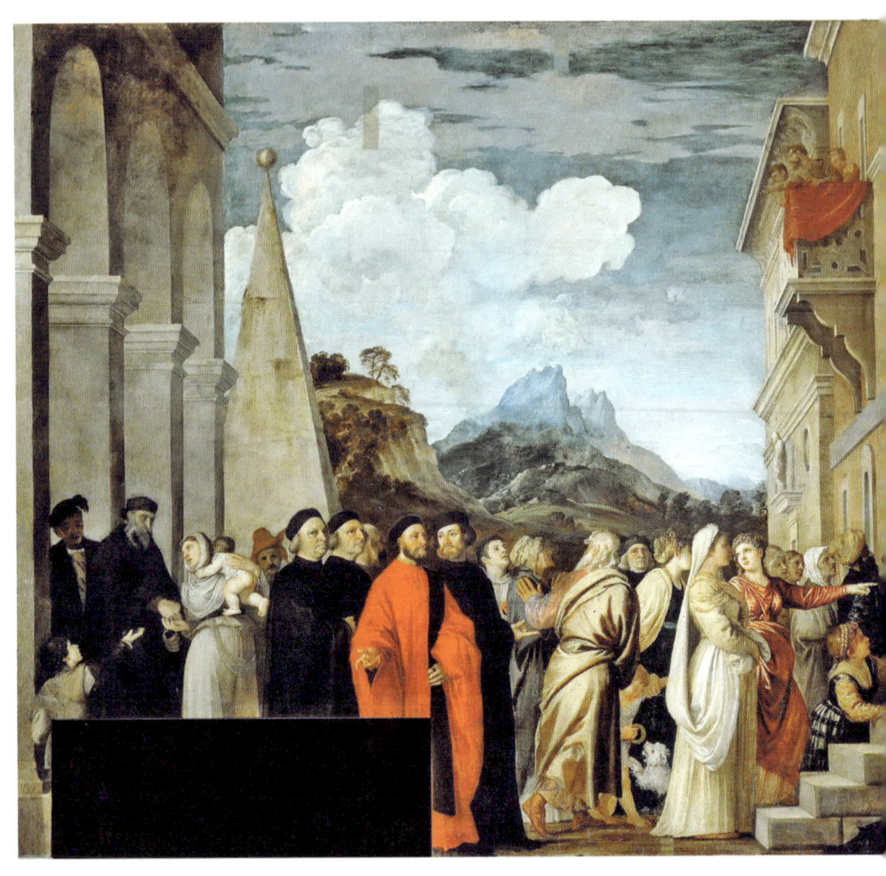

Titian, *Presentation of the Virgin in the Temple*, 1534–1538. Galleria dell'Accademia, Venice, Italy. Heritage Image Partnership, Ltd./Alamy Stock Photo.

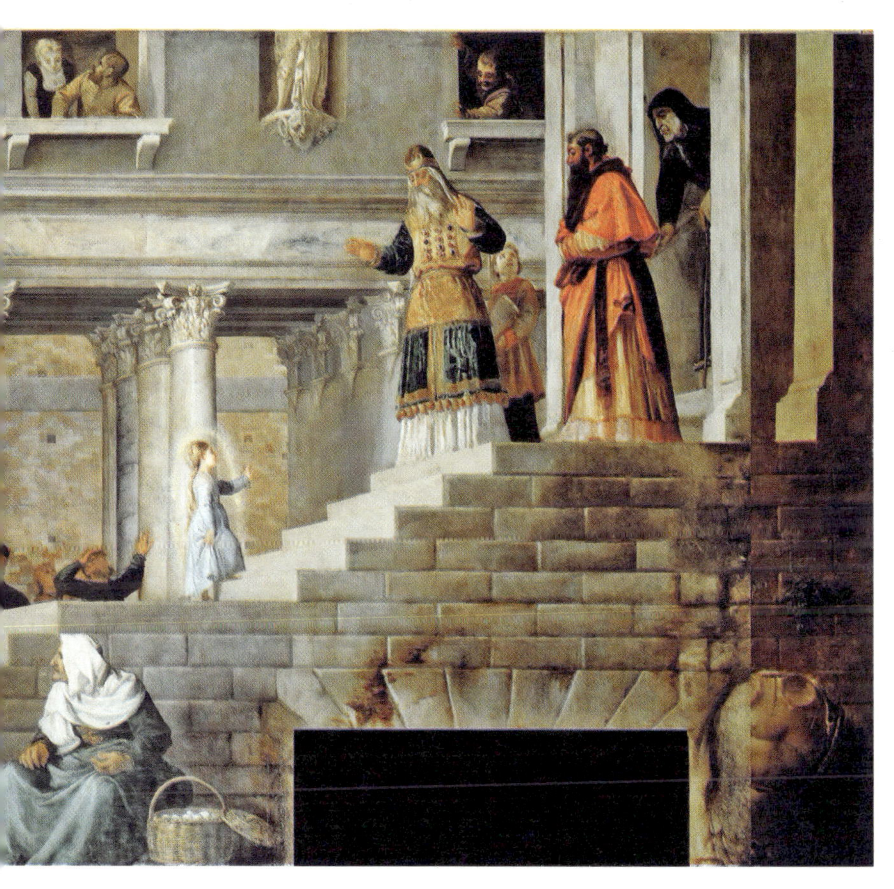

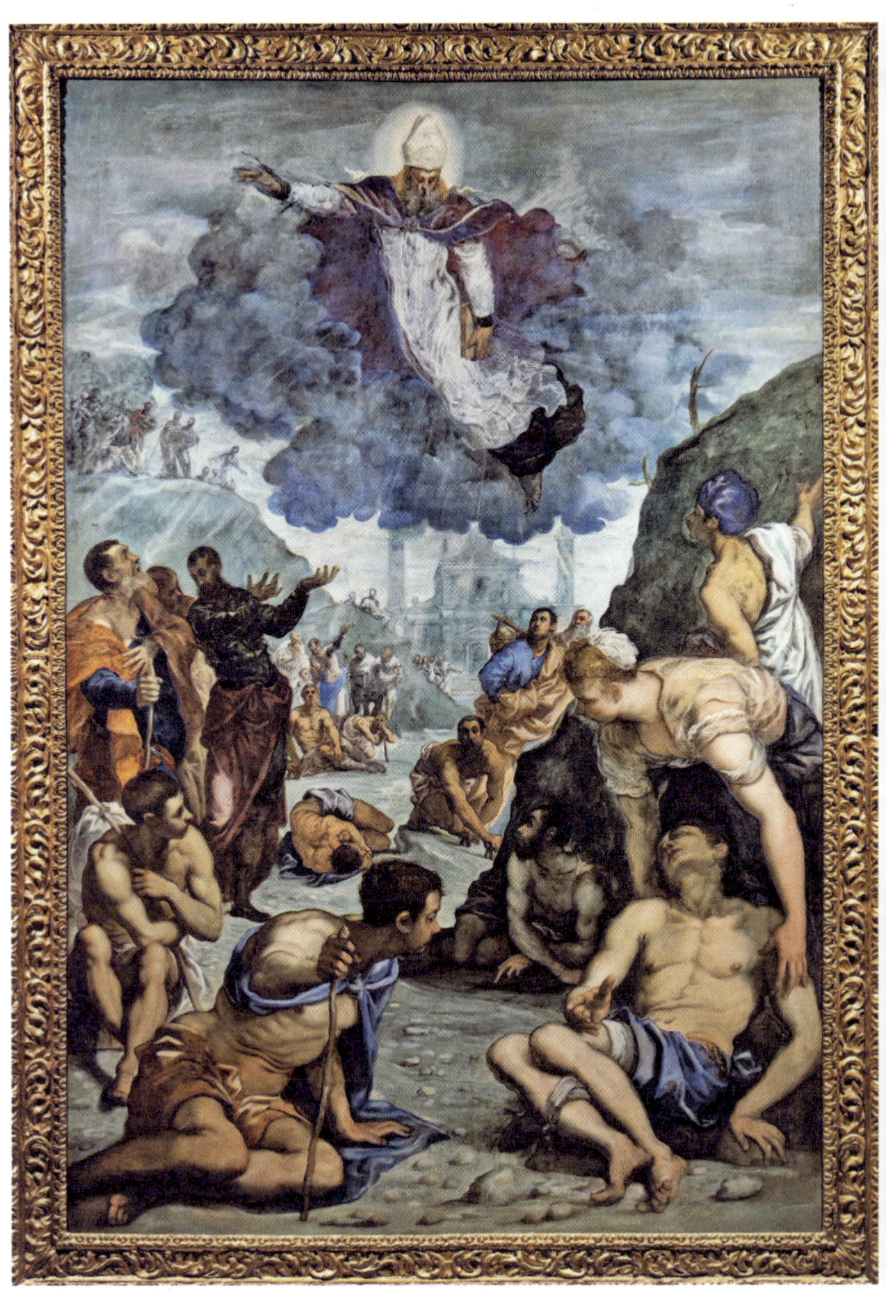

Jacopo Robusti, called Tintoretto, *Saint Augustine Healing the Lame*, circa 1560. Museo Civico Palazzo Chiericati, Vicenza, Italy. Ghigo Roli/Bridgeman Images.

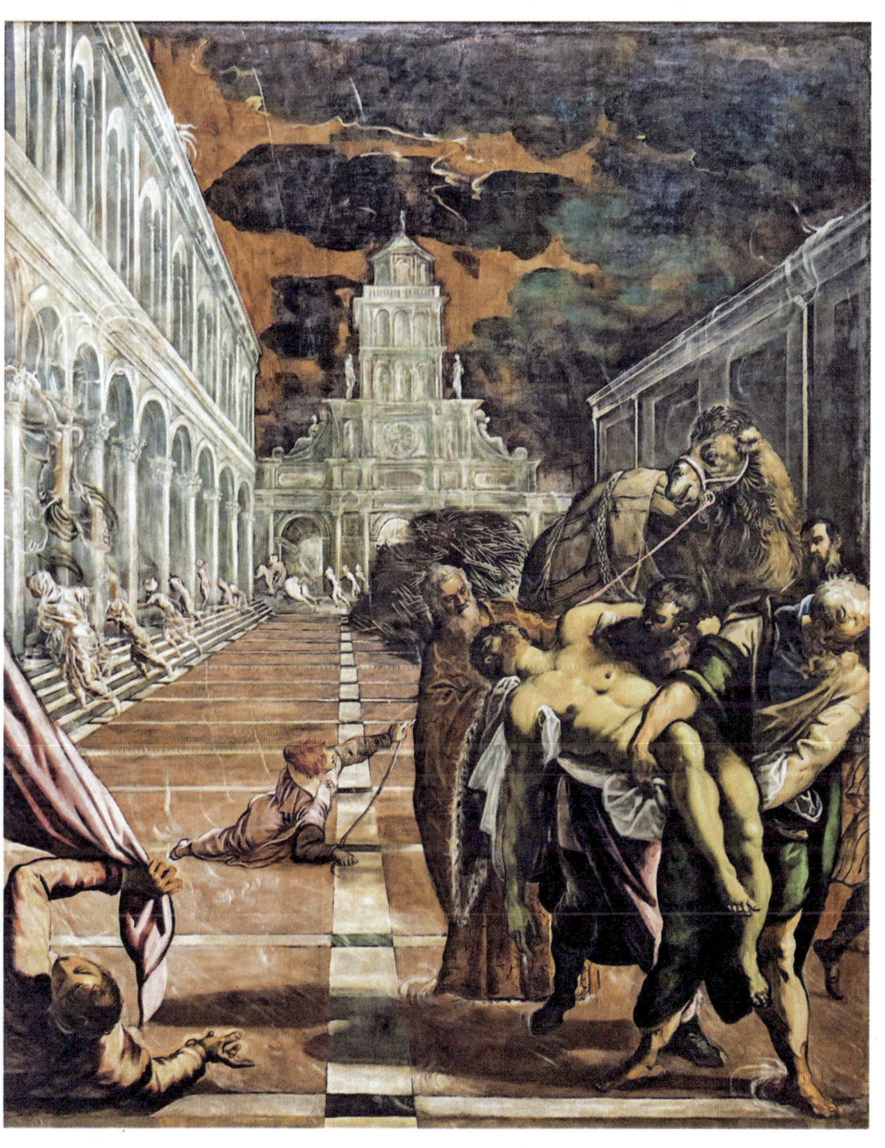

Jacopo Robusti, called Tintoretto, *Transport of the Body of Saint Mark*, 1562–1566. Galleria dell'Accademia, Venice, Italy/Bridgeman Images.

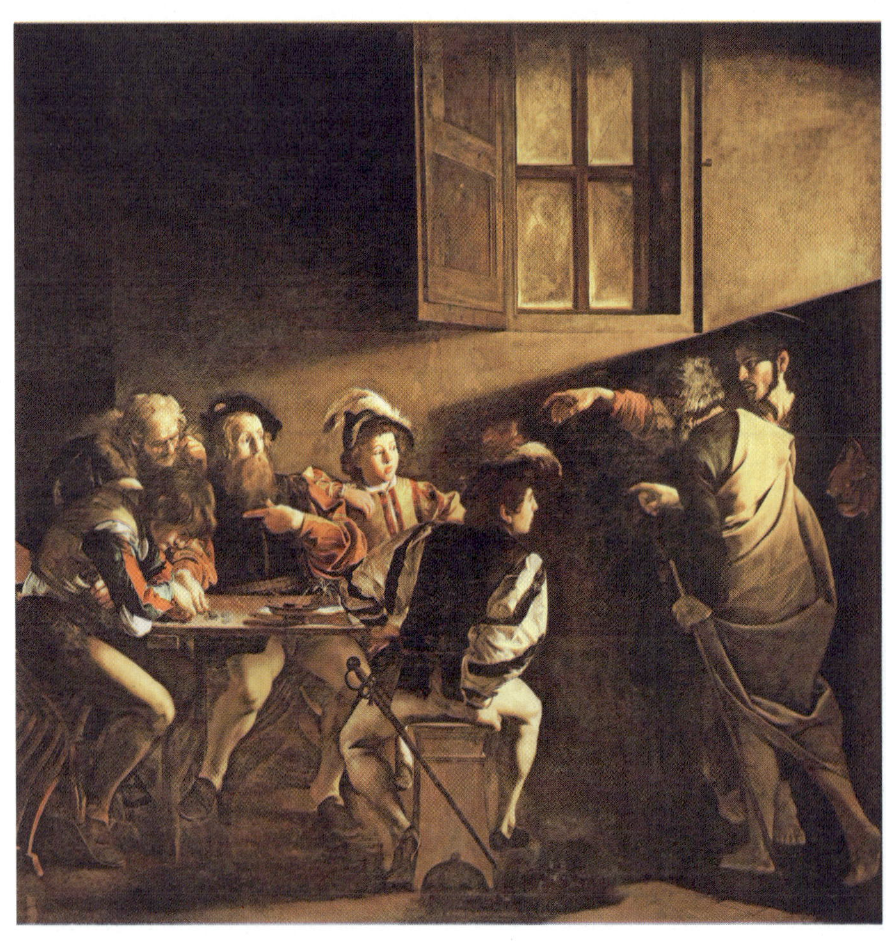

Michelangelo Merisi da Caravaggio, *The Calling of Saint Matthew*, 1600. Contarelli Chapel, San Luigi dei Francesi, Rome, Italy/Bridgeman Images.

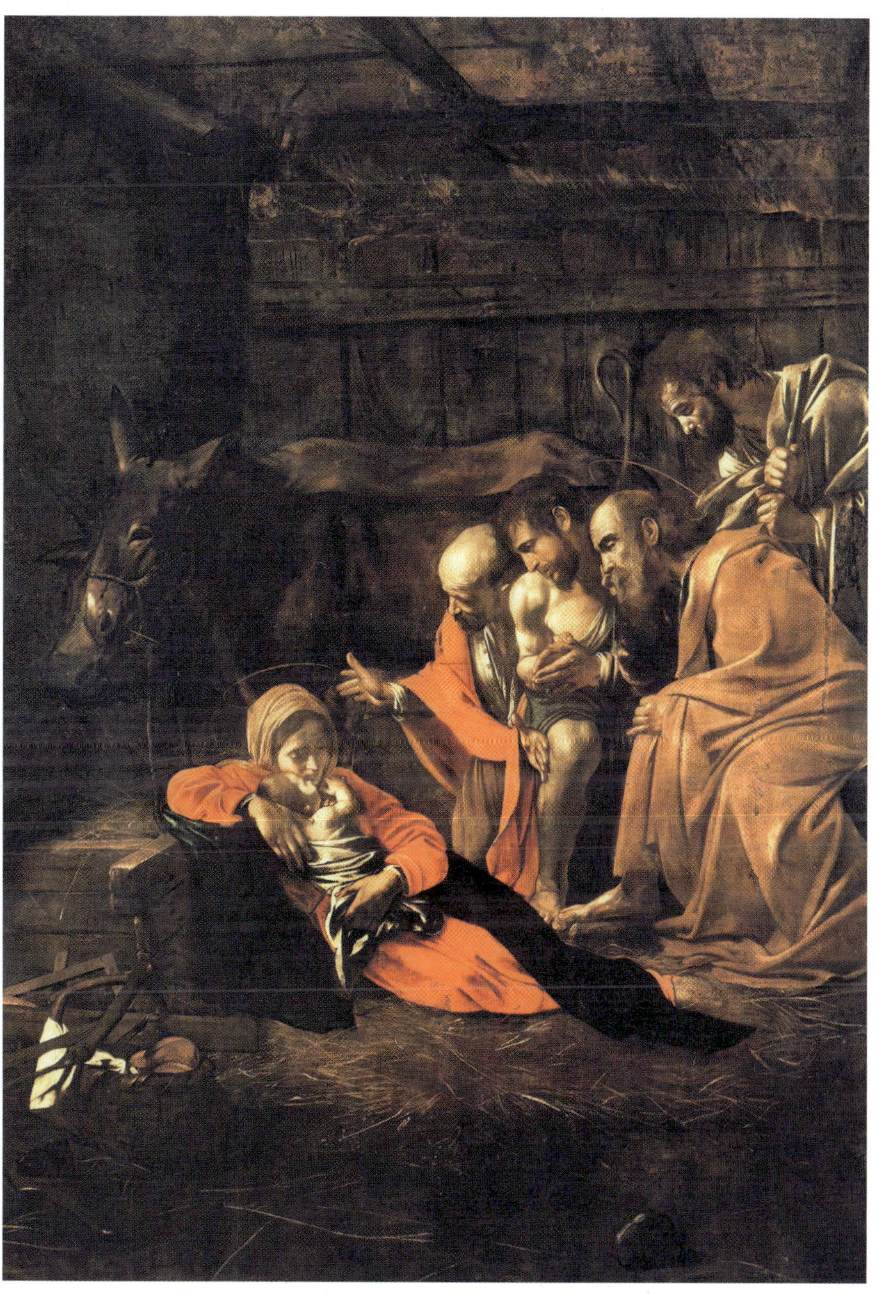

Michelangelo Merisi da Caravaggio, *The Adoration of the Shepherds*, 1609. Museo Regionale Interdisciplinare, Messina, Italy. Artefact/Alamy Stock Photo.

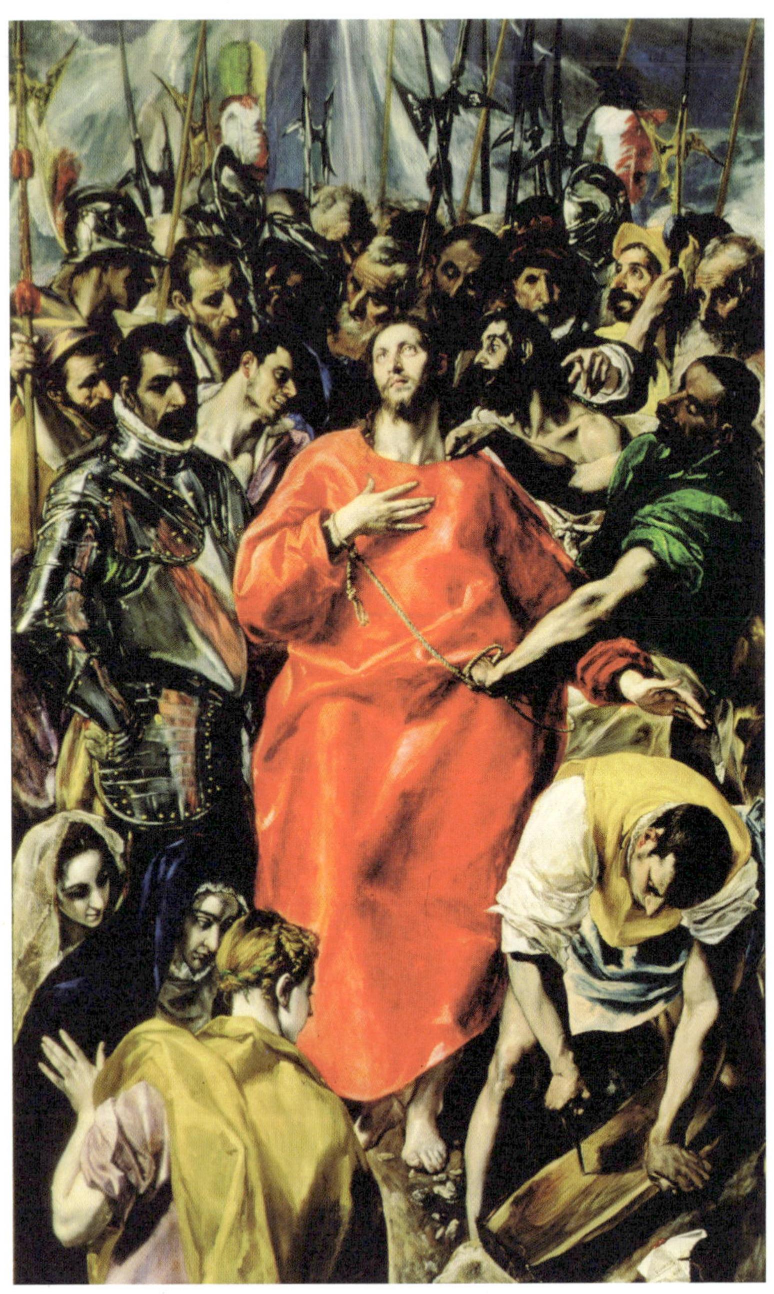

El Greco (Domenikos Theotokopoulos), *The Disrobing of Christ*, 1577–1579. Toledo Cathedral, Toledo, Spain/Bridgeman Images.

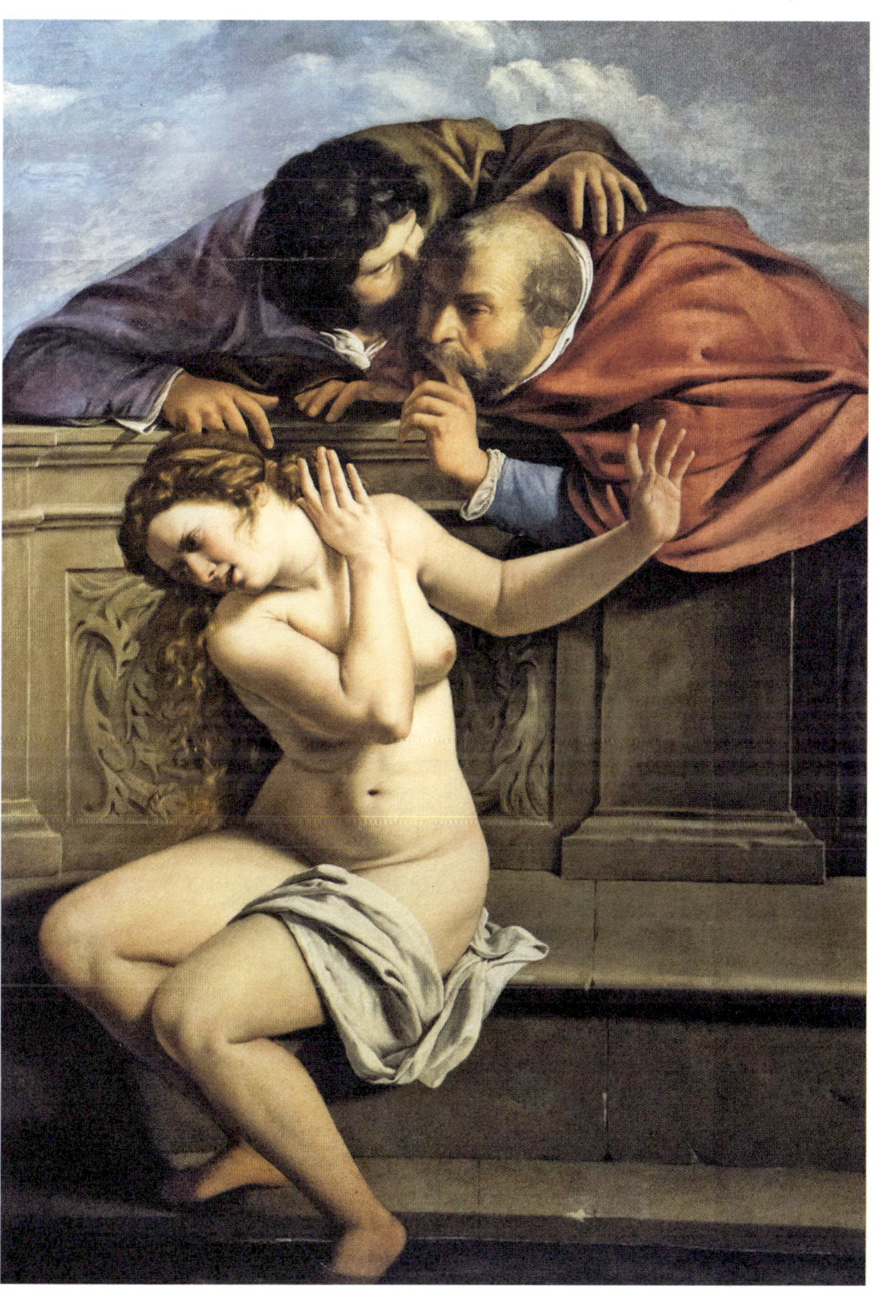

Artemisia Gentileschi, *Susanna and the Elders*, 1610. Schloß Weißenstein, Pommersfelden, Germany. Artexplorer/Alamy Stock Photo.

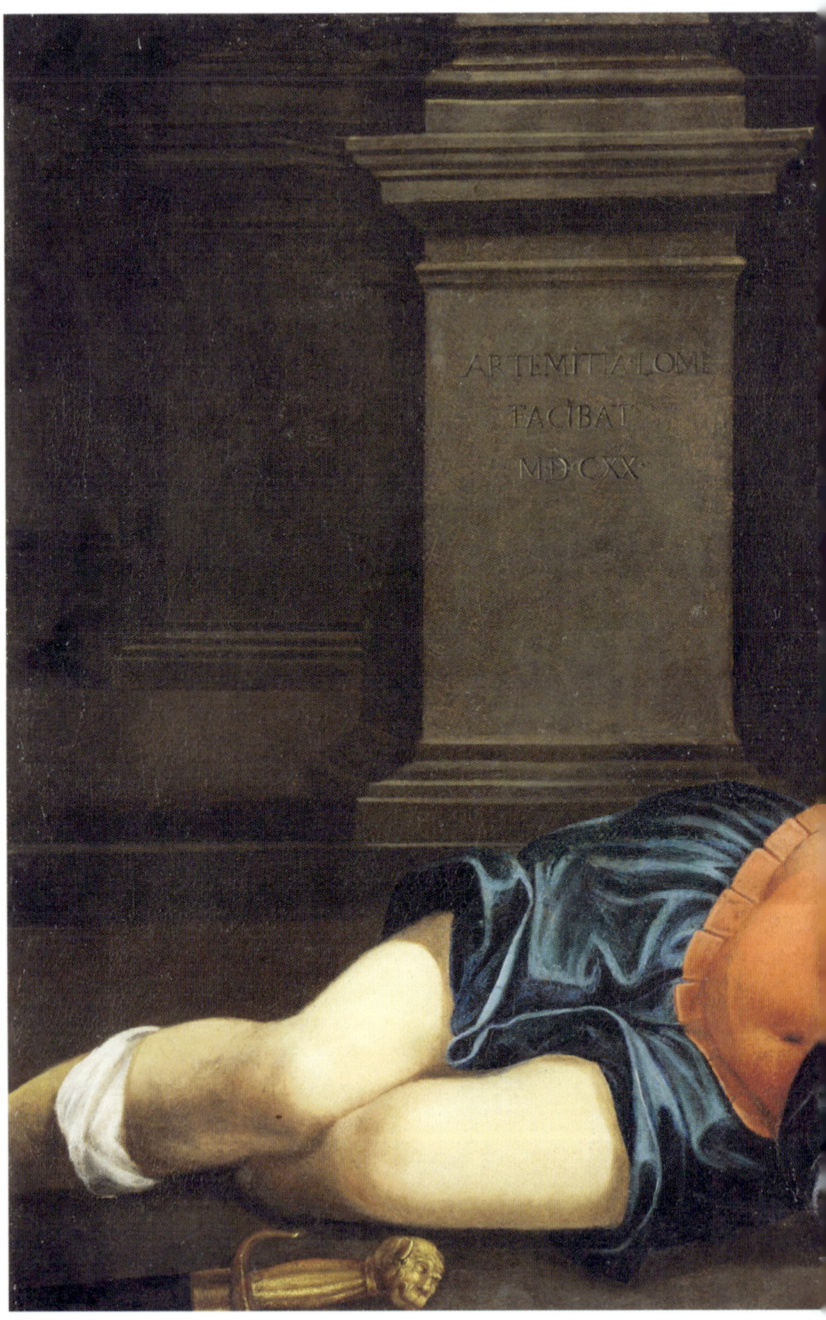

Artemisia Gentileschi, *Jael Killing Sisera*, 1620. Museum of Fine Arts (Szépművészeti Múzeum), Budapest, Hungary. Photo © Fine Art Images/Bridgeman Images.

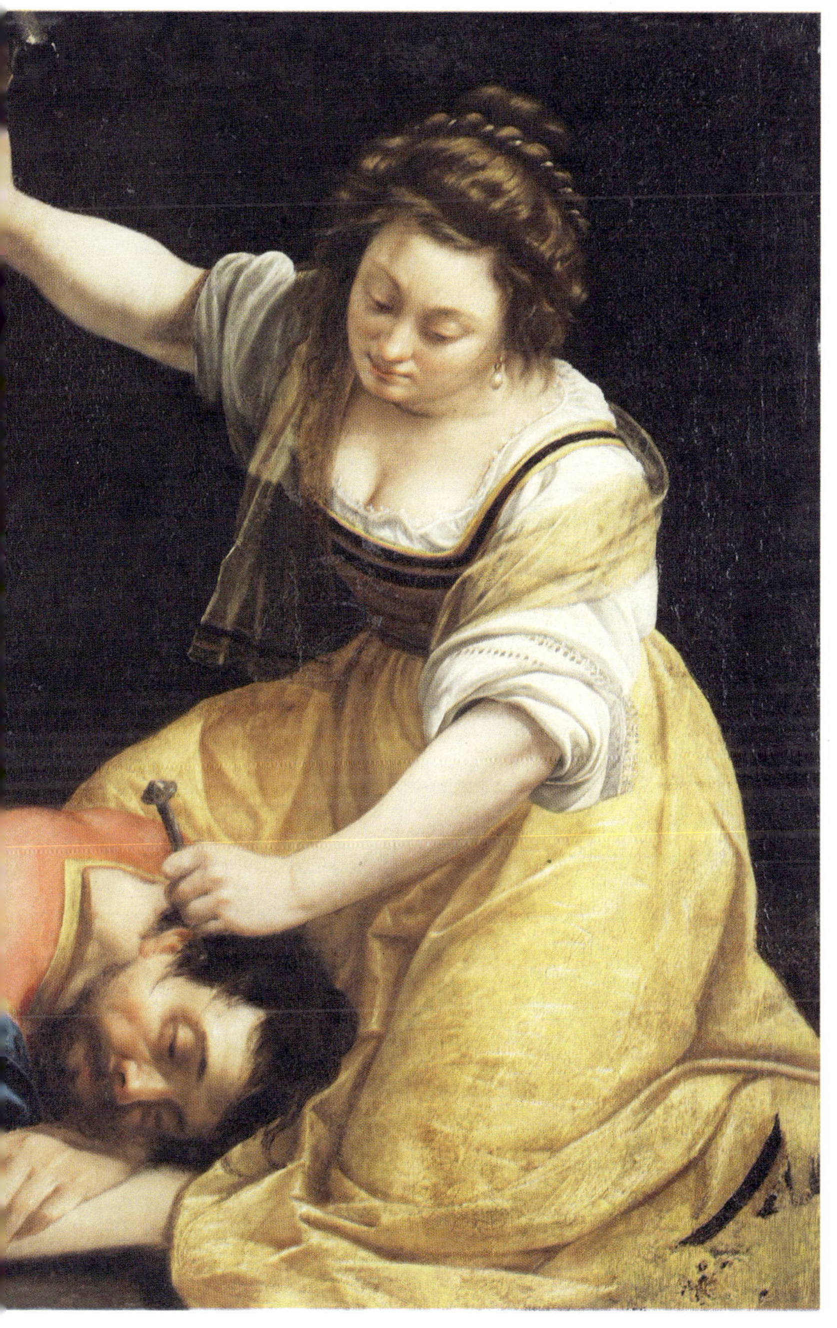

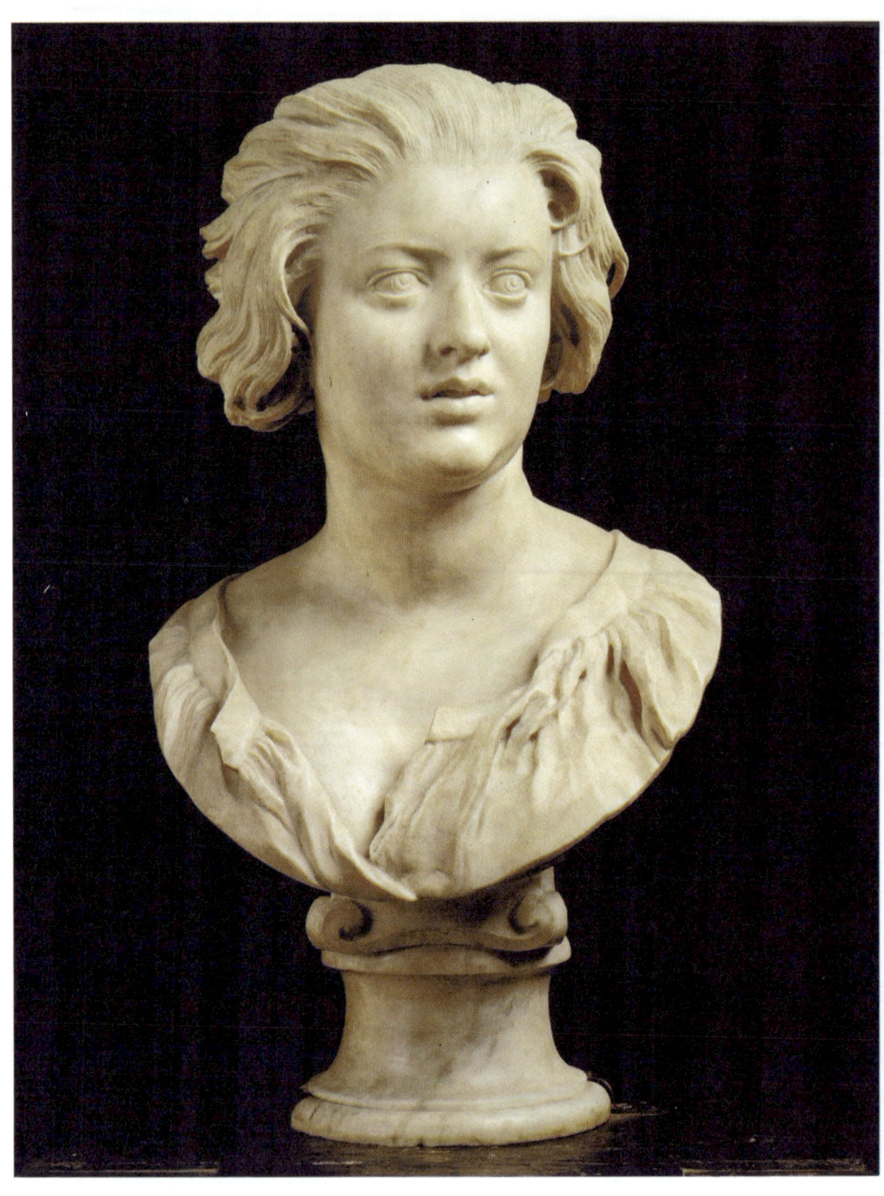

Gian Lorenzo Bernini, *Bust of Costanza Piccolomini*, c. 1637–1638. Museo Nazionale del Bargello, Florence, Italy. Photo © Raffaello Bencini/Bridgeman Images.

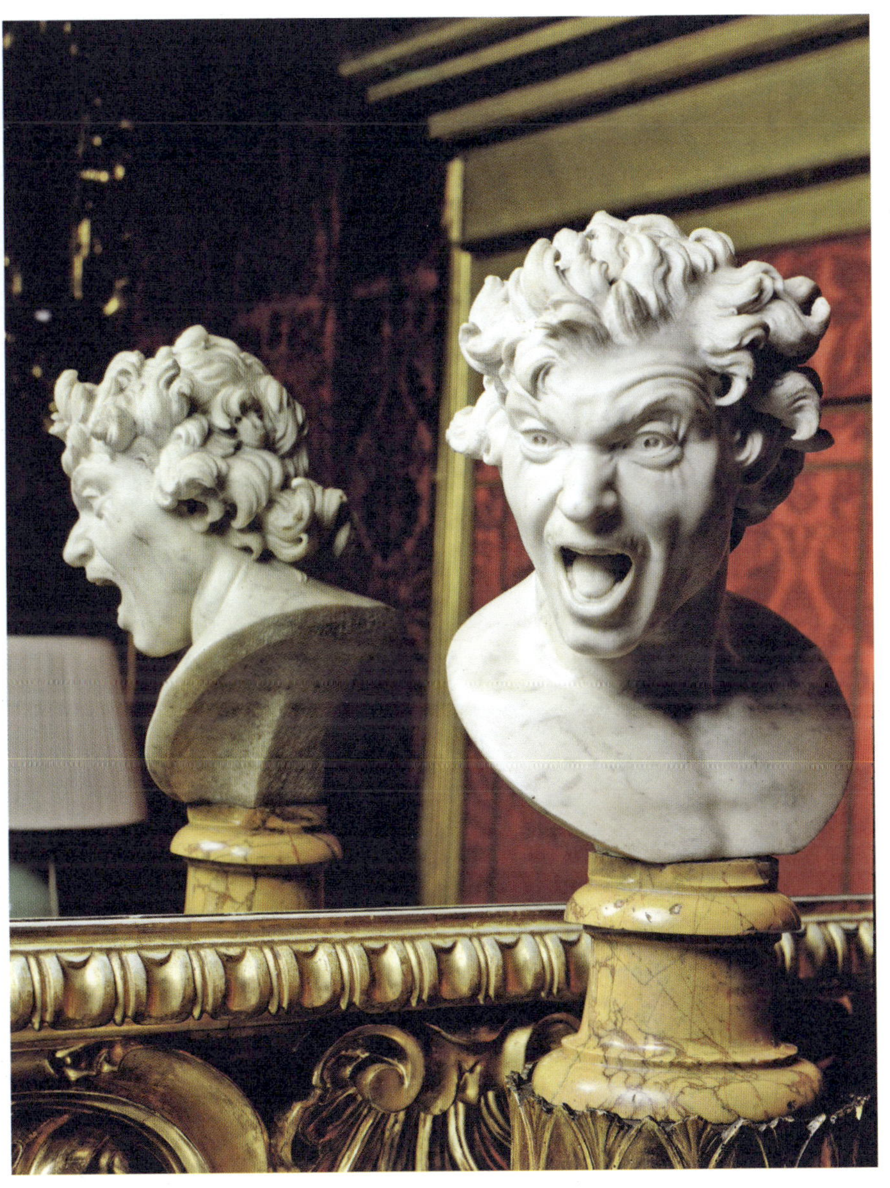

Gian Lorenzo Bernini, *Anima dannata (Condemned Soul)*, 1619. Spanish Embassy, Rome, Italy/ Bridgeman Images.

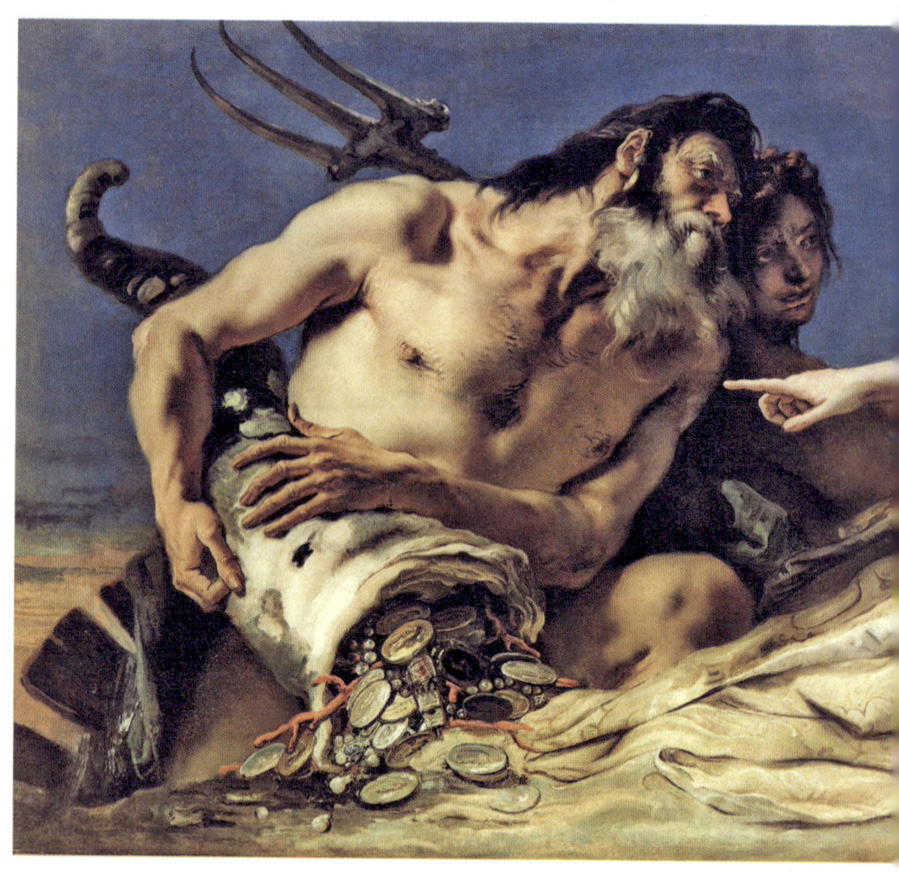

Giovanni Battista Tiepolo, *Neptune Offering Gifts to Venice*, before 1758. Palazzo Ducale, Venice, Italy. © Francesco Turio Bohm. All rights reserved 2023/Bridgeman Images.

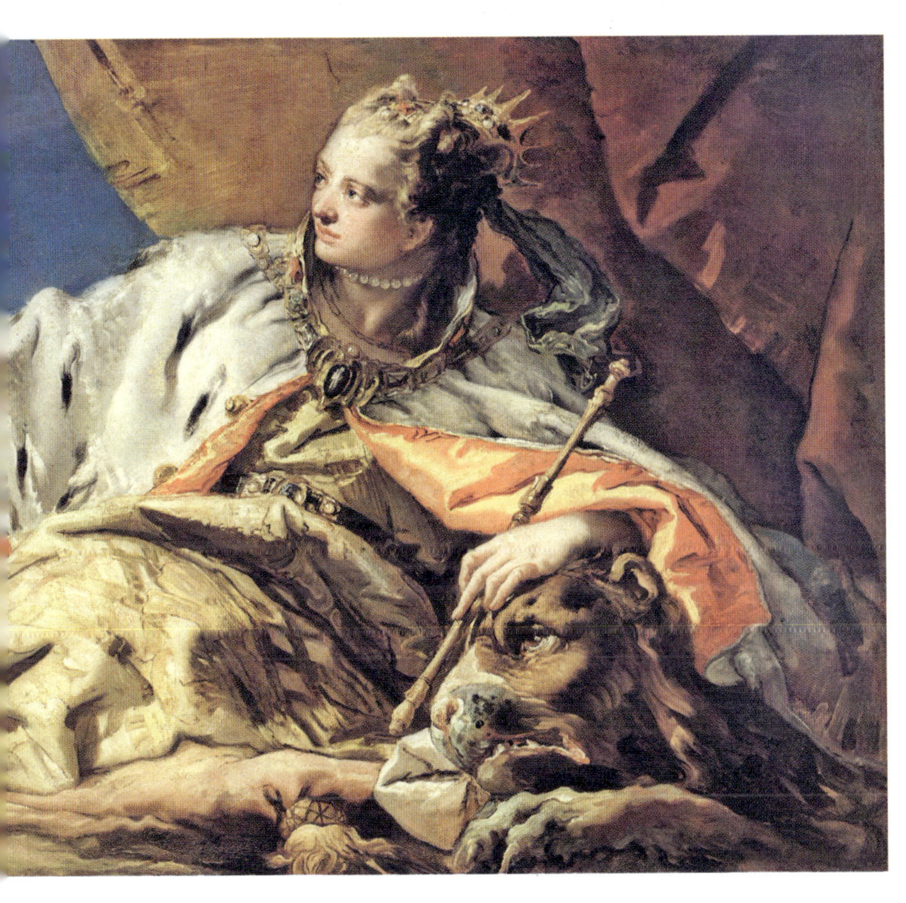

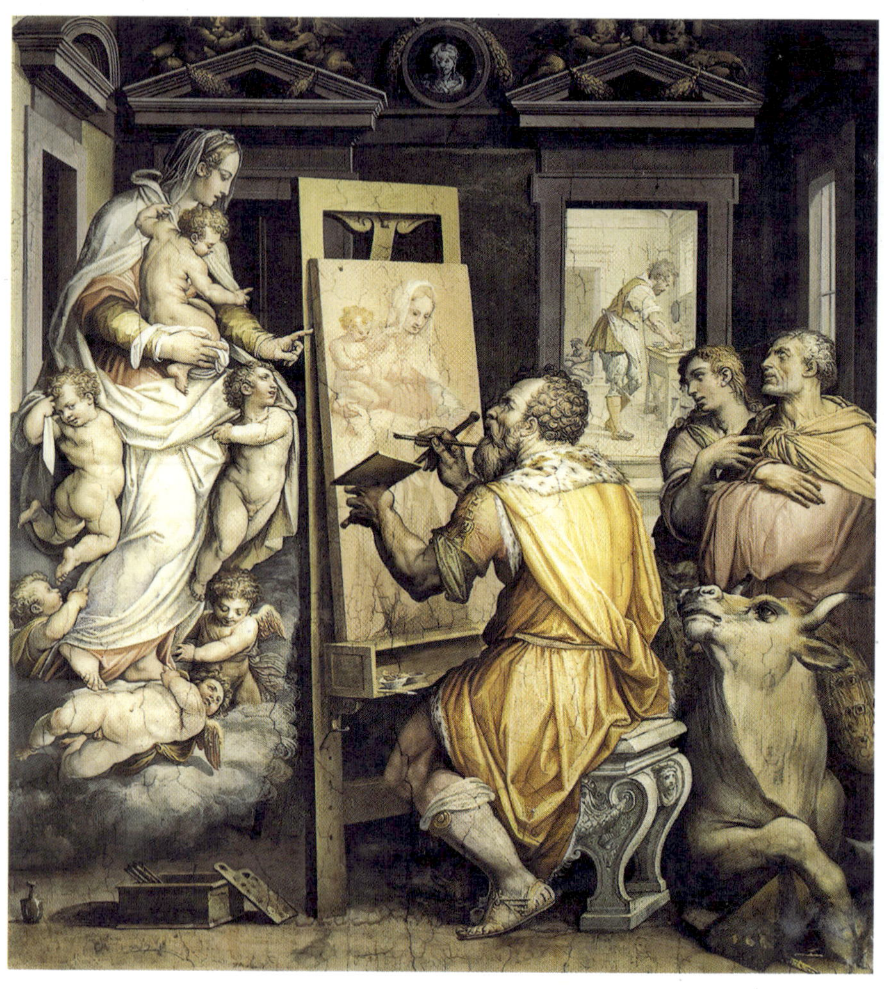

Giorgio Vasari, *Saint Luke Painting the Virgin*, after 1565. Saint Luke Chapel, Santissima Annunziata, Florence, Italy. Artefact/Alamy Stock Photo.

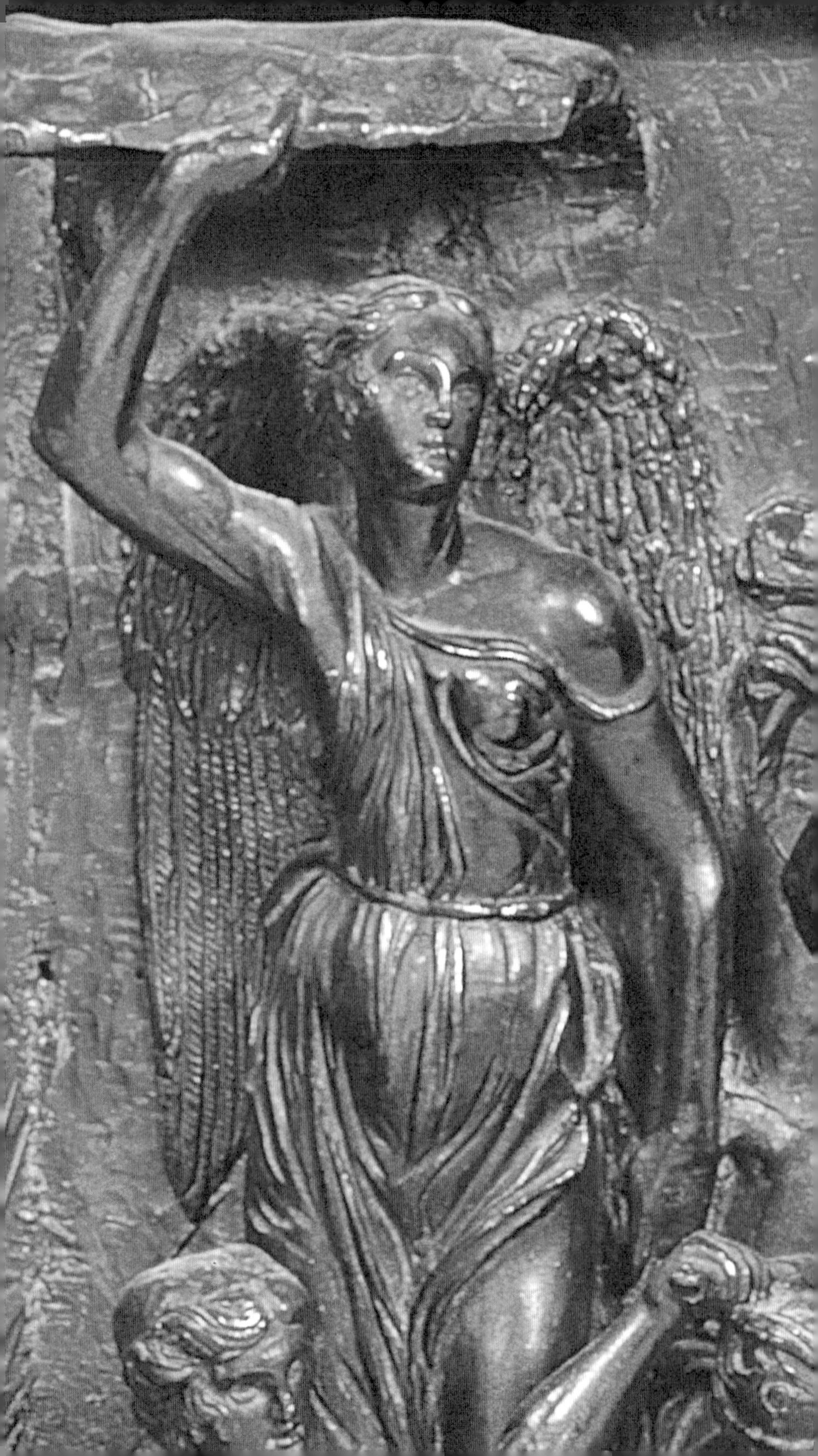

1   *Bronzes for the Ages (Bertoldo di Giovanni)*

New York's Frick Collection famously gathers beautiful artworks in a range of sizes, from ambitiously scaled paintings to smaller works such as Limoges enamels, medals, and tabletop statues, the kinds of objects that were crafted to be held as well as seen. This reduced, intimate scale was the one at which the Florentine sculptor Bertoldo di Giovanni (c. 1440–1491) excelled. Virtually unknown today except to specialists, he was eclipsed in his own lifetime by more epic figures like his teacher Donatello, his contemporary Andrea del Verrocchio, and above all by a young man who haunted the Medici family gardens where Bertoldo served as caretaker: Michelangelo Buonarroti. Bertoldo, in other words, spent his days among some of the great masters of the Italian Renaissance, in the Florence of Lorenzo de' Medici, and his own creations richly reward a closer look. With quiet insistence, Bertoldo's beguiling little masterpieces invite us to feel our way back into the texture of life in fifteenth-century Florence, with

Bertoldo di Giovanni, *Battle between Romans and Barbarians*, after 1478, detail. Museo Nazionale del Bargello, Florence, Italy/Bridgeman Images.

its bustling commerce, its vicious feuds, and the gossamer dreams its residents spun of worlds beyond their Tuscan cityscape and their daily pursuit of money.

Bertoldo cast those dreams in metal, carved them in wood, and modeled them in clay and stucco, producing Arcadian visions of gods, nymphs, and shepherds who never toiled for a living, sculpting Old Testament heroes and virtuous Christian saints, turning ordinary Florentines into knights and ladies from a mythic age of chivalry. Unfortunately, for all his skill, he often failed to pay the rent on real estate too grand for his earnings. Fifteenth-century Tuscans loved nothing more than a good lawsuit, and Bertoldo eventually attracted a small army of landlords who pursued him in court until Lorenzo de' Medici decided to settle the sculptor's debts and take him in as a *familiare*, a member of il Magnifico's extensive household.

Bertoldo's legal trail through the Florentine archives is especially precious, for he makes only two fleeting cameo appearances in our usual sourcebook for Renaissance artistic biographies, Giorgio Vasari's *Lives of the Most Excellent Painters, Sculptors, and Architects* (first published in 1550 and revised in 1568). Vasari describes Bertoldo as the "foster child" of the great sculptor Donatello, an apt description for someone who probably began his apprenticeship as a young boy.[1] After more than a decade of close association, Bertoldo had learned to imitate his master's style so closely that he attempted to clear up some of Donatello's incomplete comissions after the artist's death in 1466. Vasari reports that the similarity of their technique "can be seen in a bronze battle among horsemen, very beautiful," which Bertoldo executed for Lorenzo de' Medici, and in the bronze pulpits for the church of San Lorenzo (although these were finally completed in the sixteenth century).[2]

The "bronze battle among horsemen," once on display in Palazzo Medici alongside the family's collection of antiquities, now resides, like many former Medici possessions, in the Museo Nazionale del Bargello in Florence. Bertoldo based his writhing tangle of handsome men and handsome horses on the relief decoration of an ancient Roman marble sarcophagus he saw in Pisa, every missing head and limb a stimulus to his own artistic imagination. With a fine-tuned sense for composition, he turned the original subject, a struggle between Romans and barbarians, into a show-case for every kind of anatomy, animal, human, and divine (two sinuous winged victories in clinging dresses and a nearly nude personification survey the deadly struggle with godlike indifference). The bodies contort so ingeniously in three dimensions that we can hardly believe that Bertoldo has managed to compress the whole maelstrom into a space less than two inches deep. Vasari's assessment of the panel as *molto bello* is a rare compliment, but then he must have seen Bertoldo's marvel many, many times (he first came to Palazzo Medici at the age of eleven, to study with two young members of the family).

Donatello's mastery of bas-relief was one of the greatest legacies he passed on to Bertoldo, who created bronze reliefs on Christian themes to guide private prayer as well as classical scenes to excite other kinds of fantasy. Donatello was one of the first sculptors to produce plaquettes, bronze miniatures designed to suit customers who, like Bertoldo himself, struggled to balance high-flying tastes with middling incomes. And, as Vasari reminds us, Bertoldo "cleaned up" Donatello's magnificent pulpits for the Medici-sponsored church of San Lorenzo, designed by Donatello's friend Filippo Brunelleschi (a friend who nonetheless had Donatello cast into debtor's prison in 1412—Bertoldo was hardly the only artist who struggled to make ends meet).

"Cleaned up" is a revealing phrase: a Renaissance sculptor's work was nowhere near done when a cast bronze was freed from its mold. The metal still needed to be chiseled, chased (that is, pushed into shape), polished, patinated, and often colored, and the traces of that meticulous process are as evident in a statuette as they are in a colossus. Bertoldo carved his bronze work after casting it, and he seemed to gravitate to that medium the way other members of Donatello's workshop were drawn to marble. It is irresistible to wonder whether his parents—immigrants from Germany, the home of the foremost metalworkers in Europe—had something to do with this preference. His father, Giovanni di Bertoldo, and his mother, Barbara, were weavers by profession, attracted to Florence by the city's deliberate efforts to recruit skilled cloth workers from abroad (not just from foreign countries but from neighboring city-states such as Siena). In Florence, the family joined other German immigrants in Oltrarno, the section of Florence "across the river," and Bertoldo would continue to favor German neighborhoods as an adult, perhaps to please his mother, who lived with him after her husband's death.

But Bertoldo's bronze work also had a tantalizing local pedigree. Florentines were well aware that their city had been founded as a Roman military camp; the rectangular blocks of the ancient street plan survived in the centermost part of the city, and ancient Roman artifacts were a familiar sight: marble sarcophagi, coins, gems, vases, statues in bronze and marble, and bronze miniatures. Even more intriguing to Florentine eyes were the Etruscans, the people who gave their name to the region of Tuscany and once ruled much of what is now central Italy before the Romans subdued them. In the fifteenth century, when the population of Florence greatly exceeded that of Rome, the Etruscans provided an ideal rallying point for Tuscan patriotism, in pointed contrast to the imperial Roman symbolism of the papal state. Lorenzo de' Medici therefore sought out Etruscan antiquities to display alongside works of ancient Roman art in every shape, size, and medium. Many of the artists he fostered, like Bertoldo and Michelangelo, were evidently captivated by Etruscan bronze figurines, with their wiry physiques and exotic poses, just as Alberto Giacometti would be several centuries later.

The Etruscans nourished a special devotion to the Greco-Roman hero Hercules, whom they called Hercle, and so did the people of Florence. The city happened to adopt two ancient heroes as its mascots, Hercle from the classical world and David from the Bible—both of them, like Florence, small but mighty. (Hercules/Hercle also had a special association with cattle, and with those huge slabs of sizzling meat now known as Florentine beefsteak.) Bertoldo's statuette of *Hercules on Horseback* draws inspiration from ancient bronze figurines, but like his battle relief it sets out to better the ancients at their own artistic game. Normally, Hercules carries a club and dresses in a lion skin. He may herd cattle on Greek vases, but he is never shown doing something as sophisticated as riding a horse; in addition to being small, he was not very bright. But Bertoldo's Hercules is entitled to an extra degree of refinement; rather than the rough-and-ready, dimwitted strongman of classical myth, this rather unbrawny hero commands the obedience of his magnificent horse by force of character and intelligence—the horse has neither bridle nor reins, and Hercules is looking back over his left shoulder as his mount prances ahead. The skin of the slain Nemean lion is knotted by its paws around his neck, a typical detail, but this lion's majestic head is something special. Portrayed in three dimensions rather than as a flattened skin, it rests on Hercules's right thigh. The hero has turned his own head away from the lion's pelt, but he knows where it is; his right hand rests inside the creature's open jaws. With his left hand, Hercules grasps his club as usual, but also a garland of flowers and fruits, which is extraordinary. Another flower garland crowns his head, and despite his wild hair, both his beard and his luxuriant moustache are carefully trimmed. His marvelous mixture of crudity and refinement makes him endlessly enigmatic, and the same is true for many of Bertoldo's statuettes, from his dancing *Orpheus*, clad in socks and sandals as he twists in the ecstasy of playing his *lira da braccio*, to the two faunlike *Shield Bearers*, with their traces of gilding. The jaunty little goat tail on the Frick *Shield Bearer* is Bertoldo's work, but the shields and clubs that give the figures their modern titles turn out to have been added in 1908 rather than the Renaissance. Bertoldo was one of the first artists to create statuettes in the antique style, and his workmanship certainly lacks the supreme finesse of Benvenuto Cellini two generations later—but so do most of the ancient bronzes that served as his models. Like his teacher Donatello and his contemporary Andrea del Verrocchio, Bertoldo was a pioneer, eager to express new forms in new media. He was also evidently inspired by the contrast between wildness and civilization. His *Hercules on Horseback* is almost a gentleman, whereas his *Shield Bearers*, for all their grace, are still untamed forces of nature, wrapped in vines with unkempt hair, and his *Battle* depicts the struggle that turns men into savages.

One of the most savage events in Bertoldo's own lifetime took place in Florence Cathedral on April 26, 1478, when several members of the Pazzi family, a rival clan to the Medici, conspired to assassinate Lorenzo de' Medici and his brother Giuliano during Sunday Mass. The plot had covert support from Pope Sixtus IV in Rome, one reason that the signal for the conspirators to pounce on their intended prey (at least according to some accounts) was the moment in the liturgy when the officiating priest, the Pope's nephew, raised the host to signify its transformation into the body of Christ. Lorenzo was wounded but managed to escape into the cathedral sacristy, but handsome, popular Giuliano was butchered on the spot. The attack only served to consolidate Lorenzo's command over Florence, and to reinforce that command, he commissioned a medal. One side, labeled SALUS PUBLICA ("the public safety"), shows only Lorenzo's head, facing right, rising above a vivid portrayal of his brush with death. The other, with the motto LUCTUS PUBLICUS ("public mourning"), has Giuliano's head, facing left, above a crowd of swordsmen converging on his prostrate body and a second scene showing his body carried aloft out of the cathedral. The medal is roughly two and a half inches in diameter, and its two sides are, like so much of Bertoldo's work, quirky and original, remarkable for their convincing portrayal in miniature of violent action within an architectural space.

Bertoldo was no less ingenious when he worked in plaster and clay. Art historians now believe that he executed the plaster roundels that decorate the courtyard of Palazzo Medici, each one of them bearing a scene from one of Lorenzo's collection of ancient cut gems and cameos (many of them inscribed with his name). His life-size statue of a stark naked Saint Jerome was carved in wood and then modeled in gesso (a type of plaster) before he painted it, a startlingly vivid presence with piercing brown eyes that until recently were buried under a layer of plaster from a subsequent restoration. Along with ascetic saints, Florentines loved images of chubby winged babies, which they called *spiritelli*, little sprites. Bertoldo was a masterly crafter of fat baby thighs in bronze, painted plaster, and terra-cotta, this last a medium in which the Etruscans had been masters in antiquity.

The Medici villa at Poggio a Caiano outside Florence was designed in a fifteenth-century version of Etruscan style, with a pedimented temple front drawn from the description of Etruscan temples supplied by the ancient Roman architectural writer Vitruvius, with a terra-cotta frieze of white-painted figures on a blue background, somewhere between a marble relief and a giant cameo, on which we can admire a whole succession of ancient divinities, including a hook-nosed character with a hammer drawn straight from an Etruscan tomb. He may be the deity Demogorgon, who was not a real Etruscan god but rather an invention of the writer Giovanni Boccaccio, the author not only of the ribald stories of the *Decameron* but also of a *Genealogy of the Gods*. These primeval immortals, designed for one of the most refined patrons of the Renaissance, are the perfect terrain for Bertoldo's particular genius, inspired by the oddities of the ancient world as well as its classics, and ever ready to take contemporary art in ambitious new directions.

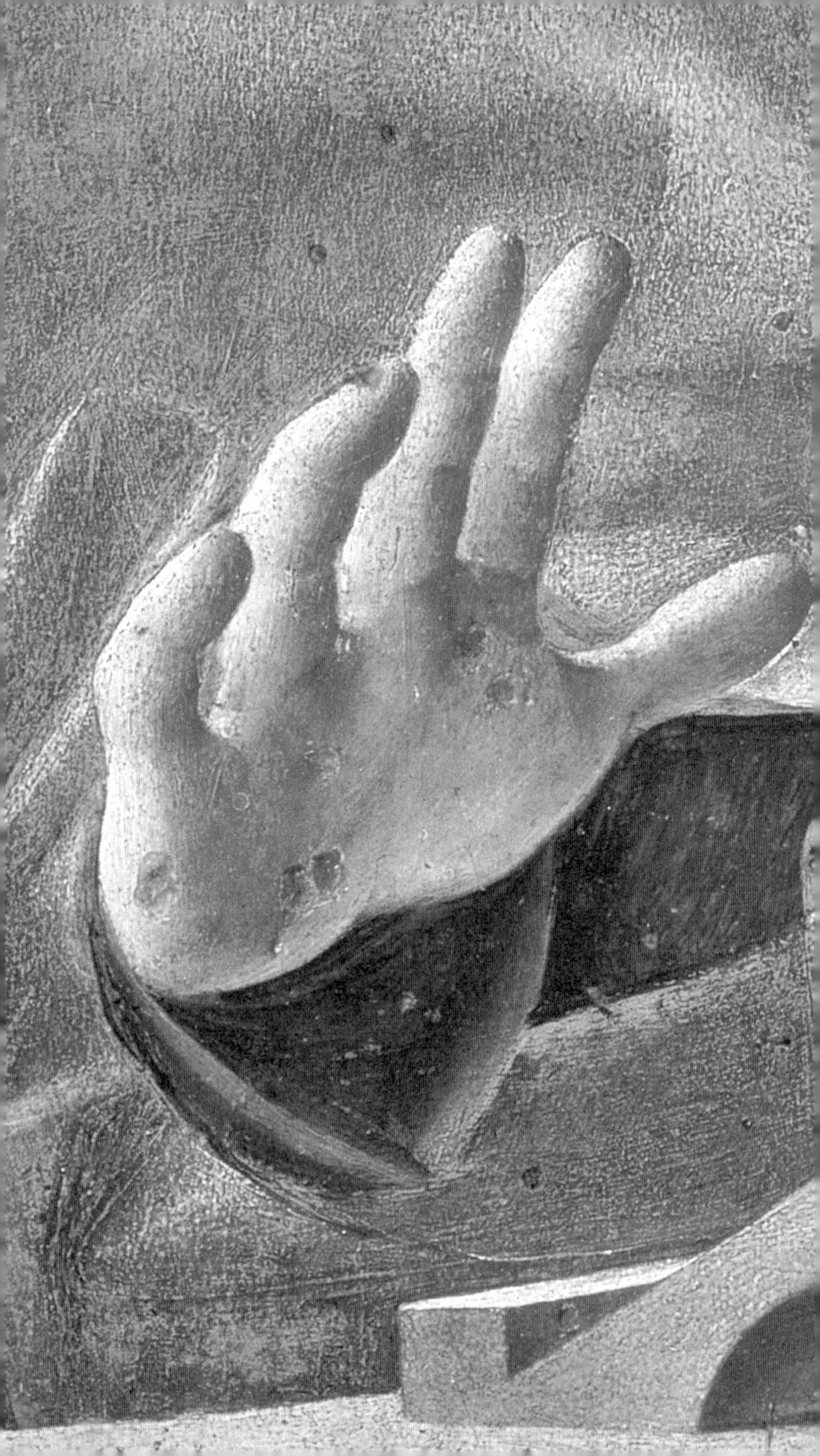

2 *"A Painter Not Human" (Antonello da Messina)*

In October 1608, the fractious painter Michelangelo Merisi da Caravaggio made a daring escape from a Maltese prison and set sail for the Sicilian port of Messina. Perhaps he chose Messina because he could count on a network of friends and protectors there, but perhaps, as the Italian art historian Mia Cinotti has suggested, he went for an entirely different reason: to see the works of a long-dead artist named Antonello, who in his radically different way shared Caravaggio's obsessions with light and with the fathomless depths of the human soul.[1] There can be no doubt that Caravaggio saw Antonello's paintings in Messina. We can see their influence on two of his own paintings now in Messina's Regional Museum: a *Raising of Lazarus* (commissioned by a man named Lazzari) and a poignant *Adoration of the Shepherds* that echoes both Antonello's resplendent blues and the older artist's exceptional gift for conveying the intimate bond between mother and child.

Antonello da Messina, *The Virgin Annunciate*, 1474–1475, detail. Galleria Regionale della Sicilia, Palermo, Italy/Bridgeman Images.

Caravaggio was hardly the only painter to fall under the spell of Antonello da Messina. When Antonello left Sicily for Venice in 1475, the Venetian artist Giovanni Bellini is said to have dressed up as a nobleman and sat for a portrait, just so he could spy on the newcomer's dazzling technique. Thirty years before Leonardo da Vinci developed his famous *sfumato* modeling and immortalized Lisa Gherardini del Giocondo with an enigmatic smile, Antonello had already mapped the highlights and shadows of the human face as abstract patterns in themselves and as clues to the puzzle of character.

His best-known portrait is that of a smirking Sicilian whose image was vandalized long ago by deep scratches through the man's eternally mocking eyes and smug mouth, but other portraits by Antonello convey mirth by the subtlest of touches: a half-closed eye, a quizzically cocked eyebrow, a sober cap defeated by a sidelong glance and a feather of obstreperous hair. The highest tribute of all to Antonello's artistry, however, comes from his son, who trained in his father's workshop and carried out their unfinished commissions after Antonello's death. One of these paintings, a Madonna and Child, is signed "Jacobello, the son of a painter not human" (filius non humani pictoris). Jacobello was more than competent in his own right, but as he recognized, Antonello belonged to another category altogether: immortal, heroic, divine.

Antonello painted only a handful of subjects (as far as we know), and always people: Madonnas, saints, businessmen, and the suffering Christ, crucified between the two thieves, alone and crowned with thorns, or dead. It is a strangely limited mix (no portraits of contemporary women, for example). He presents these persons, sacred and profane, in a way that is utterly individual, unlike what any other artist was doing in his time or ours. In some ways his meticulous detailing, influenced by Flemish masters like Jan van Eyck, draws heavily on medieval precedents, but the paintings themselves are as fresh today as when he painted them, modern revelations rather than relics of a bygone culture, despite the fact that they are images of men in archaic clothing and Christian holy figures, cracked, rubbed, worm-eaten, sometimes ruined beyond hope.

Antonello's real subjects are universals rather than particulars: love, despair, sorrow, amusement, and, above all, light. No one, not even Leonardo or Piero della Francesca, has ever paid such penetrating attention to the way light works. He knew nothing of photons or electromagnetic waves, but he understood, and recorded with uncanny penetration, the differences among beams, rays, reflections, glow, luminosity, and radiance. At the same time, he was a master of psychological detail and of nature, taking care to paint the reflections of infinitesimal ducks on a distant pond, or to set Saint Jerome at ease in his study by surrounding him with a scholar's ideal company: a placidly loping lion and a sleeping tiger cat.

There are several reasons why Antonello is not as well known today as artists like Leonardo, Michelangelo, or Caravaggio, though he is undoubtedly their equal. First of all, a frustratingly small sample of his work still exists, for his beautiful city, founded by Greeks in Homer's time (circa 730 BCE), sits on one of the Mediterranean's major fault lines and has paid the price for that precarious location many times over. Since Caravaggio's visit in 1608, Messina has been leveled by two catastrophic earthquakes, one in 1783 and another in 1908, when thirty seconds of seismic shaking toppled more than nine tenths of the city's buildings. Ten minutes later, a forty-foot tsunami crashed down on the devastated port, while a pelting rain continued off and on for miserable weeks, complicating rescue efforts and destroying many of the books, documents, and works of art that had survived the quake, the wave, and the aftershocks (almost three hundred of them).

Only one of Antonello's great projects in Messina managed to withstand this series of disasters (not to mention the Allied bombing in World War II): the altarpiece for the church of San Gregorio, crushed under its ruins in 1908 and rain-soaked for weeks afterward. In total, a little over thirty of this great artist's works survive, a disproportionate number of them painted during his year in Venice. Considering that between August 1475 and August 1476, Antonello completed at least ten works (one of them the imposing San Cassiano altarpiece in Venice), we could be missing more than 90 percent of his legacy.

Second, that paramount maker of early modern artistic reputations, Giorgio Vasari, never traveled to Sicily; he went no farther south than Naples (two hundred miles, or two days' sailing, north of Messina). Vasari knew some of Antonello's Venetian works, but by the time he made his own trips to Venice, in 1541–1542 and 1566, the minute brushwork and clarion colors of Antonello and Bellini were distinctly old-fashioned. Instead, Titian reigned as king of Venetian painting, with his huge canvases and paint applied in daring dabs and slashes. Furthermore, because Antonello spent only a year in Venice, in 1475–1476, the barest scraps of information about him survived in local memory several decades later.

As a result, Vasari's biography of the Sicilian is almost entirely made up, an attempt to account for Antonello's distinctive artistry by a Tuscan who basically regarded Sicily as off the map. Like many of Vasari's fictitious anecdotes, it is suitably dramatic: after seeing a painting by Jan van Eyck in Naples, Antonello reportedly put aside every other thought of business and went to Flanders, and in Bruges "became well acquainted with [the artist], making him a present of drawings in the Italian style and other things, until . . . he agreed to let Antonello see how he painted with oils."[2]

Not long afterward, Vasari continues, Jan died, and "Antonello returned from Flanders, eager to see his homeland again and let Italy in on such a useful, beautiful, and convenient secret."[3]

It sounds like a plausible explanation for the way Italian painters shifted their preference between the fifteenth and sixteenth centuries from working in egg tempera to working in oil, but it is patently untrue. Jan van Eyck died in 1441, when Antonello was probably about eleven years old, and Italians had already known about oil painting since at least the fourteenth century. On the other hand, a gradual change in taste is much less fun to read about than the adventures of a randy Sicilian descending on the fleshpots of Venice, which is Vasari's version of Antonello's life story. After his return to Italy, he stayed a few months in Messina, then went to Venice where, because he was a person greatly given to the pleasures and everything else to do with sex, he resolved to spend the rest of his days, having found a way to live that was exactly according to his tastes.[4]

Vasari's regional biases have persisted through the course of modern Italian history, and they continue to color contemporary views of Italian art. Messina is still assumed to be a bit of a backwater, and yet for Caravaggio, as for Shakespeare, the setting for *Much Ado about Nothing* bore a name to conjure with, no less than Venice and Verona. Despite the repeated ruination of the city (which has been rebuilt since the devastation of 1908 in a lovely early twentieth-century "Liberty"—i.e., art nouveau—style), its Regional Museum preserves evidence of a vibrant and distinctive local culture in Antonello's day, when the Mediterranean was a thoroughfare as much as a barrier, and Messina was a privileged spot on every nautical chart.

Nevertheless, we know very little today about the life of Antonello di Giovanni di Antonio. At the turn of the twentieth century, two Sicilian scholars (collaborators at first and then bitter rivals), Gioacchino Di Marzo and Gaetano La Corte Callier, transcribed and published a series of documents regarding Antonello preserved in the State Archive in Messina. All but two of these papers were lost in 1908 when the earthquake, tsunami, and rain destroyed the archive building and most of its contents, and dashed virtually all hope of finding anything more about him among the bureaucratic papers of his native city.

Antonello drew up his testament in 1479, when he was forty-nine years old; two months later he was dead. Fifteenth-century estimates of age are not always accurate, but on this evidence 1430 remains the best guess for his date of birth. Other records show that his father hired a ship to bring the painter and his family back to Messina after he executed a commission on the Italian mainland in 1460, that he gave away a daughter in marriage, and that he shared his era's penchant for lawsuits. Gaps of several years in the paper trail suggest that Antonello may have worked somewhere aside from Messina in those years (as he undoubtedly did before his return to the city in 1460), but he almost certainly never took the grand tour of northern Europe that Vasari's biography ascribes to him.

Instead, the young Antonello traveled from Messina to Naples sometime around 1445, to apprentice with a local Neapolitan master named Colantonio. Under the cosmopolitan reign of King René d'Anjou, Colantonio could draw from a wide range of European artistic traditions, including those of Spain, the Low Countries, France, Byzantium, and Italy itself, and he made the most of that broad opportunity. He worked extensively in oil paint like northern artists but placed his figures within Italian-style perspectival spaces, and he passed on this spirit of eclecticism to his talented pupil. Medieval Italian panel painters turned their raw powdered pigments into paint by mixing them with egg, which dried quickly, stuck stubbornly to a surface, and provided excellent, opaque coverage. Pigments suspended in linseed or walnut oil, on the other hand, glistened with an oily sheen, took much longer to dry (and could therefore be reworked), and could be diluted to produce a nearly transparent glaze.

Antonello, rather than adopting the oil techniques of northern Europe, adapted traditional Italian methods to recreate the appearance of Netherlandish art, with its lustrous surfaces and microscopic detail, but not its painstaking, time-consuming process: he often painted his figures in tempera, added oil glazes to lend them a Flemish sheen, and put in final highlights—the glint of an eye, a shiny fingernail, or a luminous pearl—as tiny applications of white lead. The rapid drying times of tempera allowed him to work much more quickly than a painter who relied exclusively on oil, and the large number of paintings documented for his year in Venice suggests that he may have maintained an impressive rhythm of productivity throughout his career.

Experiments, of course, do not always succeed, as Leonardo learned when he painted his *Last Supper* in dry plaster on white lead rather than using standard fresco, and lived to watch it flake away. The cracked condition of so many of Antonello's surviving paintings may have something to do not just with the natural disasters to which they have been subjected but also with their unusual composition: successive layers of egg and oil paint that have aged—that is, decayed—in different ways, at different rates. In his use of one pigment, however, Antonello was absolutely typical of his era: early in his career, he made his blues from azurite, a copper compound that can turn green with time. As his reputation grew, so did his resources, and he could afford the very best blue: powdered lapis lazuli, shipped from Afghanistan, the true blue that never fades. Its brilliant huc still blazes forth from the mantles of the Madonnas he painted in the latter part of his life.

Of all Antonello's paintings, the most remarkable, perhaps, is his *Virgin Annunciate*, a young woman who pulls a glorious true-blue mantle close around her as she takes in the message the angel Gabriel has just delivered: she is to bear the son of God. Her right hand stretches out as if to pause the angel's headlong announcement—or time itself—a brilliant exercise in foreshortening and a still more brilliant exercise in light, shade, luminosity, and the minute highlights that distinguish what art historian Giovanni Carlo Federico Villa calls "the greatest hand in Renaissance art."[5] Most strikingly of all, Antonello has put us, the panel's viewers, in the position of the angel.

Many of Antonello's Madonnas are plain-featured, with relatively short, small noses, in dramatic contrast to their aquiline-featured Byzantine counterparts or the long, haughty pointed profiles favored by the Dalmatian sculptor Francesco Laurana, who worked in Palermo from 1465 to 1471. (Today, in Palermo's Regional Gallery of Art in Palazzo Abatellis, Laurana's icily remote marble portraits provide a particularly suggestive foil to the warm energy of Antonello's Virgin.) But as two women passed by the *Virgin Annunciate* in Palermo recently, I heard one say to the other, "Now that's a real Sicilian face. She's *siciliana, siciliana*. I have a niece who looks just like her." This Madonna, and her counterparts, for their very ordinariness, manage to create something more marvelous than transcendent beauty: the miraculous illusion of reality, as if she were really there before us.

As for the smirking rogue with the curly hair and the elaborate shirt, we know how real he must have been to the person who attacked his face with a sharp instrument all those centuries ago. Five hundred years later, the Sicilian novelist Leonardo Sciascia still recognized him, and so do we:

Who does the unknown man resemble? A mafioso from the countryside or one from the best neighborhoods, the member of parliament who sits on the right, or on the left, the peasant or the lawyer? He looks like the writer of these notes (it's been said), and he certainly looks like Antonello. And just try to pin down the social status and the individual human nature of this personage. Impossible. Is he a noble or a plebeian? A notary or a farmer? A gentleman or a lout? A painter, a poet, an assassin? "He resembles." There you have it.[6]

Antonello could have become the court painter of Milan's lord, Galeazzo Maria Sforza. He made a visit, was suitably wined and dined, but in the end declined the offer. Galeazzo Maria may have had exquisite taste in art, but he was also a capricious tyrant, and Milanese fog was no substitute for the sun of Messina.

As a result, however, much of Antonello's work perished, preserved most memorably now in the notebooks of one of his most influential admirers, the Venetian-born writer and critic Giovanni Battista Cavalcaselle (1819–1897). Cavalcaselle's passion for Antonello developed in 1859–1860, when he began wandering from city to city in Sicily, on the Italian mainland, and in the rest of Europe, seeking out collectors and pictures to examine and record, his few possessions bound up in a peddler's pack. A fiery progressive, Cavalcaselle had joined Giuseppe Mazzini's short-lived Roman Republic in 1849 and took refuge in England when it fell a few months later, a death sentence in absentia hanging over his head. There he perfected his English and, together with the English journalist and diplomat Joseph Archer Crowe, spent the rest of his life producing a series of pioneering books in English on the history of art. *The Early Flemish Painters* came out in 1857. Following its success, Cavalcaselle went to Sicily to conduct research for their next project, *A History of Painting in Italy*. There, the exile could travel safely because his death sentence only applied in the Papal States, not in the Kingdom of the Two Sicilies. By the time *A History of Painting in Italy* was finally published, in 1871, both countries had been incorporated into the new Kingdom of Italy, so that Crowe and Cavalcaselle's title, with daring novelty, referred to a nation-state as well as geographical artistic expression. Cavalcaselle himself was free to move about in Italy, no longer a subversive but a patriot.

Cavalcaselle was a superb draftsman as well as an intent, insightful observer, his sketches capable of capturing every nuance of Antonello's portraits and sacred works—his smug Sicilian, for example, is almost as cockily obnoxious as Antonello's original. The records Cavalcaselle kept of works he saw in Sicily are especially precious now for their descriptions of paintings that perished in the 1908 earthquake, but there are also trenchant and often poetic observations about surviving works. He notes, for example, that the hands of Saint Jerome in Antonello's *Saint Jerome in His Study* "have suffered," by which he really meant that the paint itself was distressed, but somehow the phrase also suggests that the hands of the hermit saint, the Jerome who inspired the painting, have themselves lived through many an ordeal. The painting itself is a small marvel. Jerome's reading desk is a wooden structure set within an airy basilica with the same deep shadows, surprising light sources, and graceful lines of the cathedral of Messina, and the sunlit landscape on view outside the windows (which casts its own reflected light back into the interior) is undoubtedly local. Jerome, like Machiavelli, has dressed in his very best clothing (a cardinal's scarlet robe) to meet his manuscript, but he has also taken off his shoes before mounting the stairs to his seat; he combines respect with comfort. As a hermit in the desert, Jerome was said to have removed a thorn from a lion's paw and made a lifelong friend of the fierce beast; as Antonello's saint concentrates on his book, the lion quietly patrols the premises, while Jerome's little cat takes a nap next to two potted plants, a tiny peaceable kingdom by the sea.

Cavalcaselle was bothered, however, by the "vulgar" features that Antonello repeatedly used for his paintings of the suffering Christ. Rather than a handsome, regal figure, Antonello, aside from a youthful devotional image of a fine-boned blond with a wisp of beard, presents Jesus as a blunt-faced, almost homely man, his reddened eyes brimming with tears and his mouth downturned in desolate sadness. The most lacerating of these paintings is an *Ecce Homo*, showing the moment when the Roman procurator Pontius Pilate displays Jesus to the crowd in Jerusalem as the people who hailed him a few days earlier cry for his crucifixion. Critic Giorgio Montefoschi reminds us that we have no record anywhere in the Bible of what Jesus looked like, "but if his face is the one that Antonello has depicted—the face of suffering and of the lowliest—he is the one we want to love, and do love."[7]

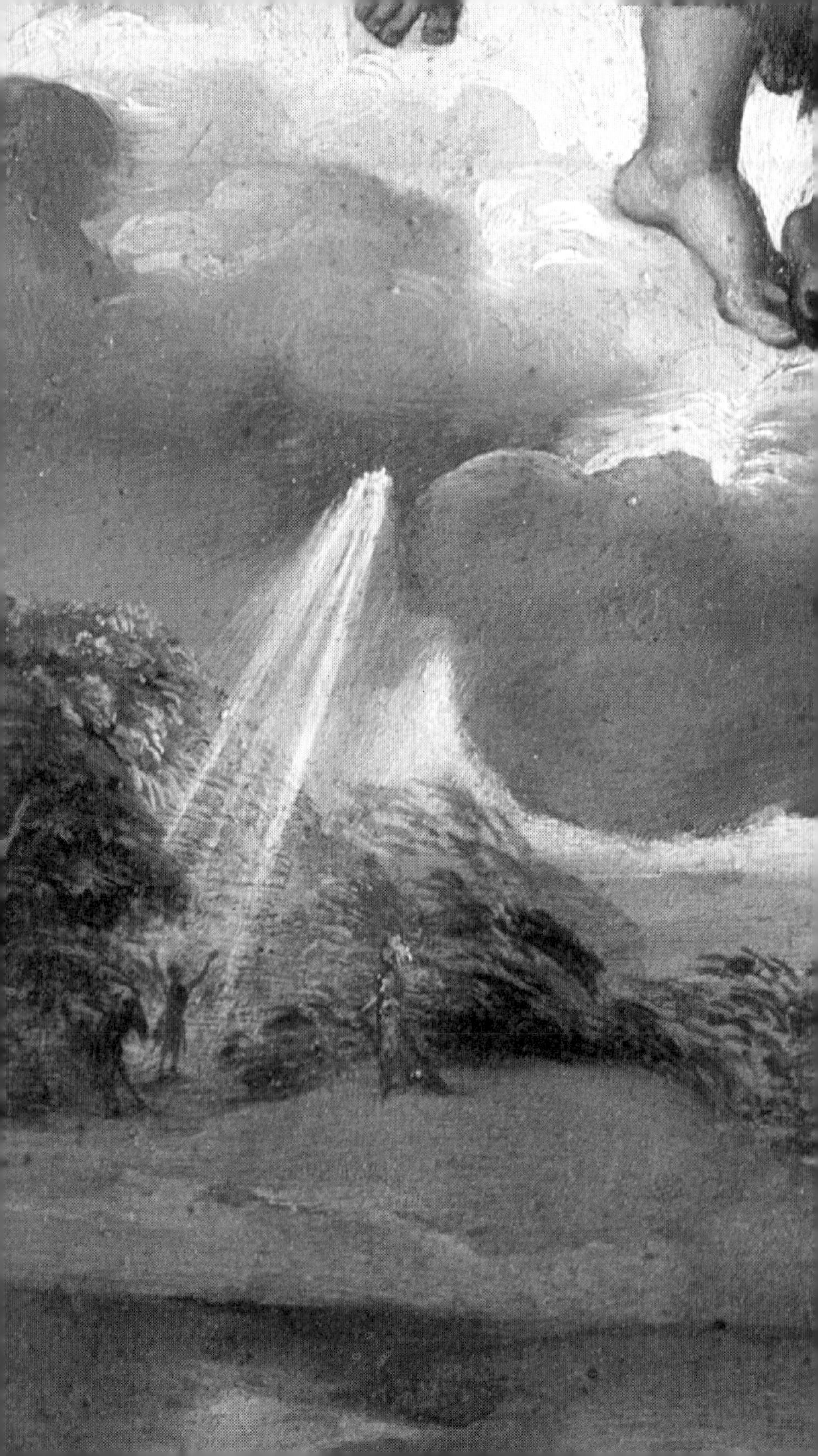

In its normal setting on a wall of the Galleria Palatina in the Pitti Palace in Florence, *The Vision of Ezekiel*, painted partly by Raphael, partly by Giulio Romano, is one small work in a multitude, most of them clamoring loudly for attention: Titian's *Bella* and Raphael's *Donna velata* vie for the crown of voluptuous textures—velvets, silks, pearls, hair, living flesh. Nearby we see both Raphael's portrait of Tommaso Inghirami in wall-eyed rapture, the veins all but pulsing beneath the surface of his skin, and the circular compactness that lends the same artist's *Madonna of the Chair* its intimacy.

Amid all this beautiful clamor any viewer can probably be forgiven for missing what *The Vision of Ezekiel* has to offer beneath its strange image of God descending in a cloud of apocalyptic monsters: an infinitesimal landscape with a tiny Ezekiel in the foreground, no larger than a silverfish, transfixed by a burst of heavenly light. But what a landscape! Its lazy river recedes back

Raphael, *The Vision of Ezekiel*, c. 1518, detail. Galleria Palatina, Florence, Italy/Bridgeman Images.

into endless depths between steep wooded hills. In the space of perhaps two inches by eight, the painting takes us on a dizzying flight straight up the Tiber valley to the green heart of Umbria, to the road that still leads from bustling cities like Florence and Perugia to Rome. It is a landscape as gently softened by the slow action of wind and water as Leonardo's famous drawing of the upper Arno valley is stark and spiky, and it is a vision no less evocative of nature's omnipresence, of perspectival depth and the artist's commanding eye—yet all contained within the lower margin of a painting that is largely taken up with a bizarre, and entirely unnatural, celestial vision.

A large tapestry showing the same arresting subject was woven on Raphael and Giulio Romano's design in Flanders by the Fleming Pieter van Aelst to adorn Pope Leo x's canopy bed in the Vatican Palace. In its textile version, Ezekiel's mystic amalgam of God, cherubs, and apocalyptic beasts floats on clouds in the pure blue-gray air, free of all earthly ties, including Ezekiel himself. Van Aelst, a master of his craft, evokes the radically diverse textures of divine flesh, fur, bursts of light, and vaporous clouds by minutely adjusting the color of his woolen filaments; in its effect, the tapestry is both a monument and a miniature.

In the painted *Vision of Ezekiel*, however, the most captivating passage is the most incidental: this incomparable, and incomparably tiny, miniature landscape. All of Raphael's preparatory drawings (and those of his assistants) concentrate exclusively on the airborne vision. The landscape seems to have been painted almost as a whimsy, but if so, it is the whimsy of a master. In its perfection this painted portrait of a place flies in the face of conventional art historical wisdom, which says that the old masters who managed large workshops entrusted this kind of background detail to assistants and concentrated their own efforts on the faces and hands of the major figures.

Certainly, artists' contracts often stipulated that the masters themselves would deal with hands and faces, but his works show that Raphael painted whatever part of a picture he chose: foreground, background, top, bottom, middle, everything, and, often enough, nothing at all after supplying the basic design. The only way to know what part of a painting he really touched is to look at it, carefully, in every detail. There are paintings in which the background steals the show, on a small scale like the Tiber valley at the bottom of *The Vision of Ezekiel*, or on a monumental scale, like the landscape that basks in sunlight behind the cold gray rocks where a painfully young *John the Baptist in the Wilderness* sits for a moment, stretching out a long shapely leg.

In *The Madonna of Divine Love*, a peaceful Madonna and Child rest at twilight with the infant John the Baptist while Joseph stands guard well behind them, almost out of the way, keeping watch over his family from a place within the crumbling vaults of an ancient Roman ruin, plunged into sudden darkness as a winter twilight shifts abruptly to night. If you stand at the right vantage, the ruin suddenly snaps into three dimensions as only Raphael's paintings can do. He worked this figure of Joseph, and this background, with his own hand, and it is impossible to stop looking at them.

When it comes down to it, why should a master painter be interested only in foregrounds, or figures? From the beginning of his career to the end, Raphael exploited every bit of the surface available to him. He also exploited the physical position of his viewers. To achieve its full effect, for example, his last painting, the *Transfiguration*, needs to be seen from a distance that can only be achieved under present circumstances by standing in the door to the neighboring room of the Vatican Picture Gallery. Then the upper half of this tall, two-tiered painting turns into a whirling vortex, a wind from heaven that presses down two of the three apostles who bear witness to the scene, and yanks the third one upward as it pulls Jesus, Moses, and Elijah up into its vacuum.

The spiral effect of the *Transfiguration*'s divine tornado is as forceful as an El Greco, and El Greco must have seen this painting, with its gyrating space and its silvery glow, on the high altar of the Roman church of San Pietro in Montorio; the future Pope Clement VII, who had ordered the painting for his bishopric in France, could not bear the prospect of never seeing it again, with the luxuriant (and arsenic-laced) silver yellows and serpentine greens that only Raphael could create by applying layer after layer of pigment, incorrigibly limited to two dimensions. But Raphael's red chalk preparatory drawings for the original *Transfiguration* stand by his associates' copy of his great panel painting as a reminder that his chief means of sparking their enthusiasm was the exuberant force of his talent.

Raphael and his contemporaries seldom worked in isolation. They learned their trade as artists by joining a workshop in late childhood, eventually becoming assistants, then collaborators, and at last, if they were sufficiently lucky and sufficiently talented, masters in their own right. Raphael himself managed a big, diversified workshop that may have included as many as fifty people at one time, from young boys to mature specialists who were dominant figures in their respective fields. Thus, under the general label of "Raphael," Giulio Romano and Gianfrancesco Penni (among many others) carried out drawings and paintings, Marcantonio Raimondi concentrated on engravings, Giovanni da Udine on stucco, still life, grotesques, and animals, Lorenzetto on sculpture, Luigi de Pace on mosaic, Antonio da Sangallo on architecture, each of them at the highest level of quality.

At the heart of it all, Raphael bound all their different sensibilities into a coherent group that produced huge quantities of art in virtually every medium, at the same time maintaining a distinctive, consistent style across the board. Sustaining this level of quality and consistency was an achievement in itself, but the most interesting aspect of the workshop was its harmony: in this brash, violent age, Raphael apparently deployed his forces with the utmost gentleness. As a leader and manager of fractious human beings under tremendous pressure, he provides a model for the ages. One wonders what the artist learned about management from his most important private patron, the wily Tuscan banker Agostino Chigi, whose Rome-based business extended its tentacles from London to Constantinople. Artistically speaking, Raphael's relationship with Chigi was one of the most important in the course of his career.

Most contemporaries called Raphael's associates his "boys," both because many of them were so extremely young, and because Raphael treated them with such affection.[1] In his 1550 biography of Gianfrancesco Penni, fellow artist Giorgio Vasari reported that

Raphael "took [Gianfrancesco] into his home, and together with Giulio Romano always treated them as if they were his own sons." Fatherly Raphael had lost his own father at the age of eleven, but Giovanni Santi must have been an affectionate parent as well as a wise mentor, at least to judge from his son's portrayals of Saint Joseph as the kindest of fathers.

Like an observant father, Raphael seems to have continued to put his hand everywhere and anywhere in the workshop, even when his interests had spread outward to encompass archaeology and ancient literature and his commissions poured in from all sides. These direct interventions seem to have been as essential to establishing his artistic authority as his sense of organization, his creative energy, and his agreeable personality, for when he does apply his hand to a painting no one can come near him, not even Giulio Romano, his most gifted associate.

Perhaps because of his own supreme talent, Raphael was not a jealous master. Like his distant uncle and mentor Donato Bramante, he was as competitive as any of the rivals he moved out of the way, but no anecdotes or documents record snide comments from either of these two gentlemen from Urbino about other artists' work. Raphael's rivals, on the other hand, could be vicious, none more so than Michelangelo Buonarroti and Sebastiano del Piombo, the Venetian painter who had come down to Rome with Agostino Chigi in 1511 and quickly lost the assignment of frescoing Chigi's villa to Raphael.

Sebastiano apparently cherished a grudge as persistently as his irascible Florentine friend Michelangelo. A revealing example is the letter he wrote on July 2, 1518, to Michelangelo in Florence. He had just been to see the public display of Raphael's *Saint Michael* and *Holy Family of François I*, two of the painter's early experiments with sharp contrasts of light and shadow, both destined for the king of France. Both Sebastiano and Raphael were inspired to try chiaroscuro—stark contrasts—by the example of Leonardo da Vinci, who was living in Rome during this period and had the *Mona Lisa* and some of his drawings with him. Raphael's chiaroscuro style was phenomenally influential, both in France and in Rome, and it is his example, rather than Leonardo's, that probably convinced Caravaggio to adopt the chiaroscuro style that quickly made him famous. But Sebastiano, himself a master of moonlit effects, was unimpressed by Raphael's results:

> It pains my spirit [he wrote to Michelangelo] that you weren't here to see two paintings that have been sent off to France by the Prince of the Synagogue. . . . I won't say any more than that they look like figures that have been standing in smoke, or iron figures that glow, all bright and all black.[2]

The epithet "Prince of the Synagogue" expresses more than simple anti-Semitism (though it expresses that too). Several of Raphael's friends maintained close associations with Jews, including Agostino Chigi and Giles of Viterbo, the influential head of the Augustinian order and friend of Popes Julius II and Leo X, who hosted a rabbi in his house for several years. For the Augustinian mother church of Sant'Agostino, Raphael had painted an image of the prophet Isaiah in 1512, in which he flaunted the powerful muscles and brilliant pastels that Michelangelo had just brought into fashion on the Sistine Chapel ceiling (unveiled in 1512), all, however, done with his own incomparable delicacy of technique. Michelangelo, who had worked across the Sistine ceiling with huge sweeps of a very large brush, could not have missed either the reference to his own work or Raphael's sublime dexterity in mimicking it.

Furthermore, *Isaiah* was the second time that Raphael had openly imitated Michelangelo: the first occasion was in 1511, when he inserted a sulky portrait of Michelangelo himself into his *School of Athens*, playing the part of the dour Greek philosopher Heraclitus. This tribute advertised not only the fact that Raphael could ape Michelangelo's style, but also—more mortifying by far—that he had obtained a sneak preview of the Sistine Chapel ceiling. Between 1508 and 1512, the space was supposedly off limits to nearly everyone, but Bramante and Raphael slipped in for a look in 1510, and the younger painter's treatment of Michelangelo flaunts the escapade, as well as his own ability to suggest a velvety texture that no one else, least of all Michelangelo, could achieve in fresco.

Raphael reserved the most velvety surface of all for his painted Michelangelo's suede dogskin boots, the one article of clothing the Florentine master truly loved. As for *Isaiah*, it is tempting to see him as a portrait of Giles of Viterbo's rabbinical friend and Hebrew teacher Elias Levita, because the darkly handsome prophet carries a scroll written in perfectly legible Hebrew. The "Prince of the Synagogue" was the Prince of Painting in Rome, however relentlessly Sebastiano tried to unseat him.

Between about 1513 and 1517, Raphael's drawings and paintings show a certain amount of confusion. His life was certainly complicated enough to confuse anyone. Orphaned by the age of eleven, now in his early thirties (he was born in 1483), he must have realized by 1513 that he had become the dominant painter in papal Rome, at the very pinnacle of an energetic, competitive heap. Then he lost two of his greatest allies and father figures in short order. His first great patron, the fiery, driven Pope Julius II, died in 1513, followed by Raphael's great-uncle and mentor, Donato Bramante, in 1514. Bramante, a close friend of the late pope, had been the architect who convinced Julius not simply to reinforce the thousand-year-old St. Peter's Basilica, but to replace it. In 1514, responsibility for this monumental project passed to Raphael. To supremacy in painting, he was suddenly compelled to add supremacy in architecture. He immediately set to work studying the *Ten Books on Architecture* of the ancient Roman writer Vitruvius, which meant learning Latin, archaeology, and construction technique while still managing the busiest artistic workshop in Rome.

The way he chose to face this impossibly challenging position provides another clue to Raphael's success, and indeed his greatness: he placed implicit trust in his young associates, confident that they would work to his standards even before they were mature enough to do so reliably. Antonio da Sangallo was twenty-nine in 1513, but Giulio Romano was probably in his teens, and Gianfrancesco Penni either seventeen or twenty-five. Raphael inspired his precocious "boys" by his own example, and also by keeping a close watch on every stage of execution, as works of art passed from the stage of commission to sketch to model to completed object. He gave everyone on his team ample room to experiment, and, above all, he let them make mistakes. For the most part, the results were good enough to pass muster with patrons, and morale within the group was evidently high; Giovanni da Udine and Penni, especially, were never as productive alone as they were under Raphael's direct guidance.

Gianfrancesco Penni was the son of a Florentine weaver, a painter whose work achieved something of the softness of Raphael's textures for flesh, drapery, and landscape, but as time went on Raphael used the youth more and more as a personal assistant; his nickname, "Il Fattore" ("the Agent") means that he probably managed the master's accounts. Raphael's death in April 1520 was especially traumatic for the twenty-four-year-old Penni, who quickly revealed his limits as an artist in the absence of constant direction from his mentor. A faithful translator of Raphael's complex compositions and an eager observer of northern European artists like Dürer, he never quite found his own bearings in the eight years he spent on his own (he died in 1528 at the age of thirty-two).

Penni was not the only artist whose creative fire seemed to fizzle out after April 1520. Giovanni da Udine's power of invention runs riot in the years around 1518. After close study of the surviving examples of ancient Roman decoration and a look at the instructions on pigments and stucco supplied by Vitruvius, he had succeeded in recreating the ancient Roman recipe for stucco in 1518 (the magic ingredient was powdered travertine). Soon Rome blossomed with his fanciful decorations, in stucco relief and in swift strokes of fresco. He peopled the Vatican Palace with grotesques, plants, animals, and mythological figures, in the loggia leading to the papal suite, in the suite of Pope Leo's associate Cardinal Bibbiena, and in the entrance loggia to Agostino Chigi's villa (the Loggia of Cupid and Psyche).

After Raphael's death, however, Giovanni's creative energy begins to slow: his work in the Medici villa now known as Villa Madama is dazzling, but less clever than his work a few years earlier, and the loggia he painted just beneath the loggia of Leo X is equally limited for a painter who once seemed to notice, and exult in, every detail of art and nature.

For one member of the workshop, however, originality was less of a problem after Raphael's passing than it had been before. Giulio Pippi, universally known as Giulio Romano, "the Roman," was Raphael's most talented, most privileged, and most unruly associate. He clearly loved Raphael, but his mentor's death also freed him in many ways, including the liberation of his ribald sense of humor (proof, many Italians would say today, that Giulio was a real *romanaccio*). It was only after Raphael died in 1520 that Giulio dared team up with the engraver Marcantonio Raimondi to produce a set of explicit erotic engravings in vaguely classical settings known as *I modi* ("ways to do it"). First published in 1524, *I modi* became an underground hit and a public scandal.

To be sure, Raphael had given the boys fairly free rein when it came to decorating the entrance hall for Chigi's suburban villa, where Giovanni da Udine produced some of the world's most suggestive fruits and vegetables, including an obscene coupling of a long green gourd and an overripe fig right above the entrance to Chigi's study. Just below this impudent assemblage, Gianfrancesco Penni supplied a flying Mercury who looks more stark naked than heroically nude, and throughout the rest of the room Giulio provided a bevy of buxom goddesses who wear no more than elaborate hairdos, no two of them alike. Chigi and Aretino, both on hand in 1518, no doubt provided appropriate commentary, but these exchanges were private, not public.

Giulio Romano found a similarly sympathetic patron when he moved north in 1524 to join the court of Federico II Gonzaga, Marquess of Mantua; in fact, *I modi* may have begun in that Lombard city rather than in Rome, as a series of salacious drawings for the nobleman's private enjoyment. But when Raimondi committed those drawings to engraving and mass distribution, private amusement became a public statement about Roman tastes. *I modi* mounted a less than ideal defense against the scathing anti-Roman pamphlets produced in Germany by another master of the printed page, Martin Luther, and for a brief time Pope Clement VII cast Raphael's former engraver into prison, ostensibly for violating copyright.

Recently, scholars have increasingly agreed that the famous double portrait of Raphael and a younger friend shows Raphael and Giulio Romano. The identification has much to recommend it, although there are some significant differences between the features of the young man and Titian's later portrait of Giulio in his prosperous maturity (unless the older Giulio had begun plucking his eyebrows and Titian ignored the shape of his ears). Infrared reflectography reveals that the two figures in the Roman painting were once posed almost side by side, but Raphael eventually thought better of it and moved his own figure higher, so that he could clap his friend paternally on the shoulder—another reason to suppose that the friend might be restless, ambitious Giulio.

The younger man's sword and the sober dress of the pair indicate that they are two gentlemen; in effect, Raphael is passing his hard-earned and still novel status as gentleman artist on to his protégé. Giulio knew how to accept the lesson; he was the one member of "the boys" who came from well-born parents, and in Mantua he became exactly the kind of gentleman artist this painted letter of recommendation assumes he will become. Men of consequence normally dressed soberly in early sixteenth-century Rome, favoring dark hues like the black the sitters wear in most of Raphael's "friendship" portraits. (Hence middle-aged Leonardo made quite an impression in his pink cloaks and pink tights.) The young Florentine banker Bindo Altoviti, on the other hand, sat for Raphael in 1511 clad in a mantle of deep blue, the better to bring out his limpid blue-gray eyes, bee-stung lips, and luxuriant blond hair (soon to fall victim to male-pattern baldness, just like the young Giulio Romano's raven curls).

We can only be grateful to Bindo and Raphael for choosing to privilege beauty over conventional sobriety. And it is hard to feel entirely sober in the presence of Raphael's portrait of his friend Baldassarre Castiglione, clad in muted gray and black, but in what sensuous textures, and with what scintillating points of red and blue adding life to the fabric. This was a painter who saw beauty in every part of his friends, from their character to their choice of clothing. It is a pity that no portraits of Agostino Chigi survive (apparently they existed).

Raphael pays homage to friendship of another sort in his *Donna velata*, both the portrait of a beautiful sleeve and of a beautiful woman, every stroke of it from his own hand, from the tendril of curling hair that barely brushes her face to the provocative finger that plays with the fastening of her bodice. The *Donna velata* hangs under normal circumstances in the same room in Florence as Titian (in the Galleria Palatina), with Rubens just down the hall, and they make perfect company: the three men whose love affair with women and oil paint reached the ultimate pitch of jubilation.

Raphael's assistants could never quite reach this level, though Giulio sometimes came close. Nonetheless, the gentle master consistently brought out the very best in the members of his workshop, as their creations with him and without him reveal consistently and unequivocally. In his own day, only Leonardo, Michelangelo, and Titian could rival his infectious exuberance and impeccable control. But neither Leonardo, nor Michelangelo, nor Titian could have produced the little vignette of the upper Tiber valley beneath the feet of Ezekiel's apparition. The bird's-eye view and the deeply receding space may well owe an essential debt to Leonardo (they may well have been inspired by the valley behind the *Mona Lisa*), but the sun-soaked colors belong to Raphael alone.

The panel is normally attributed to Giulio Romano, working from a drawing by Raphael. Surviving preparatory drawings, however, show only the apparition itself, a white-haired man perched somewhat awkwardly among the clouds on a quartet of flying beasts. The exquisite little landscape must have been added freehand. Giorgio Vasari, writing in 1550, assumed that the landscape was by Raphael himself.[3] So can we.

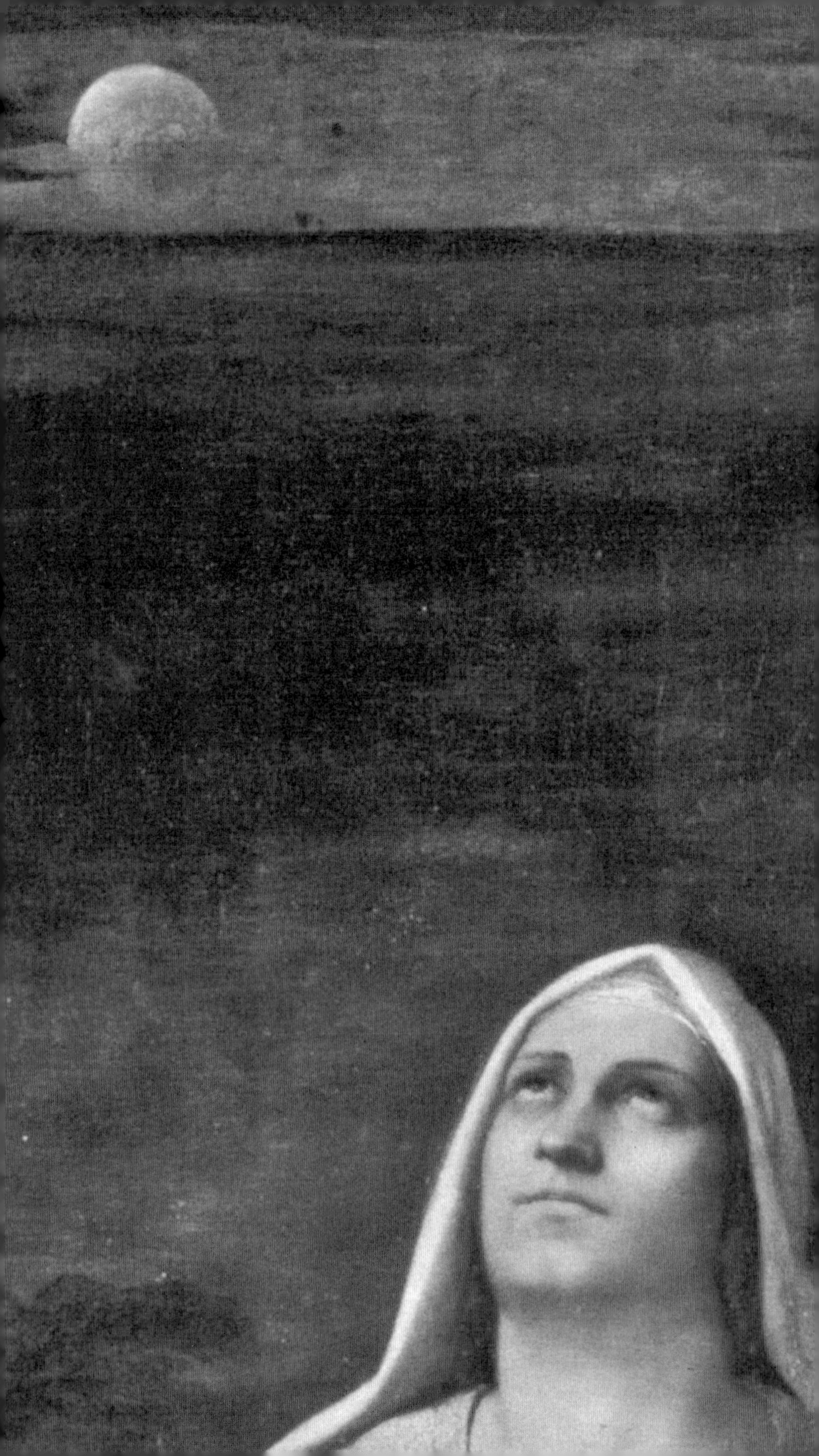

4 *Roman Rivalries (Sebastiano del Piombo
and Michelangelo)*

In theory, they were the perfect combination: a Florentine sculptor and a Venetian painter, a master of line and a master of color, Michelangelo Buonarroti and Sebastiano Luciani. The pair met in Rome, perhaps as early as August 1511, when Sebastiano arrived in the entourage of Agostino Chigi, a banker, diplomat, industrialist, and international power broker, triumphant after six months of negotiations in Venice involving France, the Holy Roman Emperor, and the papacy. Along with the hard-won treaty that linked these four powers in a Holy League, Chigi returned to Rome with 30,000 ducats pledged from the Venetian state treasury, a painter (Sebastiano), a Greek typographer, and the daughter of a Venetian greengrocer, his latest mistress. He set Sebastiano to work painting frescoes for his new suburban villa in Trastevere, "The Pleasure Garden" (*Viridarium*), the deceptively idyllic headquarters for his international banking operation. (Designed by Baldassarre Peruzzi, a disciple of Bramante, it was acquired

Sebastiano Luciani, called Sebastiano del Piombo, *Pietà*, c. 1515, detail. Oil on wooden panel. Museo Civico, Viterbo, Italy. Luisa Ricciarini/Bridgeman Images.

in 1579 by the Farnese family and has since been known as the Villa Farnesina.)

Michelangelo had also been painting frescoes in Rome, on the vast ceiling of the Sistine Chapel, a project that had engaged him since 1508 and would occupy him until 1512. Ironically, both artists would rather have been doing something else. Michelangelo, who claimed that he had drunk in marble dust with the milk of his wet nurse, longed to carve stone rather than stand for hours every day on a sky-high wooden scaffold, craning his neck as he swept his huge brushes overhead. Sebastiano had almost always painted with oil on wood or canvas rather than applying water-based paint to fresh plaster; fresco was not an ideal technique in the damp salt air of the Venetian lagoon, and he had little experience with it. He had probably carried out only one serious fresco commission before coming to Rome: a joint project with his teacher Giorgione and another young assistant, Tiziano Vecellio—Titian, the artist Chigi had truly hoped to lure away from Venice.

Sebastiano may have left Titian behind, but he soon learned that he had another rival in Rome itself. Raphael, two years older than Sebastiano, had just completed two large frescoes in the papal apartments, *The School of Athens* and *The Triumph of Theology* (conventionally, if inaccurately, known as *The Disputation of the Holy Sacrament*), large public commissions that revealed an unparalleled mastery of the difficult medium. Within a year, Sebastiano was no longer painting frescoes for Agostino Chigi's "Pleasure Garden." He had just finished one section of a wall in the summer dining room when Chigi suddenly passed the whole assignment to Raphael, who rose to the challenge with a fresco of the nymph Galatea scudding across the Aegean in a dolphin-drawn seashell chariot, nymphs and mermen gamboling around her in a sparkling, whitecapped sea. The abrupt substitution left Sebastiano with a burning urge to redeem himself and an incandescent hatred for his charming, successful competitor.

Chigi's villa still tells the story today: Sebastiano's frescoes in the lunettes of what is now called the Loggia di Galatea show skillful brushwork, novel color combinations, and some small triumphs, like a marvelous pair of spotted hawks and a young boy hurtling down from the heavens in a striped silk loincloth (not

Icarus, but Perdix, the nephew of Daedalus, who was turned into a partridge). Fresco, however, can be a treacherous medium, because its colors change in the first hours, as wet plaster turns to dry. Rather than working with the colors they see, fresco painters must predict what those colors will become, a skill for which there is no more reliable guide than experience.

Lacking that experience, Sebastiano gave Chigi a rainbow that turned brown, golden hair that faded into its background rather than shining forth, a peacock's tail whose shimmering blues devolved into chalky gray. With oil paint, artists can change their minds, but the most effective way to alter a fresco is to chop out the original plaster and begin again. Sebastiano, like most Venetians, went straight to work on his paintings without sketching them out extensively on paper, confident that he could always adjust figures and compositions as he went along: oil paint dried slowly, especially in the Venetian damp. This spontaneity shows with particular clarity in an ambitious early painting, a *Judgment of Solomon* from 1506–1509, that time has revealed as a patchwork of experiments.

But when Sebastiano gave his frescoed figure of Juno in Chigi's villa an impossibly long pair of calves, he could only hope that the dazzle of her peacock chariot would distract critical eyes from her defective anatomy—as it may have done for a short while, before the calcium carbonate in his drying plaster dimmed the peacocks' luster. There was no question of beginning again on these frescoes, however flawed. Agostino Chigi was not a man to waste time. His grandnephew Fabio Chigi reported that "he utterly hated all lazy people" (or as Fabio put it in poetic Latin, *ociosos omnes oderat omnino*).[1] Sebastiano's lunettes and wall have stayed as they were for five centuries, imperfections and all—charming, but only a cloudy memory of what they must have looked like when the colors were still wet on the wall. Raphael's *Galatea* utterly eclipsed them, to Sebastiano's eternal outrage.

The Venetian's skill at oil painting, on the other hand, remained indisputable. Shortly after Sebastiano's disappointment at Chigi's villa, one of the banker's associates, Giovanni Botonti, commissioned a large altarpiece for the cavernous medieval church of San Francesco in nearby Viterbo, to be executed in oil on a wooden panel. Sebastiano had already struck up his friendship with Michelangelo, who provided a preparatory drawing for this new painting, a *Lamentation over the Dead Christ*, or *Pietà*.

Trained in the artistic tradition of his native Tuscany, Michelangelo prized drawing (*disegno*) as the essential preparation for creating any work of art, in any medium, from jewelry to architecture. Prodigiously talented, charismatic, and overbearing, he supplied friendly fellow artists with drawings for their own projects, imposing his muscular style on a whole generation in Florence and Rome. The drawings were gifts, but they were also assertions of dominance.

Sebastiano had several reasons for gravitating to Michelangelo, first among them the sheer power of the Florentine's artistry. His first great *Pietà*, carved in 1501 for a chapel in St. Peter's Basilica, plays out its quiet tragedy with gentle simplicity, as a mother faces the death of her child in the only way she can: with pure, steadfast love. In this early *Pietà* Mary throws up her left hand in despair as her right hand catches her son in an iron grip; in Michelangelo's last, unfinished *Pietà* in Milan, a small, stocky Mary slings an arm around Jesus to clutch him in an embrace fierce enough to last forever. Michelangelo could be stingy, grumpy, and demanding, but he knew how to communicate love in affecting details that infuse human warmth into cold stone.

Michelangelo also introduced Sebastiano to the Tuscan way of creating art. The Venetian began to refine his technique as a draftsman, concentrating on anatomy, learning to manage details in chalk on paper before committing them to paint. His surviving drawings track his progress alongside that of his mentor, but when it came to a commission as significant as the Viterbo altarpiece, Sebastiano took no chances: rather than rely on his own *disegno*, he called in the master.

Finally, the two men bonded in their hostility to Raphael. They plotted incessantly to thwart him, Sebastiano in a spirit of coruscating hatred, Michelangelo with a cooler sense of his own superiority. Michelangelo claimed to have taught Raphael everything the younger man knew about art, but their exchange evidently passed in both directions. As for Sebastiano, despite his fuming, he knew good artistic ideas when he saw them and never hesitated to put them into practice. Artists have always borrowed from other artists, and these three drew from everyone and everything: one another, Leonardo, Piero della Francesca, classical sculptures, early Christian mosaics, ancient manuscripts, Roman ruins, the human body, silk, wiggling babies, and the endless bounty of nature.

For his Viterbo *Pietà*, therefore, Sebastiano combined Michelangelo's command of anatomy with his own command of mood and color, setting the scene of Mary's bereavement in a desolate, moonlit landscape between an ancient ruin and a run-down wooden shed on the edge of a turreted city. The beautiful body of Christ, silvery in the moonglow, extends across the bottom of the painting, stretched out somewhat awkwardly on a brilliant white winding sheet. When the panel was set in place, it would have been visible just above the altar table, a reminder to the faithful that the rite of communion would transform the bread of the Host into this very same divine body (a belief that Protestant reformers would question only a few years later).

Unlike the youthful Virgin Mary of Michelangelo's Vatican *Pietà*, Sebastiano's Mary is portrayed as a plain-featured, small-headed older woman, with a sturdy body and an athlete's neck, dressed in robes of a shimmering ultramarine blue ground from pure lapis lazuli. Most striking of all is the silver-lit nocturnal landscape—there is a full moon emerging from the clouds above Mary's head—with the volcanic crags of Viterbo standing in for the limestone hills of Jerusalem. Night scenes were rare but not unknown in medieval and Renaissance art, and Sebastiano's painting also drew inspiration from the menacing cloud formations of *The Tempest*, the enigmatic painting his master Giorgione had made in Venice around 1508.

At almost the same moment as Sebastiano's *Pietà*, Raphael created his own nocturne, *The Liberation of Saint Peter*, for the Vatican Palace, concentrating, like Sebastiano, on the contrast between cool moonlight and the red-orange hints of sunlight on the horizon. Raphael, however, painted his night scene in masterful fresco. No definite evidence survives to indicate who inspired whom (and their joint source may well have been Leonardo, who was in Rome at the time). It hardly matters. Both artists would spend the rest of their careers exploring the atmospheric effects that occur in the border zone between day and night, and setting intense light against varying degrees of darkness.

From his bumpy beginning with Agostino Chigi, Sebastiano went on to a successful career in Rome. In late 1516, one of his most illustrious admirers, Cardinal Giulio de' Medici, nephew of Lorenzo the Magnificent and cousin of the reigning pope, Leo X, set him the ultimate challenge: he asked both Sebastiano and Raphael to create altarpieces for the cathedral of Narbonne, France, the cardinal's new diocese. Working in oil on monumental wooden panels, the painters would inevitably compete with each other, a time-honored patron's ploy to get the best work from each artist in the shortest amount of time.

Michelangelo had returned to Florence by then, but he and Sebastiano kept in close touch about the commission, for which Michelangelo would once again supply drawings. Some of their letters survive, and show that both artists wrote in an expansive, confident script. Sebastiano's spelling shows that he continued to communicate in Venetian dialect, and his speech must have preserved the lilting cadence that Venetians ascribe to the ebb and flow of the city's canals. Michelangelo, on the other hand, took pride in his Tuscan heritage. In Rome, therefore, they both sounded like foreigners.

Sebastiano's entry in the competition shows the moment when Jesus calls the dead youth Lazarus forth from the grave and restores him to life. As he boasted to his mentor, the final composition of this *Raising of Lazarus* involved no fewer than forty figures, as well as some vertiginous perspective effects, and exploited the sheer drama of the story itself.[2] Michelangelo furnished the preparatory drawing for the figure of Lazarus, a heroic nude still wrapped in his burial shroud, as well as sketches for some of the bystanders. The biblical description of this event (John 11:39) asserts that Lazarus still smelled of the grave when Jesus called him forth from his tomb; he had been dead for four days already. Some of the spectators to this painted miracle shrink back from the stench, but visually the young man's resurrected body is already restored to glorious perfection.

Sebastiano presented his completed painting to Cardinal de' Medici in May 1519. From one of his letters to Michelangelo, it seems clear that the outcome of the contest with Raphael was never in question. Sebastiano reports that Cardinal Giulio "told me that I had given him more satisfaction than he was expecting," confident that he had triumphed over his adversary.[3] Raphael continued to work on his entry, the *Transfiguration of Christ*, but before he could deliver it, he died of a sudden fever on April 6, 1520, his thirty-seventh birthday. Four nights later, Agostino Chigi expired in his own ebony bed with its ivory inlay, at the age of fifty-three.

Sebastiano could draw a certain satisfaction from the fact that his *Raising of Lazarus* was the painting Cardinal de' Medici decided to send to the cathedral of Narbonne. He may have been less happy to realize that the cardinal chose the *Raising of Lazarus* because could not bear to part with Raphael's *Transfiguration*, which entered his private collection. (It is now in the Vatican.) Today, Sebastiano's *Raising of Lazarus* bears the accession number NG1 of London's National Gallery, the collection's very first painting, purchased in 1824 as an outstanding example of the classically inspired painting of Renaissance Rome.

Sebastiano also excelled as a portraitist, including several portraits of Giulio de' Medici, the same Giulio who commissioned the *Raising of Lazarus* and who became Pope Clement VII in 1523. A half-length oil painting on a wooden panel shows the clean-shaven, darkly handsome (if slightly pear-shaped) pope a year or two after his election, looking off to one side as he sits restlessly on his throne, isolated against a moonlit night sky. (We do not see the moon, but we can infer its presence from the beams it casts.)

The moonlight, beyond the visual pleasure of its silvery shimmer on the velvet pile of Clement's capelet, may suggest an association with Endymion, the young shepherd from Asia Minor who, according to Greek myth, attracted the attention of the moon goddess Diana. While Endymion slept among his flock at night, she swooped down from Olympus to kiss him on the sly. Pope Clement's friend and spiritual adviser Cardinal Giles (Egidio) of Viterbo declared in one of his theological tracts that Endymion could be seen as a Christian image of the human soul, enveloped in God's love but often as dimly oblivious to its condition as the sleepy shepherd was to the caresses of his divine lover.

Sebastiano's Clement, on the other hand, is watching something attentively. This Endymion, the painting seems to suggest, is a Good Shepherd with his wits about him. Clement's taut posture—seated in an armchair in red and white papal attire—deliberately evokes Raphael's famous portrait of an earlier pope, Julius II, as a man of action eager to spring from his throne. Raphael's Julius, however, is wrapped up in his own thoughts, and some of the discomfort in his posture stems from the pains of old age. Sebastiano's Clement, by contrast, is attuned to the world around him, although he seems to regard it with a certain hauteur.

Unfortunately, Clement was not alert enough to read the signs of his turbulent times. Martin Luther may have set off the Reformation during the reign of Leo X, but the movement spread like wildfire under Clement's watch. Rome itself was caught up in the increasing violence of the conflict in 1527, when some 12,000 mercenary troops, many of them Swiss Protestants, were released from serving Holy Roman Emperor Charles V in central Italy. Rather than return home, these soldiers of fortune saw easy money to be made by ransacking the Eternal City, which they did for nearly a year of brutal mayhem (as a comparison, Alaric and the Visigoths stayed only three days in the great sack of 410).

Clement was forced to slink out of the Vatican down the fortified corridor to Castel Sant'Angelo, the huge concrete tomb of the emperor Hadrian transformed into a papal fortress. There, like an ancient Roman patrician (and like Pope Julius before him), he grew a beard as a sign of mourning. Sebastiano painted him in this penitential mood, circa 1531—a small portrait head in profile—using oil paint applied to slate, the deep, somber gray of the stone enhancing the pontiff's grim demeanor. The arrogance and self-consciousness of the earlier portrait are gone. As for the painter, he told Michelangelo, "I'm reduced to the point that the whole universe could go to ruin, but I don't care and I laugh at everything . . . I still don't seem to be the same Bastian I was before the Sack; I still can't settle my brain."[4] By painting on stone, according to the papal secretary Vittore Soranzo, Sebastiano could at least make his works last an eternity.[5]

Sebastiano experimented widely with this durable new medium, as we learn from his biographer Giorgio Vasari, a much younger contemporary (Vasari was born in 1511). He also took on a challenge that bedeviled Leonardo and Raphael before him: painting with oil on plaster. In 1516, shortly before Cardinal Giulio de' Medici set up the contest with Raphael, the newlywed banker Pierfrancesco Borgherini, a Florentine with an office in Rome, commissioned Sebastiano to decorate a side chapel in the church of San Pietro in Montorio, knowing that Michelangelo would almost certainly contribute to the project as well. Endowed by the Spanish Crown, perched high on the Janiculan hill with a panoramic view of the city, San Pietro in Montorio was one of Rome's most fashionable churches. True to expectations, Michelangelo supplied most of the drawings, but it was Sebastiano who carried out the painting, after priming the chapel wall with an experimental mixture that has successfully held the pigment in place for half a millennium. Vasari reported that the secret mix included "mastic and Greek pitch [pine resin], melted in the fire and applied to the wall with a red-hot trowel," and praised its durability.[6]

Sebastiano cleverly exploited the chapel's curvature to lend more depth to the already expert perspective of his *Flagellation of Christ*. The figure of Jesus slumped before a colored marble column clearly follows a design by Michelangelo, and local rumors quickly decreed that the Florentine had come down to Rome to paint it himself. He did not—the work, on its specially prepared plaster, was certainly executed by Sebastiano—but it represents one of the high points of the two artists' collaboration.

Michelangelo had recently carved a heroically classical *Risen Christ* for the Dominican church of Santa Maria sopra Minerva in Rome—actually, he had carved two. As he shaped the face of the first version, a dark gray vein emerged in the luminous white Carrara marble. Marble is usually veined, but this particular vein occurred in an inconvenient place—the statue's face. Michelangelo managed to reduce it to a fine vertical line just to the left of Christ's nose, so cleverly concealed as to be almost unnoticeable, but he knew the flaw was there. Ever the perfectionist, he redid the entire statue, taking the opportunity, as always, to refine every detail: the pose, the angle of the Cross, Christ's proportions. The original statue now resides in Bassano Romano, a hamlet between Rome and Viterbo, where, retouched in subsequent centuries (especially the cross), it graces the side chapel of a local monastic church. The better-known second version still stands in its original Roman setting, to the left of the high altar in the immense Dominican church of Santa Maria sopra Minerva, but the figure's heroic nudity was too much for later sixteenth-century sensibilities, and a gilded bronze loincloth now sticks to Michelangelo's resplendent Christ with improbable tenacity.

For all his skill, Sebastiano suffered from what both his mentor Michelangelo and his biographer Giorgio Vasari regarded as a mortal sin: laziness.[7] Agostino Chigi may well have come to the same conclusion as early as 1512. The banker was famous for his parties, and Vasari reports that Sebastiano always enjoyed partying more than painting. (He also tells the improbable tale of how Chigi convinced a lovesick Raphael to finish a project by locking him into the "Pleasure Garden" with his mistress until the job was done.) When Pope Clement awarded Sebastiano the lucrative post of "Master of the Lead Seals" (*maestro del piombo*), the artist, married with children, complied with the requirement that he take holy orders and earned the nickname by which we know him, "Sebastiano del Piombo."

One painting by Sebastiano del Piombo is a revelation; a dozen paintings by him are enough to reveal all the formulas by which he worked—and avoided working. His best figure drawings were Michelangelo's, not his own—and in fact it was the request for yet another drawing that finally drove Michelangelo to accuse his friend of laziness. Sebastiano's ideal figures, both men and women, all have the same straight "classical" nose with large, flaring nostrils, drawn apparently from one ancient statue, the Apollo Belvedere. Clement VII is so strikingly handsome precisely because his nose is longer and more pointed than Sebastiano's standard: it lends him character. Every single one of these noses, including Clement's, is highlighted, without exception, by a white brushstroke down the ridge and a white dot at the tip.

Portraiture gave the artist real, idiosyncratic faces to work with, real clothing, and real objects. But without competition with Raphael to sting him and reality to catch his eye, he simply repeated the same poses, the same generic robes, the same expressions. Like another famously lazy painter, Andrea del Sarto,

46

Sebastiano invariably concentrates on the center of his paintings and neglects the corners—they both painted so beautifully in those centers that we can forgive them the corners, at least until Paolo Veronese reminds us what a clever corner can do. Sebastiano's backgrounds, even the eerie Viterbo of his *Pietà*, are simplified landscapes, with at most four layers of detail as they recede into space. Raphael usually provides twice as many layers: houses, hills, rivers, towers.

His last paintings were no more than listless replicas of earlier work. Sebastiano responded to critics, according to Vasari, by saying:

> Now that I have a living, I don't want to do anything, because today there are talents in the world who take two months to accomplish what used to take me two years, and I believe that if I live much longer, which I don't expect to, we'll see everything in the world painted, and these so-and-sos are doing so much, it's better for someone to do nothing, so that they'll have something more to do.[8]

"And with that," Vasari concludes, "and other pleasantries, Brother Sebastiano went his merry way, always charming and pleasant, and in truth there was never a better companion than he."

But if it's a painter you want, Agostino Chigi was right: choose Raphael.

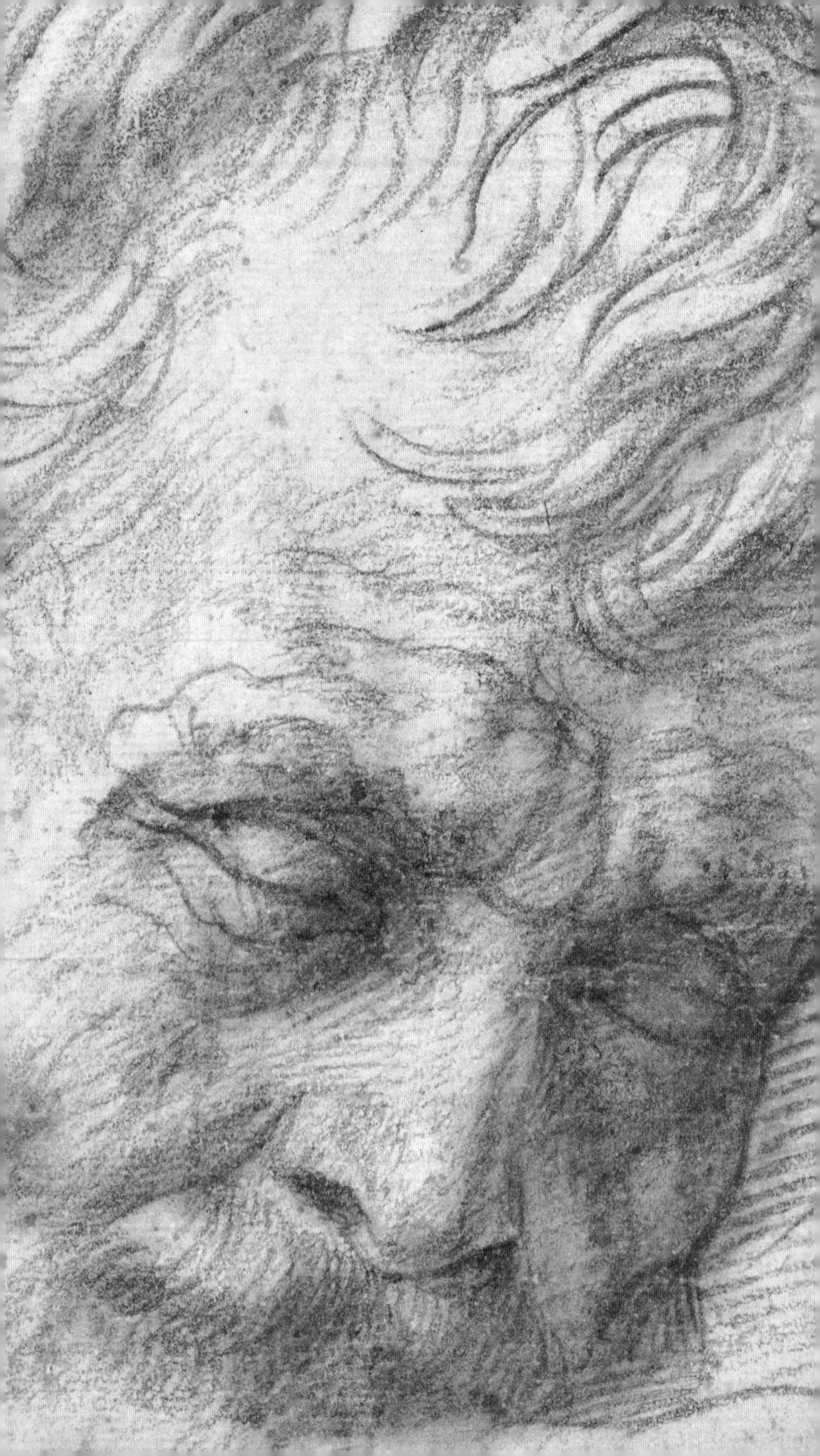

5 *Sublime, Exhilarating Andrea del Sarto*

Faced with a choice between advancing his career abroad—in Paris, no less—and returning home, the Florentine painter Andrea del Sarto chose to come home, a choice for which his ambitious student Giorgio Vasari never quite forgave him. Vasari's capsule description of his master in his *Lives of the Artists* is as sharply critical as it is memorable:

> And now we come to Andrea del Sarto, in whom nature and art revealed all that painting can accomplish in a single person through draftsmanship, color, and invention, so much so that if Andrea had been a man of a slightly more courageous and daring spirit (for he was profound in his talent and judgment), he would undoubtedly have had no equals.
>
> But a certain timidity of spirit and a certain retiring simplicity of his nature never allowed him to develop a

Andrea del Sarto, *Study for the Head of Saint Joseph* (recto), circa 1526–1527, detail. Red and black chalks. J. Paul Getty Museum, Los Angeles, USA. Penta Springs Limited/Alamy Stock Photo.

certain lively ardor, or that confidence which, added to all his other gifts, would have made him truly divine as a painter. For this reason he lacked the elaboration, grandeur, and versatility of style that can be seen in others. His figures, though simple and pure, are nonetheless well conceived, free from error, and supremely perfect in every respect.[1]

This carefully crafted account comes from the second edition of the *Lives*, published in 1568. At fifty-seven, Vasari had become an illustrious teacher in his own right, the founder of a pioneering state-sponsored art school, the Florentine Academy and Company of the Arts of Drawing (Accademia e Compagnia delle Arti del Disegno), as well as the preferred artist and architect for two competing heads of state, the grand duke of Tuscany and the pope. A man of such enormous influence had good reason to temper his words.

Twenty years earlier, a leaner, hungrier Vasari had written about Andrea at far greater length and with blistering intimacy. Nervous, struggling, and in debt, the neophyte writer had staked his career on the idea that people might want to read the biographies of artists, and hence for the inaugural edition of the *Lives*, published in 1550, Andrea del Sarto came wrapped in a cloud of gossip:

The most excellent painter Andrea del Sarto, more excellent in his life than in his art, was deeply obliged to nature because of a rare talent in painting. If he had devoted himself to a more civil and respectable life and not neglected himself and his neighbors for his craving for a woman who always kept him poor and lowly, he would have stayed in France, where he was summoned by that king [François I] who adored his work and esteemed him greatly, and would have rewarded him on a grand scale. Instead, to satisfy his own appetite and hers, he returned home and always lived in a lowly manner, and was never paid more than poorly for his work, while she, whom he regarded as his only good, finally abandoned him as he lay dying.[2]

The bitterness of this passage is the bitterness of personal experience. Like Andrea's other apprentices and assistants, Vasari lived in the master's house (which is still standing today, at the corner of Via Giuseppe Giusti and Via Gino Capponi), experiencing both Lucrezia's physical beauty and her volatile character. The first edition of the *Lives* complains:

> And although [Andrea's] assistants put up with the situation in order to learn something in his company, no one, great or small, got away without some malicious word or deed from her.[3]

Vasari lived and worked for many years in Florence, but he was not a Florentine himself; for him, home was Arezzo, another Tuscan city. If his artistic world had a center at all, it was probably Rome. But a native Florentine like Andrea del Sarto can be excused for putting Paris behind him in 1519: like many of his contemporaries, he regarded his own city as the artistic capital of the world. It was precisely his return from France, moreover, that enabled Andrea and his pupils, numerous and talented, to forge an entirely new artistic style for the new Medici rulers of a new, modern Florentine state.

For generations, drawing—*disegno*—had been the activity that best defined Florentine art. Long before they were allowed to apply color, apprentice artists were expected to hone their skills at drawing everything around them, from nature to people to works of art and architecture. Michelangelo's advice to one member of his workshop was typical: "Draw, Antonio, draw, Antonio, draw and don't waste time."[4] Michelangelo himself spent long hours in the garden of Palazzo Medici sketching works of ancient sculpture before he began to learn how to hew costly blocks of marble, just as his elder contemporary Leonardo da Vinci would draw endless plans on paper before he began to paint or build. Goldsmiths drew, embroiderers drew, architects drew, and thanks to a solid background in drawing a master in one medium could become a master in others. Filippo Brunelleschi turned his talents from the miniature scale of gold jewelry to the gigantic dome of Florence

Cathedral, Michelangelo turned from his marble *David* to the frescoed ceiling of the Sistine Chapel, and Raphael revealed a skill for architecture that equaled his command of paint. They were all trained in Florence.

Normally, drawings were only the means to an end, tools to be thrown away when they had served their purpose. Cartoons, the paper mockups for paintings, were particularly vulnerable. Pricked with holes or scored with a sharp point, they were often destroyed when their essential lines were transferred to a wall or wooden panel. Sculptors who drew their designs on a block of wood or stone inevitably hacked their *disegno* away in the act of carving.

Paper, moreover, was expensive, but it was also extemely durable (many of the fifteenth- and sixteenth-century books caught in the Florentine flood of 1966 have been restored to perfect legibility). Drawing sheets were pressed into service over and over again. On occasion, artists and architects would use more elaborate, finished drawings to present the projected design of a painting, sculpture, or building to a potential patron, and sometimes these presentation drawings were exhibited or passed around as artworks in their own right, as when Leonardo, perennially behind schedule, displayed his cartoons in public. Michelangelo sometimes supplied drawings to his friends for enjoyment and to his pupils for use in their own creations. In general, however, drawings were as likely to be discarded as kept. At the very least, the sheet of paper would be reused for more drawings until there was no room left on it.

In part because of his connection with Michelangelo, and in part because of his own ravenous curiosity, Giorgio Vasari was one of the first collectors to value drawings as legitimate works of art. He had taken to studying old master drawings as an aspiring artist, and when he gathered information about colleagues as an aspiring biographer for his *Lives*, he also sought out their drawings, binding them into a series of books. These books, unfortunately, have been lost, though isolated pages survive.

One leaf from Vasari's vanished collection centers on a pensive *Study for the Head of Saint Joseph* by Andrea. Vasari has inked a delicate frame around the figure, a black chalk study with delicate highlights of red on the cheeks. A scrolled label at the bottom identifies Andrea del Sarto as the author in elegant classical capitals. Here, at least, the pupil's awe at his teacher's talent has silenced every criticism.

Like Brunelleschi before him and Benvenuto Cellini after, Andrea, the son of a tailor (*sarto*), trained first as a goldsmith. Long before he touched gold, however, he had learned to draw with pen and ink, the standard medium for *disegno* in the fifteenth century, and also with sticks of hard red and softer black chalk. Leonardo and Michelangelo had been pioneers in the use of rust-red chalk, mined near Siena, and Andrea followed their example just as he adopted their innovations in his paintings. The hardness of red chalk provided a strong, definite line—brilliant talent that he was, Andrea normally laid out his compositions in a few flawless strokes—but chalk could also be smudged to create delicate contrasts of light and shadow. Sometimes the artist created wash effects by going over his chalk drawings with a watery paintbrush.

As a child of the late fifteenth century (Andrea was born in 1486, three years after Raphael), he learned to draw with pen and ink and to paint with egg tempera, a quick-drying medium that created hard edges and glossy surfaces, as well as fresco, which produced equally crisp outlines on chalky white plaster. By the early sixteenth century, however, Florentine painters like Fra Bartolommeo and Andrea had begun to prefer oil, which dried more slowly and could be applied in diaphanous layers to produce a softer sheen. Andrea reveled in his own version of Leonardo's *sfumato*—"smoky"—technique, which created dramatic shifts between light and shadow, but with such subtle changes in color that human flesh seemed soft to the touch and landscapes seemed to be shrouded in mist.

To these delicate textures, he added the blazing pastel colors that Michelangelo had unveiled on the Sistine Chapel ceiling in 1512 and the stately grace that Raphael was developing for his human figures in the teens of the sixteenth century. Andrea's painting is softer-edged than Raphael's, and his faces, with their deep-set eyes, have a brooding quality all their own that would inspire his pupil Jacopo Carucci da Pontormo to strive for that same intensity of expression.

Like any ambitious artist of his time, Andrea drew from ancient sculpture as well as nature; for artists of the Renaissance, the work of the ancients was nearly as divine as the work of the Creator. Sometimes the sculptural derivation of a drawing is obvious, as in the case of the red chalk *Study of the Head of an Old Man in Profile* from Berlin—this is an ancient Roman portrait of the poet Homer, and Andrea has perfectly captured the chilly sheen of light reflecting from marble. At other times, we may wonder whether the study of an arm or leg is based on the observation of stone or of skin. Amusingly, we also find Andrea's assistants pressed into service as models from classical or biblical antiquity. One kneels reverently, holding a sack that the master will turn into a lamb offered to the Christ Child for an *Adoration of the Shepherds*. A red chalk portrait of Julius Caesar sprouts an almost transparent wisp of beard; this Caesar is drawn not from sculpture but from life, and perhaps from life as it was lived in Andrea's studio.

Some of these drawings from half a millennium ago strike an uncannily modern note: the luminous figure of a young woman emerges from a densely cross-hatched shadow like the young girls in some of Picasso's Minotaur etchings from the 1930s; the black chalk drawing of a draped leg can also read as an abstract pattern of spiky, jagged lines.

The refined red chalk figure of a young girl who bows her head as tendrils of hair fall around her face may be the sketch for a penitent Mary Magdalene. For once the sitter is not Andrea's wife Lucrezia, whose gorgeous black chalk portrait makes the most of a medium that emphasizes the contrast between light and shade. Unmarked paper creates the highlights on Lucrezia's skin; the rest has been smudged to a delicate *sfumato*. In a masterful touch, tiny, almost imperceptible patches of light outline the bottom of her nose and chin to give her a lifelike glow; this is the work of a man who has looked long and lovingly at this beautiful face, perhaps while young Giorgio Vasari was looking daggers from the sidelines.

Disegno accompanied Andrea at every step of creation, from idea to paper preliminaries to painted panel (as a legacy of his tempera tradition, he preferred wood to canvas). His relentless activity of drawing and redrawing did not stop with sketches and cartoons; it continued as underdrawing on the panel itself and

54

then in incessant revisions of outlines and figures before the paint finally dried once and for all. Because pigments change with time, details that were once covered over by a layer of paint sometimes begin to emerge again; these ghosts are termed, not quite accurately, *pentimenti*, "repentances" (they are really the original sin, not the repentance).

In the *Holy Family* that Andrea painted for Ottaviano de' Medici, the painter turns out to have struggled long and hard with one of the Christ child's legs, yet after two or three tries, all of them now visible in a smear of *pentimenti*, it still seems to have come out too small. Curators can penetrate still deeper into a painting with the help of a technique known as infrared reflectography, which uses a special camera to photograph how wavelengths longer than the range of visible light reflect from its layers of pigment. In the case of the Medici *Holy Family*, the detailed red chalk drawing of a wizened elderly woman looks very much like Andrea's underdrawing for the figure of Saint Elizabeth on the painting itself. But the features of the Saint Elizabeth we see in the final painting have been smoothed and softened, her face turned into a more perfect oval, her wrinkles blurred. The unblinking detail of the drawing has been transformed into an ethereal vision.

This gauzy, ethereal softness seems to be one of the ways that Andrea del Sarto identifies his holy figures as belonging to another realm. We can see the same transformation from the exquisite black chalk portrait of a youth—who seems to be somewhat surprised that he has been taken into the artist's studio for a sitting—to the serene painted figure of a young John the Baptist in the wilderness.

Andrea's portrait of a young scholar retains its unmistakably individual features, including a cleft chin, strong nose, and brilliant eyes, the eyes and nose equally prominent in a swift preliminary sketch executed in red chalk. This youth is a scholar, not a saint, and Andrea portrays him with precision in a clear beam of light as he looks back over his shoulder in an arresting pose that owes something to Raphael's equally arresting portrait of the handsome Florentine banker Bindo Altoviti. But not everything about this precisely lit image is clear; the whitish object the young man holds has sometimes been identified as a block of marble, clay, or a brick, which would make this painting the portrait of an artist, and sometimes, as seems more likely to this viewer, as a book.

In contrast to an artist like Paolo Veronese, who paints with unrelenting intensity right to the very corners of his canvases, or Raphael, who can give a tiny background the same definition as the main event, Andrea concentrates his effort on a few central figures, or, as in the case of the scholar with the book that can also read as a block, on a face, leaving the rest in a pleasant haze. This uneven level of attention is surely what Vasari meant when he said that Andrea "lacked the elaboration, grandeur, and versatility of style that can be seen in others." His paintings, beneath their sumptuous surfaces, are rather stark and simple compared with the pinpoint detail of Bronzino, or Vasari's crowd scenes, or Pontormo's intricately interlaced compositions. We can see why Vasari could find his extraordinary master both so sublime and so exasperating.

Like his contemporary Baccio Bandinelli, a divine draftsman and a competent sculptor, Andrea del Sarto may be one of those Florentine artists for whom drawing had become an activity that Giorgio Vasari was perhaps the first to understand in all its significance: the most essential act in the mysterious process of making art, and ultimately the only act that truly mattered.

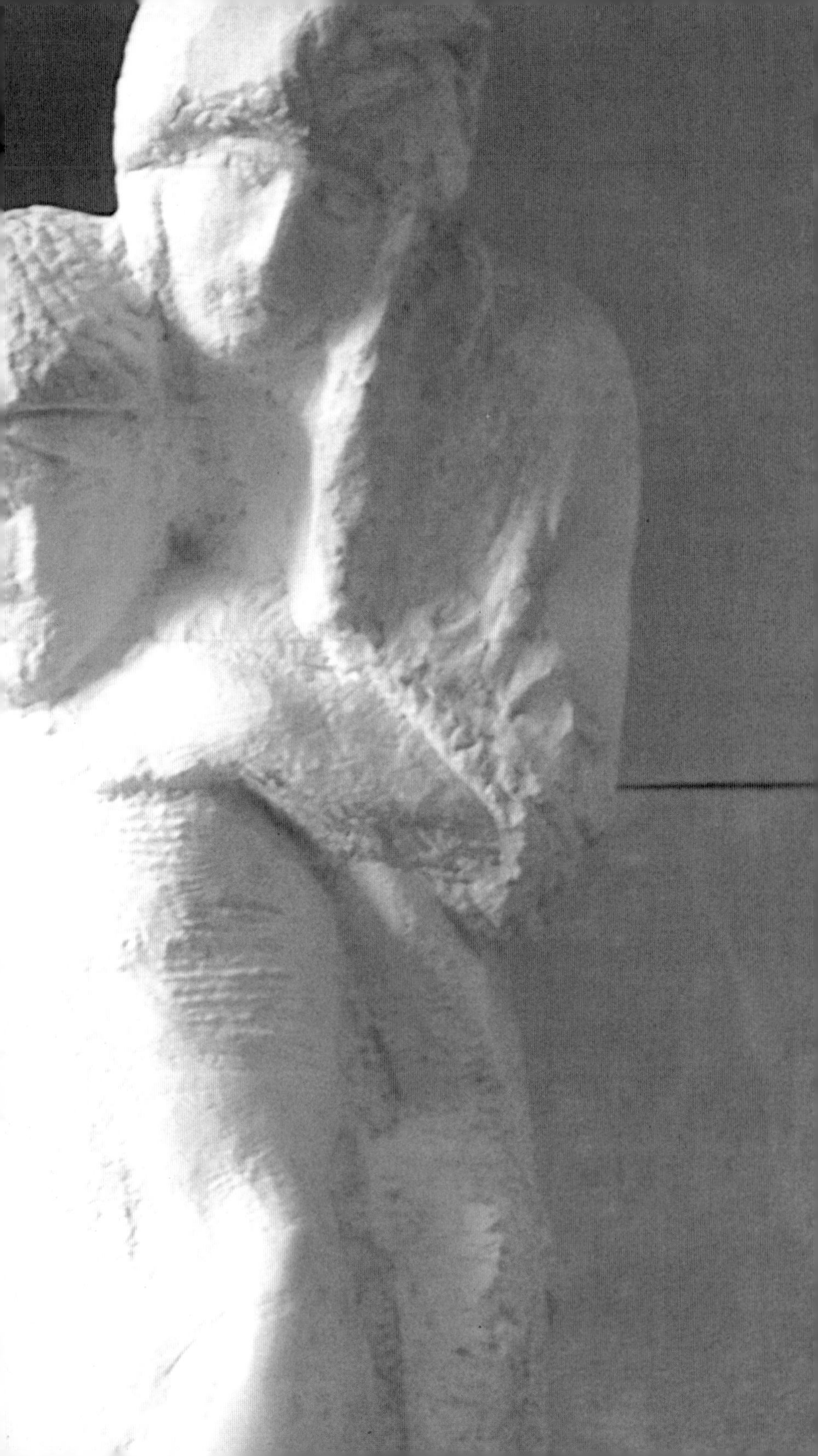

6   *He Made Stone Speak (Michelangelo)*

If Michelangelo's first biographers described his achievements as nothing short of divine, the man himself was beset throughout his life with mortal worries. They only increased with age. He was seventy-five when his protégé Giorgio Vasari described him in 1550 as sent down by Heaven to redeem art from its "endless futility," "passionate but fruitless zeal, and the presumptuous opinions of mortals, more distant from truth than darkness from light."[1] Fortunately, as Vasari saw it, God had a plan:

> The governor of Heaven . . . decided to redeem us from
> such error by sending to earth a spirit universally capable,
> by single-handed effort in every art and profession, of
> exhibiting perfection: in the art of drawing, by delineating,
> outlining, shading, and highlighting to give painting a
> sense of three dimensions; as a sculptor, to work with
> right judgment; and in architecture, to make our dwellings

Michelangelo, *Rondanini Pietà*, 1564, detail. Musei del Castello Sforzesco, Milan, Italy. 2010Stockvs/Alamy Stock Photo.

comfortable and safe, sound, cheerful, well-proportioned, and rich in the variety of their ornament.[2]

That same year, art's designated redeemer doubted in a letter that the new pope, Julius III, would need him, "given my old age."[3]

Shortly thereafter, in 1553, a closer associate than Vasari, Ascanio Condivi, published his competing account of the great man's life, apparently encouraged by Michelangelo himself. The factual errors they had found in Vasari's biography did not include discerning Heaven's role in Michelangelo's birth "in the year of our salvation 1474, on the sixth of March, four hours before dawn, on a Monday." Astrology was important in sixteenth-century Italy, not yet separate from the discipline of astronomy, and Michelangelo's father, as a minor aristocrat, took care to have a professional cast his newborn son's horoscope. Condivi remarks:

A grand nativity indeed, already revealing the greatness of this boy and his creative genius, for Mercury (with Venus in the second house), received into the House of Jupiter under a benevolent aspect, promised everything that followed: that this would be the birth of a high and noble creative genius, capable of universal success in whatever enterprise he undertook, but chiefly in those arts that delight the senses, such as Painting, Sculpture, and Architecture.[4]

When Condivi published his *Life of Michelangelo*, the "high and noble creative genius" was nearly eighty. Far from basking in the "universal success" promised him by his horoscope, he had recently become so frustrated with a sculpted *Pietà* in his studio that he took up a hammer and smashed it with thoroughly professional competence. As a visitor reported in 1549, the frail old man could still break up marble with astonishing facility:

I have seen Michelangelo, although more than sixty years old [in fact he was seventy-four] and no longer among the most robust, knock off more chips of a very hard marble in a quarter of an hour than three young stone carvers could have done in three or four, an almost incredible thing to anyone who has not seen it; and I thought the whole work would fall to pieces because he moved with such impetuosity and fury, knocking large chunks, three and four fingers thick, to the floor.[5]

Luckily, the repentant sculptor saved the broken pieces of his mangled *Pietà* and handed the wreck to one of his students, Tiberio Calcagni, with a request to repair the damage. Before he lost his temper, Michelangelo had meant for this four-person statue group to decorate his tomb, and therefore lent his own features to the elderly figure of Nicodemus, who bends protectively over the tragic tableau of the dead Christ, his mother, and Mary Magdalene, holding them all in his generous embrace.

Because all creative people start out as young people, we have a tendency to ascribe creativity to youth itself, but mature masters like Michelangelo remind us that the urge to create has nothing to do with age or the lack of it, but rather with that inventive spirit both he and Vasari called *ingegno*—inborn wit, cleverness, genius. The spirit often manifests young, but like wine and wood, it depends on age to reveal its full complexity. When Michelangelo turned seventy, he had nineteen more years to live, every one of them spent at work. As dear friends died and his body weakened, he took on a remarkable series of huge, daunting projects, fully aware that he would never live to see them completed. In his deeply spiritual vision of the world, his own limits hardly mattered; God had called him, and he had answered.[6]

Michelangelo's dilapidated Roman studio, set in an area with the inauspicious name of Macel de' Corvi (Crows' Market), fell victim long ago to the urban dreams of a nineteenth-century unified Italian state and the imperial designs of Benito Mussolini. Today a discreet plaque on the side of the mock-Venetian Palazzo delle Assicurazioni Generali on the vast Piazza Venezia commemorates the site, sacrificed in the early twentieth century to the Roman headquarters of an insurance company. Where idling taxicabs now spew their exhaust in the shadow of Trajan's Column, Michelangelo inhabited a Rome that still had a foot in the Middle Ages, surrounded by the scents of the Macel de' Corvi's butcher shops, the filthy streets, and the chestnut horse in his stable, the modest luxury of an older man who no longer walked so well. Marvelous statues peopled his studio, where he made a home amid the raw stone and the masterpieces, in the company of his kindly caretakers, the housekeeper, and the cat.

Sometimes Michelangelo climbed the steep slope behind his house to meet his aristocratic friend Vittoria Colonna, Marchioness of Pescara, at a terrace on the Quirinal Hill. There, overlooking the city, they could contemplate the view of the unfinished St. Peter's Basilica, soon to become the artist's most challenging commission of all: a man in his eighties, charged with putting the largest dome in the world on the largest church in the world, inventing a new kind of construction technique as he inspected the goings-on from a wooden scaffolding suspended 150 feet in the air, venturing, as ever, fearlessly out into the void.

Michelangelo was a man of coruscating passions, flashes of destructive temper, and affections so intense that they sometimes scared his friends away. He was introduced to Vittoria Colonna in 1536, when he was sixty-one and she was in her mid-forties. Her sprawling family castle, Palazzo Colonna, a medieval fortress on the site of an ancient temple (transformed along elegant baroque lines in the eighteenth century), loomed over Michelangelo's humble, odoriferous Macel de' Corvi, but Vittoria lived, when in Rome, in a convent. Her patrician lineage thrilled him, and so did her status as a published poet; each of them was starstruck by the other, probably to an equal degree.

Their friendship ebbed and flowed; both were complicated characters, deeply religious but prey to their vanities, warmhearted but impossibly demanding. Both of them received, and to some extent encouraged, a cultlike devotion. Neither of them quite fit into their hierarchical society, and nor did their friendship. Colonna would summon her new friend for a conversation and then, as the flatteries flew back and forth, remind him that they should be fixing their thoughts on religion; her way, perhaps, of keeping the artist's epic emotions at a comfortable distance. Theirs was not a romance in the conventional sense; Michelangelo reserved those feelings for another younger friend, Tommaso de' Cavalieri, and the portrait drawing he presented to Tommaso is a more polished work in every way than the devotional drawings he produced for the pious marchioness.

Vittoria Colonna was not a beautiful woman, and perhaps that is why she took such peculiar pride in her shapely breasts. They make a conspicuous appearance in most of her portraits, in odd contrast to her proper widow's weeds, and they also figure with jarring prominence in the fulsome praise lavished on her by the writer Paolo Giovio. Michelangelo presented her with his drawing of a *Pietà*, a Virgin Mary mourning over the body of her son, dressed in a gown that emphasizes the Madonna's own monumental bosom.

Like so many of Michelangelo's close friends, Colonna died long before him, at a much younger age. One by one, his patrons, his assistants, and his friends slipped away, compelling him to find new companions. They included the strange residents of his studio: figures of heroic men and women emerging, with every blow of his chisel, from their mysterious marble shrouds. Michelangelo loved releasing these characters from their captivity. His copy of Colonna's collected poems is signed *"Michelangelo schultore"*—that was how he thought of himself. Despite the fact that his learned contemporaries regarded sculpture as the lowest of the arts because it required such hard physical labor and generated so much noise and dust, he knew their talk was nothing but talk. What could be more majestic than a colossus, and who knew better than he how to create one?

Michelangelo carved stone with matchless speed and facility, but the fact that he shaped his works instinctively rather than by careful advance preparation led him into trouble as well as success; his studio was filled with half-finished projects, some of them impossible to complete, some of them familiar if silent friends. For years, he kept his monumental *Moses* at home as he struggled to finish its companion figures for the long-overdue tomb of Pope Julius II. Reportedly he smacked it on the knee and ordered, "Speak!"; one wonders whether, in the privacy of the studio, it actually did from time to time. When Moses finally left his long residence in the Macel de' Corvi for his present home in the church of San Pietro in Vincoli, the journey was short but arduous: a gigantic

Hebrew prophet riding on a cart through treacherous, unpaved Roman streets.

If sculpture stood lowest on the totem pole of the Renaissance arts, architecture stood at the pinnacle, for it included elements of drawing, painting, and sculpture as well as its own particular specialties: shaping cities and enclosing space. And because of its complexity, architecture, more than the other arts, was an older man's game in Renaissance Italy. Most of those older men, like Michelangelo, had served out their apprenticeship in some other profession.

The guild system, with its hierarchical network of masters and apprentices, meant that only experienced men were likely to be entrusted with the large budgets, large workforces, and myriad problems involved in construction. Filippo Brunelleschi belonged to the goldsmiths' guild; Donato Bramante, Raphael, and Baldassarre Peruzzi began as painters; Leon Battista Alberti and Fra Giovanni Giocondo da Verona were educated as classical scholars and learned to draw because all gentlemen did, just as they learned to play a musical instrument. Vasari was tutored in the classics before his apprenticeship to an artist. There were exceptional people who worked as architects from the very beginning of their careers, but they entered the profession at a lower rung of the social ladder, like the Sienese architect, engineer, and theorist Francesco di Giorgio Martini, whose father had been a purveyor of chickens, and the Sangallo dynasty of architects, descended from a Florentine woodworker.

The dome of St. Peter's presented the elderly Michelangelo with challenges on every conceivable front, from the declining powers of his own body to the demands of spiritual aesthetics to the physics of construction. Simply climbing the thirteen stories to the base of the dome was an effort in itself: somewhat unsteady on his feet, he rarely made the ascent. Shortly after accepting the weighty assignment from Pope Paul III, Michelangelo realized that the basilica's rising dome had grave structural flaws. The only solution was to demolish the existing structure and rebuild it from scratch, while preserving the cavernous church on which it rested. In the middle of the sixteenth century, he had been called upon to perform a twentieth- or twenty-first-century task: dismantling the upper levels of a high-rise without compromising the rest of the building. Furthermore, this particular high-rise loomed over the horizon in plain view for miles around. No one was prepared to watch its majestic outline shrink rather than ascend to glorious new heights.

To convince the pope, Michelangelo brought forth all the social graces he had learned as a youth in Florence at the court of Lorenzo the Magnificent, and succeeded both in getting permission for the demolition and in carrying it out, driven, as he would later write to Giorgio Vasari, "by the love of God and Saint Peter."[7] The completed dome (finished after Michelangelo's death, with a taller profile, by Giacomo della Porta) proves how attentively he solved the problems the previous dome had failed to address. That driving sense of responsibility to the pope and Saint Peter kept him from ever returning to his beloved Florence.

The truth is that not one of Michelangelo's creations can be conveyed easily in a photograph. The Sistine Chapel ceiling dazzles our eyes so dynamically because it curves in a gentle arch. *David* is meant to be seen from every direction, but the camera can provide only one. Without standing inside the Laurentian Library and the Medici Chapel we can never truly feel the way Michelangelo has shaped these enclosing spaces by the careful arrangement of solid columns, statues, cornices, and consoles. But his late projects present, if anything, a steeper challenge. St. Peter's is larger than our senses can grasp even when we are standing beneath its massive dome; there is no way to reproduce that disconcerting three-dimensional discomfort on a comfortably sized page. More interesting, and infinitely more moving, are the ways in which Michelangelo's last two statues—that ravaged *Pietà* now in Florence and another, equally battered *Pietà* in Milan—strike right through to the soul by some magical trick of the old man's chisel. It doesn't matter that they are both unpolished ruins; Michelangelo has passed beyond the idea of completion to single out a universally recognizable instant through an eloquent detail.

With the "Bandini" *Pietà* in Florence, it is the figure of Nicodemus and his solicitous embrace; by carving his own portrait into the elder's face, Michelangelo has turned his act of creation into a way of caring not just for his figures and the people they represent, but also for the viewers who take the time to stay awhile in their presence. Through his art, Michelangelo, in the person of Nicodemus, has assumed the burden of caring for *us*. He cares as fiercely as Caravaggio cares, actively, irresistibly, and he shows his care by letting us experience his pain as a pledge that he, in turn, will honor ours. *David*, completed when the artist was about thirty, presents humanity in the magnificence of youth, pride, and vigor. These late sculptures present nothing so much as the stubborn endurance of love in spite of everything: weakness, injustice, and death itself.

Michelangelo's last statue, another *Pietà* (the "Rondanini"), shows a tiny, muscular Virgin Mary holding the slumped, elongated body of her son. Their faces are barely sketched. Jesus has a free-floating extra arm, the remnant of a previous composition; Michelangelo vandalized this work as he had vandalized his previous *Pietà*. It hardly matters. What survives, and what no photograph can reveal, is the tension a master sculptor can pack into the Virgin's sturdy legs, riveted to the ground as she sustains this unbearable burden, and the steadfast grip of the arm she has flung around her son's corpse. She could be Atlas holding up the world, and indeed Michelangelo's faith told him that in that moment she was clasping all of human salvation to her heart. She is a scrappy little Italian mamma performing the task of a Titan. And she will never let go.

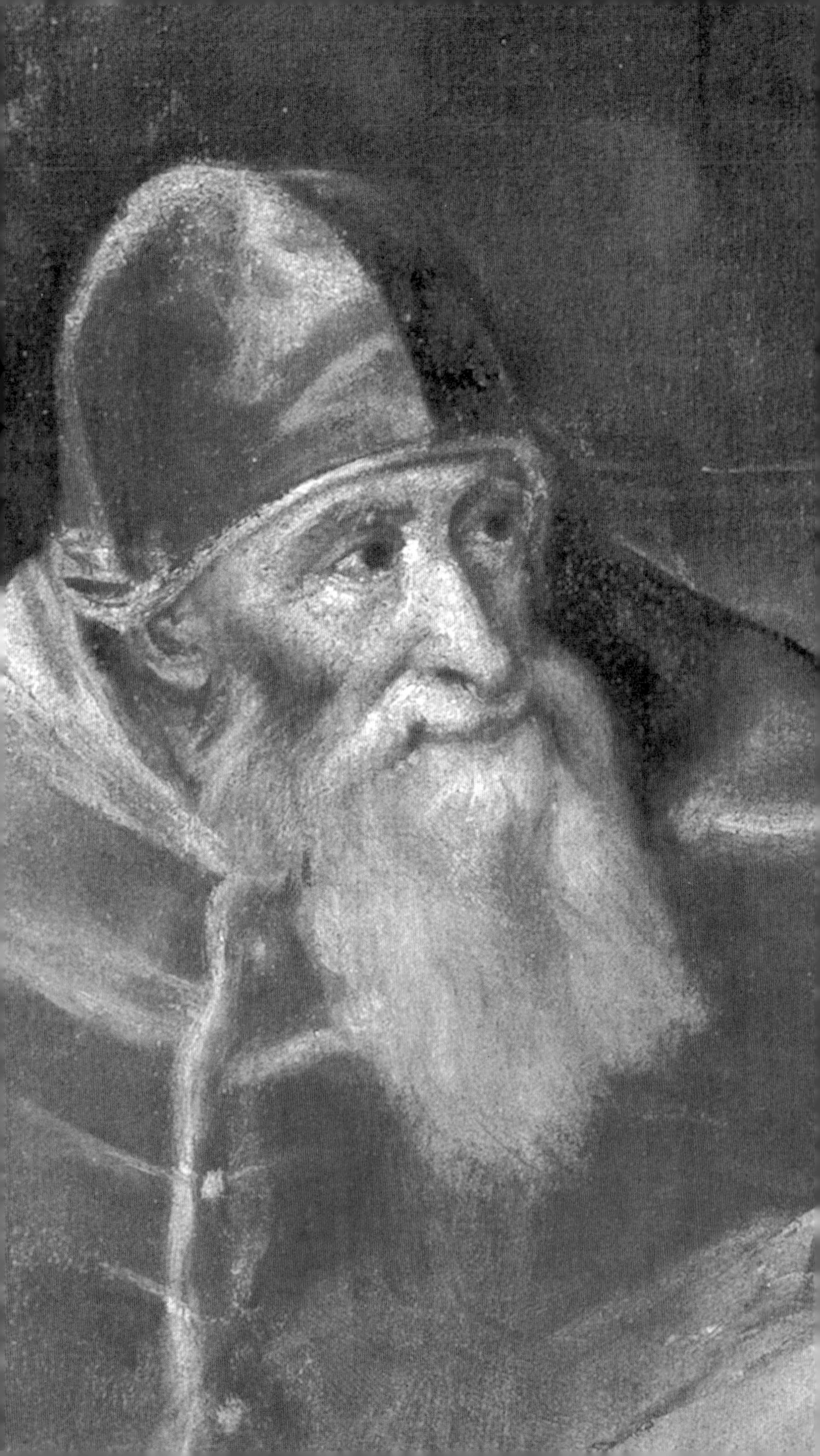

Writing an artist's biography has never been easy, for one of the most significant elements of any artistic life, the passage of an idea from eye to hand, is virtually indescribable. Furthermore, Giorgio Vasari, the pioneer of the form, struck such a brilliant balance between professional insight and juicy anecdote that writing an artistic biography in his wake can seem like trying to write epic after Homer. Vasari took egregious liberties with his *Lives*, offering up generous helpings of moral advice, tricks of the trade (normally "draw, draw, draw"), outpourings of Tuscan patriotism, and disarming hero-worship of Michelangelo. In good sixteenth-century style, Vasari also felt free to make up the occasional story when he needed one to drive home his moral point. Modern biographers, on the other hand, are expected to stick to the facts.

Aside from writing with gossipy verve, Vasari was a thoroughly respectable painter and a superb architect; he knew what he was

Titian, *Pope Paul III and His Grandsons Alessandro and Ottavio Farnese*, 1546, detail. Museo di Capodimonte, Naples, Italy. Luisa Ricciarini/Bridgeman Images.

talking about when he talked about art, and he expressed himself with firsthand expertise as well as pungent wit. Only Vasari, perhaps, could have acknowledged so openly that one of the most important things to happen in the life of the painter Tiziano Vecellio—Titian to his English-speaking admirers—was not so much an event as a long-drawn-out development, a change in the way the artist handled paint itself:

> The truth is that the way he worked in these later pictures is very different from the way he worked as a young man. The first paintings are executed with a certain fineness and incredible diligence, and are made to be seen both up close and from a distance, but these last are created out of brushstrokes laid down coarsely, and with spots of paint, in such a way that up close they cannot be seen at all and from a distance they appear to be perfect . . . and this way of working is judicious, beautiful, and stupendous, because it makes the paintings look alive and created with great artistry, disguising all the labor involved.[1]

Without that change in Titian's working method, without those abstract blobs that resolve themselves at a distance into images of startling precision, we would never have had Velázquez and Rubens, diplomats as well as painters.

With all three artists, their art has evolved into their supreme diplomatic achievement, creating quiet but powerful links between people and nations, links built and maintained in order to cherish these fragile objects of extraordinary beauty. Everywhere that Titian's paintings travel, thousands of people flock to see them, and that same exchange of art and the love of art has been taking place ever since the very young Tiziano Vecellio descended from his rugged Alpine birthplace to study painting in Venice.

It is hard to think of a painter more rooted in his environment and yet more universal in his appeal. It was an appeal he worked tirelessly to refine, for Titian was a pioneer not only in the way he painted, but also in the way that he presented his talents to an international clientele. He was a formidable, pathbreaking businessman in a century, the sixteenth, when doing business first attained a truly global scope. And like so many successful businessmen, he was a fierce patriarch, close with his money and ruthless in the ambitions he harbored for himself and his children. Titian was renowned for his impeccable manners and charming character (and he served as an unofficial diplomat on occasion), but for all that exterior charm, he kept his real feelings and his private life strictly to himself. He knew his place in his hierarchical society, even when he was subtly changing the nature of what that place might be.

Titian's afterlife is every bit as interesting as his life; his reputation, though consistently stellar, has not always been entirely wholesome. An inveterate experimentalist, he courted controversy virtually from the moment he began to assert his own artistic personality, and some of the subjects he painted have shocked later generations. In 1856, for example, the king of Naples, hoping to shore up his tottering throne, locked one of Titian's paintings away in a "Pornographic Cabinet" together with a hoard of phallic wind chimes, explicit statues, and erotic frescoes from the royal excavations in Pompeii and Herculaneum.

The sensuality of that locked-away painting, Titian's *Danaë*, is a good deal more discreet than that of those other frankly sexual objects: imprisoned in her chambers, she reclines on her bed as Jupiter appears to her in a shower of heavenly gold that pours into her lap. To the Catholic king of Naples, as he faced attack by the rebel forces of Giuseppe Garibaldi, Danaë seemed to be enjoying these unusual attentions a little too much; and the result of that golden rain was, of course, a baby: the future hero Perseus. And so Titian's *Danaë*, the lascivious ancient artifacts, and three images of Venus, by Paolo Veronese, Annibale Carracci, and Michelangelo, were consigned to a narrow room carefully chosen for its darkness and dampness, behind a door with three separate locks, their keys distributed to three different offices, and then, for good measure, the whole entrance to the Pornographic Cabinet was bricked up.

Fortunately for *Danaë*, this pious move failed to sway the forces of history. On September 11, 1860, exactly four days after entering Naples as its new Dictator (with a capital "D"; that was his official title), Garibaldi ordered that the Pornographic Cabinet of the royal collection be opened to the public. With this symbolic attack on every kind of censorship, Garibaldi announced his intent "to save the works of art from inevitable ruin." When a scramble to find the three keys to the cabinet failed, he ordered his men simply to break down the door, proclaiming, "Our revolution must be truly Italian, that is, worthy of the homeland of art and learning, and must embrace as one our glorious ancient and modern memories, fostering them all."[2]

Danaë may have languished under lock and key (just as the heroine herself did in the ancient myth), but the other Titians in the Neapolitan royal collection, a pair of portraits of Pope Paul III, retained their pride of place throughout the throes of national unification. An old pope in velvet robes evidently posed a less urgent challenge to public morals in the mid-nineteenth century than a languid young woman reclining nude on a bed. In the sixteenth century, however, when these portraits were fresh from Titian's workshop, they had been sizzling properties in their own right. According to one story (not Vasari's), Pope Paul disliked them, and it is easy to see why: Titian's brush seems to have reached deep down into the pontiff's soul to reveal attitudes, fears, and sensations that Paul surely preferred to keep to himself.

Danaë may be lolling on a bed as Jupiter rains down his favor, but because Titian shows her looking off into the distance rather than meeting our eye (or his), her thoughts remain her own. Pope Paul, on the other hand, meets us swathed in ravishing velvet robes, but Titian has laid him bare, in an individual portrait of the old man hunched on his throne, and still more so in a triple portrait that shows him with his two appalling grandsons, Cardinal Alessandro and Duke Ottavio Farnese. As suave, smooth Cardinal Alessandro looks out to the viewer from behind the pope, Ottavio, clad in white tights, white lace, and satin, doubles over in an elaborate bow, the perfect image of an oily courtier. Their ancient grandfather, with his stooped spine and shrewd old eyes, recoils with a visible shudder, his formidable will trapped in a failing body and his future wrapped up all too inevitably in this unctuous rogue. We can imagine why Ottavio's bride, "Madama" Margaret of Austria, wore mourning dress on her wedding day.

Another young Farnese scion, Ranuccio, was just a boy when Titian painted him, with the special attention this artist always reserved for the very young. His images of two-year-old Clarissa Strozzi and twelve-year-old Ranuccio Farnese are as attentive to their individual personalities as his adult portraits, and Titian's painting of the tiny Virgin Mary climbing the steps to the Temple of Jerusalem with fierce independence (*Presentation of the Virgin*, Galleria dell'Accademia, Venice) is a marvel of insight into the way children act (she may well have been modeled, body and stubborn soul, on his own daughter Lavinia).

Titian, as Vasari noted over and over again in his *Life*, was a painter of astonishing versatility, a master of landscape, of portraiture, of sacred painting, historical painting, mythology, a magician who could turn a dab of pigment into a flame, a pleat, a thunderbolt, a twinkle in the eye, a Cupid's wing. One of his last two self-portraits (Madrid, Museo del Prado, 1562) focuses on only two elements, his right hand and his face, as if to say that the essence of this phenomenally successful man depended on the mysterious partnership of that hand, those eyes, and that brain. Titian's eyes in this late portrait are like the old mirror in the poem by Cavafy "that had seen and seen"; they are clearly an old man's eyes, faded, straining, fixed somewhere off in the distance, but they are also sharp as a drill under their beetling black brows.[3] Tiziano Vecellio lived a long and largely fortunate life, but it was also a difficult life, and in this elegant, dignified picture he lets the pain of it show on his face, as clearly as he shows his own mastery of it.

In many respects, despite the painter's long, well-documented career, we know almost nothing about him, including such basic information as the number of his wives or the date of his birth. With remarkable success for so public a personage, Titian kept his domestic sphere strictly to himself. He lived in the part of Venice known as Cannaregio, near the docks and the Jewish Ghetto, in a house that he seems to have designed himself, ranged around a large garden. We can forget, in the face of all the state portraits, voluptuous goddesses, and history paintings he created over decades of activity, that Titian was also an unusually perceptive observer of nature, of trees and flowers and animals he painted from life. For a man of such enormous productivity, it is hard to imagine him simply sitting and thinking in his garden, but he clearly paid relentless attention to his surroundings, physical, spiritual, and social, and made sure that his own home provided a refuge from the metropolis in which he lived, and from his perpetually interesting times. He was a person sufficient in himself, whose artistry, thanks to his careful management, set him among popes, kings, cardinals, and emperors.

It was an unlikely destiny for a boy from an Alpine village, yet Titian never broke his ties with Pieve di Cadore, the town where he was born around 1490. The distinctive peaks of the Cadore mountain range show up again and again in his paintings, providing a background to the most disparate events: the Holy Family's flight to Egypt; a callow young lutenist's private concert for Venus (he scarcely concentrates on his music); Jupiter's abduction of Europa; Saint Jerome beating his chest with a rock in penitence; Venus blindfolding Cupid before he goes off to shoot arrows of longing into hopelessly mismatched hearts.

In Pieve di Cadore, the Vecellio family belonged to the upper ranks of a tough, hardworking mountain community: though not aristocrats, they were landowners both locally and in Venice, who made a healthy income selling timber in the city and managing a series of sawmills. Titian's grandfather Conte commanded the large Vecellio clan with the forbidding authority that Titian himself would display with his own children; the painter's father, Gregorio, stood out more for bravery and kindness than intelligence.

At the age of nine or ten, around 1500, Titian, gifted with his grandfather's wit and ambition, came down from the mountains to study painting in Venice, lodging with an uncle until he was apprenticed (so Vasari reports) to the city's most successful painter, Giovanni Bellini, whose style Vasari deplores as dry and repetitive. On the face of it, the criticism seems unfair. Bellini's paintings are stunning for the calm clarity of their composition and the brilliance of their color, sparkling, as only oil paint can sparkle, in the crisp, clean light that reflects back from the canals of Venice under a cloudless sky.

Bellini's paintings, exquisite in every detail, seem to inhabit a world in which time has been suspended, for a moment or for eternity. Vasari, that child of the turbulent sixteenth century, greatly prefers Titian, whose painting evolved with astonishing unpredictability. Like Pietro Perugino, the other late fifteenth-century painter with a hyperactive workshop, Bellini produced dazzling paintings with dazzling consistency, whereas their pupils Raphael and Titian threw themselves into one risky, exciting experiment after another and left their teachers in the dust.

Bellini would have taught Titian how to grind color and how to achieve the same piercing blues, gentle greens, and luminous whites, all of them on display in Titian's earliest paintings. But then another painter arrived in Venice from the provinces: Giorgio da Castelfranco, known immediately as "Giorgione" (Big George), an artist who could match Bellini's color in intensity, but substituted soft modeling for Bellini's hard-edged precision, the indefinite outlines of a Venetian fog for the sharp detail of the city's crisp, glittering sunlight. Titian was entranced.

That fresh enchantment shows in a very early painting, *The Flight into Egypt*. Mary, carrying her infant son, rides through a luxuriant forest meadow on a donkey, an elderly Joseph keeping careful guard behind them on foot. A beautiful young man in a white tunic leads the animal by its bridle with his right hand, while in his left he carries the family's gear in a little cloth-wrapped bundle, a wingless angel sent to watch over the refugees.

The meadow is a sea of wildflowers, and a virtual Noah's Ark looks on as the Holy Family passes through their woodland: a fox, a deer, a cow, sheep, birds, all of them as serene as the mother and child, as if an angelic spell protected them all. In the distance, Titian has painted the distinctive mountains above Pieve di Cadore: the sugarloaf mountain called Croda Cuz, and the jagged ridge of Sassolungo di Cibiana behind it. It is hard to think of this tender, gorgeous idyll as a painting of refugees fleeing an atrocity, and even harder to imagine that the young Titian painted it shortly after this region of the Veneto had been turned into a war zone, with its full share of refugees, massacres, and devastation, but so it was in 1508, when the Holy Roman Emperor Maximilian I swooped down through the Cadore, burning, looting, murdering, raping, and incidentally destroying any record of Titian's birth when his soldiers torched Pieve and its parish archives. By then, Titian, probably in his late teens, was hard at work in the relative safety of Venice, where the war created a surge of fugitives from the ravages of war, plague, and widespread poverty in the countryside.

Fifty years later, the painter of the sweet, verdant *Flight into Egypt* slashed out the harsh broad strokes of the *Martyrdom of Saint Lawrence* (Venice, Santa Maria Assunta dei Gesuiti, circa 1560), a canvas that is all browns, yellows, reds, grays, whites, and blacks, an urban scene of shocking violence from a steep, hurtling perspective. Saint Lawrence was a deacon of the early Christian church in Rome who was tied to a grill over burning coals to force him to reject his faith. Instead, legend has it, he said, with consummate aplomb, "Turn me over, I think I'm done on this side."

Titian's Lawrence is not so cool; an agonized, outstretched arm shows that he suffers the tortures of Hell—did Titian see the terrible Rialto fire that swept Venice in 1514 or some other blaze? Yet the play of color around the saint, from the sparks of his fire to the torch that blazes high above his head and the white-hot light that flashes down from Heaven to comfort him, springs off the surfaces of skin, stone, cloth, coal, and metal to weave a web of relationships that reinforce the story of heroic faith defying cruel decadence.

Some of Titian's earliest paintings already dealt with savage themes, like the episodes from the life of Saint Anthony he painted for the Scuola del Santo in Padua in 1511: a woman murdered by her husband, a man whose severed foot is miraculously reattached, and most dramatically a beautiful, plump young wife falsely accused of adultery by her husband until their baby, in the presence of Saint Anthony, speaks up to acknowledge his father's paternity. Titian captures the tragedy of the scene unflinchingly, sounding the depth of the mother's wounded pride as he dissects the suspicious father's cringing pusillanimity.

By the end of his career, Titian was painting as much for foreign potentates as he was for Venetians, although the Venetians probably paid him more reliably than the heads of state. The worst offender was King Philip II of Spain, who ordered an endless succession of paintings and paid for only a handful of them. Titian is often said to have reserved his best work for Philip, but works like *The Martyrdom of Saint Lawrence* suggest that he really did his best work for Venice, where his fiercest critic resided—himself.

Titian's late paintings confused Vasari as they confuse many modern viewers. Like Poussin and Renoir, he may have suffered from arthritis in his hands and problems with his eyesight. His brushwork grows consistently coarse, and his colors merge into a muddy brown that on close scrutiny is shot through with flashes of red and brilliant white; close up, these surfaces are as densely layered with color as a Jackson Pollock, and who is to say that they are not as carefully constructed as Pollock's compositions certainly were? And when that mud-brown is split by a bolt of electric yellow, as it is in the *Pietà* (now in the Galleria dell'Accademia in Venice), we can see how the sight of Titian's late paintings must have electrified El Greco, who would have discerned the silvery tones glistening beneath the brownish surface, just as they do in Greek icons.

The subjects of these late works are almost unremittingly harsh, none more shockingly so than the *Flaying of Marsyas* that may have been Titian's last painting, still under way when the plague carried him off in 1576. The furry satyr Marsyas had boasted that he was a better musician on his rustic panpipes than Apollo on his cithara, the carefully crafted, civilized version of the lyre (and the ancestor to guitars, zithers, violins, and all the other stringed instruments). Handsome, blond, eternally young Apollo won, of course, but the god was as mean and vindictive as he was beautiful; he condemned poor Marsyas to be flayed alive.

Titian shows the beginnings of the dreadful operation: Marsyas has been strung upside down from a truncated tree. Apollo leans in to slice into his victim's chest while a minion works on a hairy thigh. In a macabre touch, a tiny dog laps up the rivulet of the satyr's blood, just beginning to flow freely. The theme may well have been inspired in part by the 1571 flaying of the Venetian general Marcantonio Bragadin by the Turkish conqueror of Famagusta. At the same time, however, Apollo is also the universal symbol for art, so that in some terrifying sense, the handsome, pitiless god can be seen as representing Titian's bounteous, pitiless talent. It is a somber coda to a career so steeped in beauty.

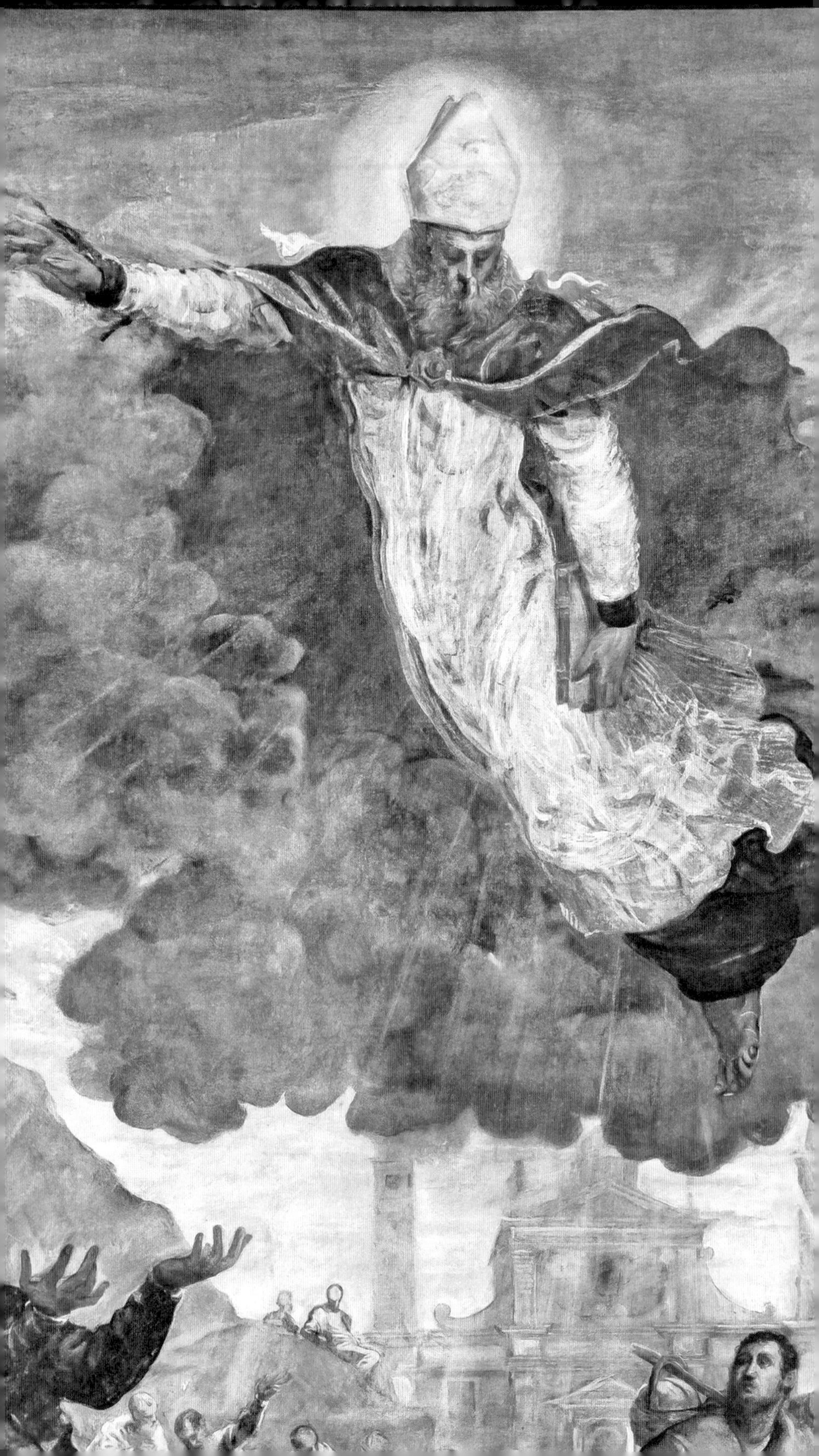

8 *The Fantastical Little Dyer (Tintoretto)*

Of the three great artists who dominated Venetian painting for much of the sixteenth century, Tintoretto was the wildest and most avant-garde. In 1568, Giorgio Vasari, who had met Tintoretto in Venice and liked him, reported that aside from the artist's musical talent and pleasant company, "he was extravagant, capricious, swift, and resolute, the most formidable brain that painting has ever known"—this from someone who had also written a biography of Leonardo da Vinci.[1]

Vasari called Tintoretto's paintings "the novel and capricious inventions and strange whims of his intellect."[2] "Whims" is really too pale a translation for Vasari's colorful term, *ghiribizzi*, which the Elizabethan writer and lexicographer John Florio defined as "sudden, humorous, fantasticall, toyish conceits," a description that seems to come close to Vasari's sense of Tintoretto's playfulness and unfathomable oddity. It is hard to believe that so fresh and inventive an artist has been with us for half a millennium.

Jacopo Robusti, called Tintoretto, *Saint Augustine Healing the Lame*, circa 1560, detail. Museo Civico Palazzo Chiericati, Vicenza, Italy. Ghigo Roli/Bridgeman Images.

In fact, Tintoretto's 1519 birthdate is just a guess. So far, scholars have recovered only the record of his death, which gives his age as 75. We do know that he was Venetian through and through, the eldest son of a man who dyed silk for a living. Dyeing was a profession the Venetians excelled at, thanks to their bountiful markets, which provided the best and most exotic raw materials. Tintoretto's father would have handled cloth from the far reaches of the Silk Road, sifting through local pigments like Umbrian woad (the chief source of blue) and exotic hues like Tyrian purple, extracted from inordinate numbers of Mediterranean mollusks. The son must have learned about pigments early, and he certainly used them in his work with uncommon mastery. "Tintoretto" is a nickname that means "little dyer" or "son of a dyer," and it passed to his artistic children (his daughter Marietta was known as "la Tintoretta"), but the painter signed his name on contracts as Jacopo Robusti.

He revealed his passion for drawing and painting early, showing enough talent to be accepted as an apprentice, presumably at the age of twelve or so, to Titian, the greatest living painter in Venice. The apprenticeship ended quickly, however. According to Tintoretto's seventeenth-century biographer Carlo Ridolfi, Titian came into the studio one day, saw some of the boy's figure drawings, recognized the first stirrings of a potential rival, "and impatiently, as soon as he had gone up the stairs and taken off his mantle, ordered his assistant Girolamo (such is the power of a little worm of jealousy inside the human breast) to dismiss Jacopo from his house immediately. Thus within a few days (they say it was ten days) the wretched apprentice was left without a master, not knowing the reason why."[3] The story may be exaggerated—early modern biographers such as Vasari and Ridolfi felt free to embroider their material to improve a tale or make a moral point—but Titian did recognize an entirely different artistic personality, and one that aroused all his defensive instincts. He kept his distance from Tintoretto in later life, even though both men were famous for their social graces as well as their artistic skills.

Thereafter, Tintoretto seems to have taught himself. Ridolfi says that the young artist was still reeling from Titian's rejection when he first tacked a piece of paper to his studio wall with the statement: "Michelangelo's line, Titian's color, the two ingredients for an ideal painting." As a Venetian, Tintoretto may never have seen a real work from Michelangelo's hands, but he knew them from engravings and clay models. He also knew, as every ambitious artist did in the sixteenth century, that Tuscan-trained artists such as Michelangelo saw drawing, *disegno*, as the essential foundation of art, whereas Titian and other Venetians were captivated by the relatively new medium of oil paint on stretched canvas (easy to come by in a city with so many sailmakers at work—the shipyards of the Venetian Arsenal could apparently construct and outfit an entire vessel in a single day). Unlike egg tempera, the preferred medium in Tuscany, oil paint dried slowly, making it easy for artists to revise their work. Rather than produce endless preparatory drawings, Venetian masters could sketch out their designs directly on the prepared canvas, in paint or with the blunt end of a brush. But Tintoretto, bent on achieving "Michelangelo's line," drew incessantly in an energetic style all his own, made up of a dense collection of short, shimmering lines rather than the long "serpentine" curves favored in Tuscany and Rome. As for color, he could learn about pigments at home, and he picked up the rest by studying the wealth of paintings, fabrics, and colored stones on display in Venice, still one of the world's great showcases for art in every medium.

Until the nineteenth century, painters mixed their own pigments, and Tintoretto, as his paintings demonstrate, was a master at creating exotic colors from the vast bounty of materials available to him. Those colors have inevitably altered over the centuries: greens and blues, in particular, tend to darken, much less so if the blue is "true blue," made from lapis lazuli, much more so if it is mixed from cheaper copper sulfate. Venetian oil paint, pigment suspended in linseed oil, also becomes more transparent with time, so that the brownish undercoat of the canvases begins to show through in paintings that are almost five centuries old. Tintoretto's works are especially vulnerable to these effects of aging because he painted more thinly and sparingly than his contemporaries; it was part of his distinctive, self-taught style. His human figures also differ significantly from those of his fellow Venetians, the result of his long study of Tuscan drawing and especially of Michelangelo: both men and women are slender, muscular, with rather small heads. If Titian's women are plump and voluptuous, Tintoretto's are positively athletic, lithe partners for men brawny enough to have jumped straight to Venice from the Sistine Chapel ceiling.

But what most disconcerted Tintoretto's contemporaries was his evident brushwork, the slashes of brilliant paint that created contours and highlights with such economy that he could cover huge swathes of canvas at an incredible speed. Titian, also experimenting with the same effects, greatly annoyed his friend Pietro Aretino by painting a portrait with zigzags of paint across Pietro's prominent paunch to indicate the sheen on his velvet robes. Aretino had the same reservations about Tintoretto—in one letter he admonishes the painter to "rein in the rush of his carelessness"—but he was also one of Jacopo's early patrons, commissioning a ceiling painting showing the *Contest between Apollo and Marsyas* in 1545.[4]

The painting for Aretino is a little bit clumsy, with only some dazzling pink and green fabrics and a magnificent tree to hint at the transformation that would come three years later, when Tintoretto painted an unequivocal masterpiece for the prestigious Venetian confraternity known as the Scuola Grande di San Marco. That painting, *The Miracle of the Slave* (1548), led to a whole series; *Saint Augustine Healing the Lame* (1549–1550), for example, shows how completely the painter had mastered the convincing portrayal of figures in space, from a distant church to the crippled men reclining in the foreground. The African saint, his bishop's miter glowing within a radiant halo, flies to the rescue of suffering humanity on a fantastic cloud of iridescent purple, its striking hue echoed in several places throughout the composition. The color has been applied in thin, thin layers, and we can see where Tintoretto has changed his mind about the placement of Augustine's right hand and the outlines of his nearly transparent white robe. The lame man crouching in the center of the painting has taken the pose of a famous ancient statue from Rome, the *Knife Sharpener* (originally in the house of the magnate Agostino Chigi, now at the Uffizi Gallery in Florence), a reassuring classical touch in a painting that otherwise upends most of the expectations sixteenth-century Venetian viewers would have had for a religious work.

And who but Tintoretto would try to capture a phenomenon as changeable, violent, and evanescent as a thunderstorm? *Transport of the Body of Saint Mark* (1562–1566), yet another masterwork for the Scuola di San Marco, shows the Christians of Alexandria taking advantage of a blinding downpour in the year 828 to spirit away the body of the martyred saint and bring it to Venice. A sturdy camel shows us that we are in the Egyptian capital, though the nearly transparent architecture, ghostly beneath pelting sheets of rain, suggests the saint's final destination: a sodden, wintry, ineffably beautiful Venice that comes around every year but rarely occurs in art—for this magical Egyptian piazza is an evident foreshadowing of Piazza San Marco. Its gossamer architecture looks barely substantial and utterly real: well-dressed ladies in pearl necklaces still fall victim to rain-slick marble pavements as fast as young men in a hurry, like the falling boy in the foreground who tugs on a pink curtain, theatening to bring down Tintoretto's whole canvas with him. Amid the chaos and comedy, a tiny group of believers performs a solemn miracle.

Tintoretto also exhibited an exceptional skill at portraiture, including two self-portraits. One shows the nervous, no-longer-young artist staring intently at himself (and hence the viewer) with huge, ravenous eyes, his curly black hair and beard as unruly as his spirit. His plain black jacket tells us nothing about him or his status; all we have is that curious, questing face, so joltingly lifelike that it looks like a real person, although we can also see that this person, and this face, have been created from dabs of paint. In 1588, Tintoretto painted himself again, his hair and beard now white, his face wrinkled, his eyes still large and brilliant, but strangely sad. His paintings, as Vasari said, covered most of Venice, but the most significant commission the city had to offer, painting the centerpiece for the Hall of the Great Council in the Ducal Palace, damaged by fire in 1577, had gone to his brilliant rival Paolo Veronese. In 1588, however, Veronese died unexpectedly, and the coveted commission passed at last to Tintoretto. Does the expression in the eyes of this late-life portrait reflect the artist's disappointment at not receiving the greatest assignment Venice had to offer, or the fear that comes with responsibility for painting Paradise, no less, at the end of a vast chamber with a ceiling that spans

25 meters? (The entire room is more than half the length and more than half the width of a football field, with not a single interior column to support the span of its immense ceiling.)

Tintoretto's preparatory sketch (now in the Thyssen-Bornemysza Collection in Madrid) reveals that the final version of this epic canvas differs from its initial study, but both display how he turned his formidable intelligence to imagining the infinite reaches of heaven: as banks of golden clouds, peopled with a dazzling multitude of saints and angels. In a realm beyond the firmament, Christ crowns the Virgin Mary queen of heaven; far beneath them, a funnel of heavenly light beams down to the doge's throne, which sits directly under the painting. The huge canvas could easily have slipped into chaos, with its pressing crowds of blessed souls and the complex hierarchies of heavenly space, but the whole composition is organized to convey a magnificent sense of order. Heaven, Tintoretto seems to suggest, must resemble nothing so much as Venice.

No matter how swiftly Tintoretto could paint, this was a project that required a team. The lonely boy who had once been expelled from Titian's workshop had long since turned into the impresario of a major studio, in which his children played a significant role, not only his son Domenico but also his daughter Marietta, one of the few professional women artists of her era. The execution of individual figures in this *Paradise* is not always up to Tintoretto's own standard, but the masterly design represents the supreme challenge, and the supreme triumph, of his career. In his own way, he, too, was a conceptual artist.

No one responded to Tintoretto more enthusiastically than a young immigrant from Crete, a colony of Venice from 1205 to 1669. Domenikos Theotokopoulos started life as an icon painter, but ambition took him to Venice and finally to Spain, where his neighbors simply called him El Greco—the Greek. With eyes trained on the gold leaf and glittering mosaics of Byzantine art, El Greco responded enthusiastically in his own work to the peculiar iridescence of Tintoretto's colors, and under the turbulent skies of Toledo he remembered the Venetian's fantastic heavenly halls, creating a free-form cloud architecture to portray the deep reaches of celestial space. Tintoretto's influence is nowhere more evident than on El Greco's *Christ Cleansing the Temple*, painted during the younger artist's two-year stay in Venice (1568–1570). But in all their works, the two painters share a profound passion for sensuous colors, elongated figures, dignified portraiture, and uncannily modern visions of heavenly space. What could be better than that?

For many of the four hundred years since the death of Domenikos Theotokopoulos, the artist known to his Spanish neighbors as El Greco, his work was regarded with the same disdain as that of his younger contemporary Caravaggio. If Caravaggio's detractors vowed that, as Nicolas Poussin put it, he had "come into the world to ruin painting," others found the Greek who made his career in the land of Don Quixote to be "contemptible and ridiculous, as much for the disjointed drawing as for the insipid colors."[1] In the nineteenth century, El Greco's monumental *Burial of the Count of Orgaz* lay rolled up and despised in a basement of the Toledan church of Santo Tomé, the venue for which he had painted it in 1586–1588 (and where it hangs again today in glory).

In the early twentieth century, the Benedictine sisters in the convent of Santo Domingo de Silos sold their altarpiece, an El Greco *Assumption of the Virgin*, to a Chicago art collector, just like many other Toledans who decided to unload their ugly, inconvenient

El Greco (Domenikos Theotokopoulos), *View of Toledo*, c. 1597–1599, detail. Metropolitan Museum of Art, New York, USA/Bridgeman Images.

canvases on wealthy foreigners just before the tides of taste began to turn. One Castilian count liquidated his El Greco to invest in a collection of contemporary art—yet it was modern painters who first began to open their eyes, and ours, to the color, the fantastic imagination, and the supreme elegance that "the Greek" brought to his work. By 1914, the three hundredth anniversary of his death, he could count admirers like Delacroix, Manet, Picasso, Miguel de Unamuno, Rainer Maria Rilke, and Benigno de la Vega-Inclán, who created the Museo del Greco in Toledo in 1911. The *pintor extravagante*, no longer an embarrassment, had become a guiding light.

If El Greco is still an acquired taste for many people, the best place to acquire that taste is in Toledo, the city where his artistry reached its full development, from his shimmering, phantasmagoric painting to the solid, surprisingly classical works of sculpture and architecture to which he also put his hand. El Greco's imagination needs to be matched against the colossal scale of Toledo's buildings, and only in Toledo can we see how carefully his fantastic cloudscapes, in heaven and on earth, drew from the shifting drama taking place in the atmosphere above his head.

Yet a man who spent the first half of his life on Crete could never erase the memory of the sun-saturated colors of the Greek islands, and they recur in his work: the aquamarine of Aegean waters, the incandescent yellow of the wild daisies that carpet Cretan fields in early summer, the delicate violet of crown anemones that he transferred to the shawl that wraps around a redheaded Mary Magdalene in a gorgeous early painting that dies when it is reproduced: no printer's ink can reproduce that fantastic mauve (or the cornflower blue of the sky above it) with anything resembling accuracy. El Greco in Toledo is irresistibly, simply glorious, an immigrant who fit as well as any other immigrant into a city built from the mingling of Arab, Jewish, and Christian cultures.

Despite his nickname, the Greek never called himself a Greek; he signed his paintings as "Krês"—Cretan. At least since the Bronze Age, the largest of the Greek islands has always been a world unto itself, culturally and politically. In the sixteenth century, with most of the mainland under Ottoman rule, Crete stood out as a venerable colony of Venice, ruled since 1212 by a military garrison that may have made up one tenth of the island's population in El

Greco's day. By then, centuries of coexistence had blurred many of the initial distinctions between the resident Venetian aristocracy and the native Greek middle class, creating a remarkable blend of arts, music, customs, languages, and religious rites, especially in Candia, the capital city, where the artist was born into a merchant family, most probably in 1541 or 1542.

His elder brother Manuel, nicknamed Manousos, served the Venetians as a tax collector, at least until bankruptcy drove him late in life to seek refuge with his brother in Toledo. El Greco painted him then as an elderly man swathed in lynx with a silver hoop dangling from his left ear, an exotic presence among the black-clad Spaniards with their carefully tended goatees above elaborate ruffs of starched and pleated lace. The Theotokopoulos brothers seem to have set up house on their own fairly early, suggesting that their parents must have died when Domenikos was still a young man. They belonged to a native Cretan bourgeoisie that lived comfortably, though clearly not without financial risk.

Set among remnants of the Byzantine past on the route that linked the Sublime Porte of Istanbul with the Italian West, sixteenth-century Candia created its own distinctive culture, what is sometimes called the "Cretan Renaissance." The Venetian governors built their forts and public buildings in Italian style; books and prints spread Italian ideas about art and architecture. But the islanders of Crete also cultivated the legacy of Byzantine Greece in art, poetry, church architecture, and religious rites, painfully aware that the Ottoman Empire might take them over as Constantinople had been taken in 1453. Navies swarmed the seas around Crete, flying the flags of Venice, Genoa, the Sublime Porte, and the Knights of Malta, and in the middle decades of the sixteenth century there was no way of knowing which side would win.

The Cretan Renaissance blossomed, then, with all the urgency of imminent doom, producing eminent scholars, most of whom emigrated to Venice, and two individuals of transcendent talent: the great artist Domenikos Theotokopoulos and the greatest Greek writer of the period, Vintzentzos Kornaros (1553–1613/4). Kornaros, despite his Venetian name (Vincenzo Cornaro), almost certainly spoke Greek as his first language, and his most important works are two long, beautiful poems in the Italian-inflected

Cretan version of that language, incorporating echoes of Ariosto and Vergil (and perhaps even Giordano Bruno), as well as Homer, into a Byzantine poetic meter.

His ten-thousand-line epic romance, *Erotokritos*, composed around 1600, would become an enduring symbol of Greekness when Crete finally did fall to the Ottomans in 1669. Set to a characteristic instrumental accompaniment of lute and Renaissance viol that combines Venetian instruments with Byzantine tonalities, *Erotokritos* was still sung by Cretan resistance fighters in World War II in the same way that classical Greek soldiers once sang the *Iliad*, and is recited from memory today by Greek rappers as well as traditional balladeers.[2] But Vintzentzos Kornaros also wrote poetry in Italian and Latin, and his brother Andreas established an Italian-style gentleman's academy in Candia that counted the Neapolitan poet Giambattista Marino among its members when Marino served as a mercenary soldier for the Venetian Republic.

The *litterati* of Candia inhabited a different world from the artists and artisans, separated by the gap between a scholarly, philosophical education and practical training in a professional skill. Yet the unknown Cretan icon painters who instructed the young Domenikos Theotokopoulos in their sacred craft also took part in the Cretan Renaissance, experimenting with new ways to combine Byzantine grace with a Western spatial sense, scouring the marketplace of Candia for exotic new colors to apply to their gilded panels of poplar wood: teal blue, terra-cotta pink, varying shades of gold leaf.

Cretan icons are nearly always recognizable for their experimental quality, but they seldom look alike. These borrowings seem to be largely a matter of form rather than underlying ideas, and for good reason; in 1439, at the ecumenical Council of Ferrara, Orthodox and Catholic Christians had agreed to continue going their separate ways. El Greco, on the other hand, wanted to understand Western style from the inside out: its philosophy, its religion, the principles, implicit and explicit, that underlay artistic creation. As a precocious inductee into the Cretan painters' guild, the younger Theotokopoulos brother may never have had access to the humanistic education of Vintzentzos Kornaros, who learned ancient Greek, Latin, and modern Italian vernacular in school alongside his own Cretan dialect, but El Greco had something just as good: a penetrating curiosity that would lead him in the same directions, to the same realms of the spirit and intellect. In the Venetian hinterland, his Italian friend Andrea Palladio was following a similar self-educated path with similar success.

One of the three surviving icons signed by the young Domenikos Theotokopoulos shows Saint Luke, the patron saint of artists, finishing a portrait of the Virgin Mary in a formal Byzantine style, with fine gilt lines to emphasize the folds in her wine-red mantle and the highlights of her long-nosed, aristocratic face. Luke, on the other hand, shifts on his chair, moving in three dimensions like the miniature angel who hovers before him, unfurling a banderole with a faint inscription. At the very beginning of his career, then, El Greco is already playing two artistic traditions and two moods against each other: heavenly calm and earthly agitation contend with each other as distinctly as West and East. These are contrasts to which he will return again and again, in different materials, different styles, and different media.

If some of the Greek's exceptional cultural curiosity came from his Cretan heritage, so, in all probability, did his lifelong love of litigation. Candia, as a stop on the route from the Levant to Venice, was a hotbed of hagglers, for exotic commodities and for the captives that Ottomans, Venetians, Genoese, and Knights of Malta brought ashore for ransom (or sale into slavery). One of the handful of documents that survive from El Greco's Cretan years settles a lawsuit by arbitration. Another records him as an icon painter (*sgouraphos*), and a third suggests that he had already established a household in his early twenties. By 1568, another document shows that he has moved to Venice. He could have seen at least one painting by Titian in Candia; in Venice, he met Titian face to face.

Icon painters work with egg tempera on gesso-coated, gilded wooden boards, a technique that permits minute strokes of tiny brushes and produces hard, smooth surfaces with the suggestion of an inner glow. Titian excelled at fresco and panel painting, but he mostly worked with oil paints on coarse-woven canvas, using his fingers as well as a range of brushes to create peaks and blotches of paint that sometimes resolve into intelligible figures only when seen from a distance.

The luster of oil made it an ideal medium for conveying the sheen of velvet or the twinkle of an eye, though El Greco's three early icons already show him striving to achieve the same effects in tempera, experimenting with silvery white highlights on drapery and exposed flesh. His icons are exquisite miniatures, but in Venice painters like Titian, Veronese, and Tintoretto were working large, on huge altarpieces and their monumental decorations for the doge's palace.

The Greek adapted, first to the new medium of oil and then to the change in scale. He experimented early on with two small, detailed versions of an agitated Western-style scene, depicting Christ driving the moneychangers from the Temple in Jerusalem. In both paintings, the sacrificial pigeons and rabbits have taken advantage of the chaos to escape as Jesus flails away at the shopkeepers with a whip; in the lower right-hand corner of one panel, a lone lamb lies placidly, still trussed for slaughter, a harbinger of what will happen shortly to Jesus himself.

In the other version of the work, the portraits of four men occupy the lamb's place: Titian, Michelangelo, the Dalmatian miniaturist Giulio Clovio, and a clean-shaven younger man with long hair who looks rather like the surviving self-portraits of Raphael. This youth, with coarser features and a longer nose than handsome Raphael, is probably meant to be the Greek himself, paying homage to the artists he regarded as his new teachers (though he may have been thinking of Raphael as well). Michelangelo had died a few years before, in 1564, but Titian and Clovio were very much alive and paying close attention to the young man from Candia, who uses this little panel to announce both his sensational ambitions and his sensational abilities.

Titian may have been El Greco's chief influence, but the Cretan's adventurous handling of oil paint also reflects his close study of Tintoretto, whose bold, brilliant slashes of paint could even imitate the falling rain. The painter of icons tried his hand at portraiture, exchanging the supernal faces of Christ and his All Holy Mother (as she is called in Greek) for the imperfect details of personality. His skill as a Western painter swiftly proved as exceptional as his skill as a creator of holy images, for which every movement of the brush had been an act of prayer. From Tintoretto, especially, he learned to use black, to darken his reds, and to model figures in three dimensions. Icon painters worked up from pure color to light; in Venice, El Greco began to paint darkness as well.

Venice must also be the place where he began to collect books, most of them in Greek and Italian. His library numbered more than 130 volumes, more than ten times the number of Caravaggio's, half the number owned by Gian Lorenzo Bernini, one fifth the size of the library amassed by the architect Francesco Borromini. El Greco not only bought books; he also read them carefully, writing his own thoughts in their margins, providing a uniquely intimate glimpse into the artist's working methods.

The purchases are those of an intellectually ambitious all-around artist, not simply a painter. El Greco bought a copy of the new revised edition of Giorgio Vasari's *Lives of the Most Excellent Painters, Sculptors, and Architects* (1568) and filled its margins with notes written in Italian. He also bought Daniele Barbaro's edition of the *Ten Books on Architecture* by Vitruvius with illustrations by Andrea Palladio (1567), as well as Palladio's own treatise, the *Four Books on Architecture* (1570). He clearly met Palladio, for he painted (and signed) the architect's portrait: a black-clad, middle-aged man standing with elegant aplomb as he rests his left hand on a fat little parchment-bound volume, stuffed with bookmarks, and extends his right hand in a courtly gesture. The Cretan must have felt an immediate sense of kinship with this man who had begun life as a stonecutter and only began to acquire his literary education at the age of thirty; with great sensitivity, El Greco paints him not as an architect, with a tradesman's compass and set square, but as an author. The little book, as art historian Lionello Puppi first observed, must be Palladio's guide to Rome rather than the big, lavish folio edition of the *Four Books*, as yet unpublished.

El Greco, however, also admired Palladio's buidings, with their clear classical lines and the suggestion of titanic forces surging just beneath the surface. Like Michelangelo before him, Palladio knew how to bring architecture to life by throwing in a curve, an asymmetry, an oversized ornament, some element just strange enough to transform a placid, predictable design into something uncanny. In his own copy of the *Four Books*, El Greco praised "el mayor arquitecto de nuestro tiempo," and eventually designed a series of the huge ornamental Spanish frames called *retablos* in the same spirit.

In Venice, too, the Greek could examine sculpture, both antique and contemporary, an art form virtually absent from Byzantine churches. He must have seen ancient statues in Candia, but we have no idea what they might have been, and he knew nothing at all about the Minoan civilization of Bronze Age Crete, however closely many of the women he eventually painted seem to share their pert profiles, their raven hair, and their captivating grace. It seems strange now that a Greek, of all people, should have had to discover the classical world in Italy.

From Venice, El Greco moved on to Rome in 1570. There, on Clovio's recommendation, he joined the entourage of Cardinal Alessandro Farnese, taking up residence at Palazzo Farnese in the center of the Eternal City. For the next seven years, he made good friends in Rome but failed to please the cardinal. To be sure, the Farnese were an old aristocratic family, wealthy, powerful, intellectually inclined, and supremely generous as patrons, but their collective taste ran to big, ostentatious displays; they owned the Baths of Caracalla and its colossal statuary as well as much of the Palatine Hill overlooking the Roman Forum, and their palazzi could be as gaudy as any ancient Roman emperor's. The Greek may also have made an unsatisfactory courtier, accustomed as he was to the comparatively egalitarian principles of the Venetian Republic and the Greek Orthodox Church.

Cardinal Farnese may have failed to see the point of El Greco, but Fulvio Orsini, his librarian, certainly did. Orsini owned at least seven paintings by the Greek, including the affectionate portrait of Clovio that hangs in the Capodimonte Museum in Naples. In 1572, the Cretan painter joined the prestigious artists' guild of Rome, but in the next few years he received no major commissions, and eventually Cardinal Farnese dismissed him. By the spring of 1577, he was bound for Spain, the wealthiest power in Europe, and the court of King Philip II, hoping, clearly, that this famous admirer of Titian might feel the same way about the master's recent protégé.

Philip failed to respond, but the Greek made an impression on Diego de Castilla, dean of Toledo Cathedral, and in Toledo the wandering Cretan finally found his home.

Toledo offered El Greco a steady stream of commissions, but the peculiarities of the place also stimulated his development as an artist in ways that might have been impossible elsewhere. The city's dramatic physical setting on a promontory above the River Tagus provided him with an endlessly suggestive play of sky, cloud, and landscape, commemorated in his two painted portraits of the city, both of them willfully distorted to serve artistic ends.

The majestic scale of the city's churches demanded, and received, a majestic response from the new arrival. The chancels of Spanish churches of the era had developed a distinctive architectural backdrop, the *retablo*, that rose to dizzying heights behind the main altar, and was divided into a series of compartments for displaying paintings and sculpture. On a smaller scale, side chapels and freestanding altarpieces also required their own elaborate frames. El Greco therefore designed his own *retablos*, picture frames, and sculptural decoration as well as paintings, contrasting the stately solidity of his classical architecture with the wild exuberance and airborne lightness of his painted visions, the warm golden glow of his gilded frames with the cool shimmer of his silvery pigments.

Against massive whitewashed interiors, he could let his palette run wild, as in the cathedral sacristy, where his *Disrobing of Christ* shows Jesus in a dazzling crimson robe that dominates the room. Furthermore, El Greco's famously elongated figures turn out to have been perfectly calibrated to the monumental spaces around them. Seen from a distance beneath a lofty vault they look graceful, stately, elegant rather than distorted; it is an old trick perfected by Byzantine mosaicists centuries before El Greco applied it to the churches of Toledo.

The low ceilings and horizontal spaces of so many modern museums end up cramping the refined artistry of this supreme master of light, form, and color. El Greco's *Assumption of the Virgin* must have been even more magnificent in its intended venue, the soaring, sunlit, whitewashed chancel of Santo Domingo, than it is in a dark, squat, windowless gallery of the Art Institute of Chicago. It is a privilege, therefore, to see the intact chapel of San José in Toledo as El Greco designed it, with its *retablo*, its statues, and the touching image of Saint Joseph with Jesus as a young boy, embracing his tall, kindly father with simple affection.

Fatherhood seems to have been the most deeply felt relationship in El Greco's life. He was captivated from the outset by the beauty of Toledo's women, and within a year of his arrival, in 1578, one of them, Jerónima de las Cuevas, had borne him a son, Jorge Manuel, whose double name honored both his grandfather, Giorgos Theotokopoulos, and his uncle Manousos. The couple never married, and Jerónima seems to have died not long after Jorge Manuel's birth. El Greco had high hopes for his son's career as a painter, but Jorge Manuel wanted to be an architect. It is a father's wishful thinking, then, that animates the portrait of Jorge Manuel, painted when he was about twenty-five (circa 1603), a handsome, sweet-faced dandy, holding the palette and brushes he himself would gladly have exchanged for an architect's rule and compass. And it is a father's incomparable skill that registers the shadow Jorge Manuel's right hand has cast across his black velvet doublet, a triumph of black on black.

Jorge Manuel also appears in the foreground of the painting that is usually acknowledged as El Greco's masterpiece, *The Burial of the Count of Orgaz*, a fourteenth-century grandee who was miraculously accompanied into the grave by Saints Stephen and Augustine, who appeared in epiphany to take up his body. Like so many of El Greco's works, this one was designed for a specific architectural setting, another lofty whitewashed chapel whose spare expanse helps to concentrate the effect of the blacks, silvers, and yellows of this huge, solemn painting. The figures of the lower register meet us eye to eye, rendered with a startling immediacy.

And then strange things begin to happen. In the midst of the funnel-like cloud formation that dominates the center of the painting, the count's tiny pale soul moves upward toward an assembly of holy figures: Christ, the Virgin, and a company of saints, all of them as diaphanously unreal as the figures below seem to be made of solid flesh, tucked into cloud formations that call to mind the Gospel of John (14:2): "my father's house has many mansions." El Greco was a consummate painter of a reality beyond our own, who never forsook the icon painter's task of committing heavenly visions to a play of colors distilled from earth.

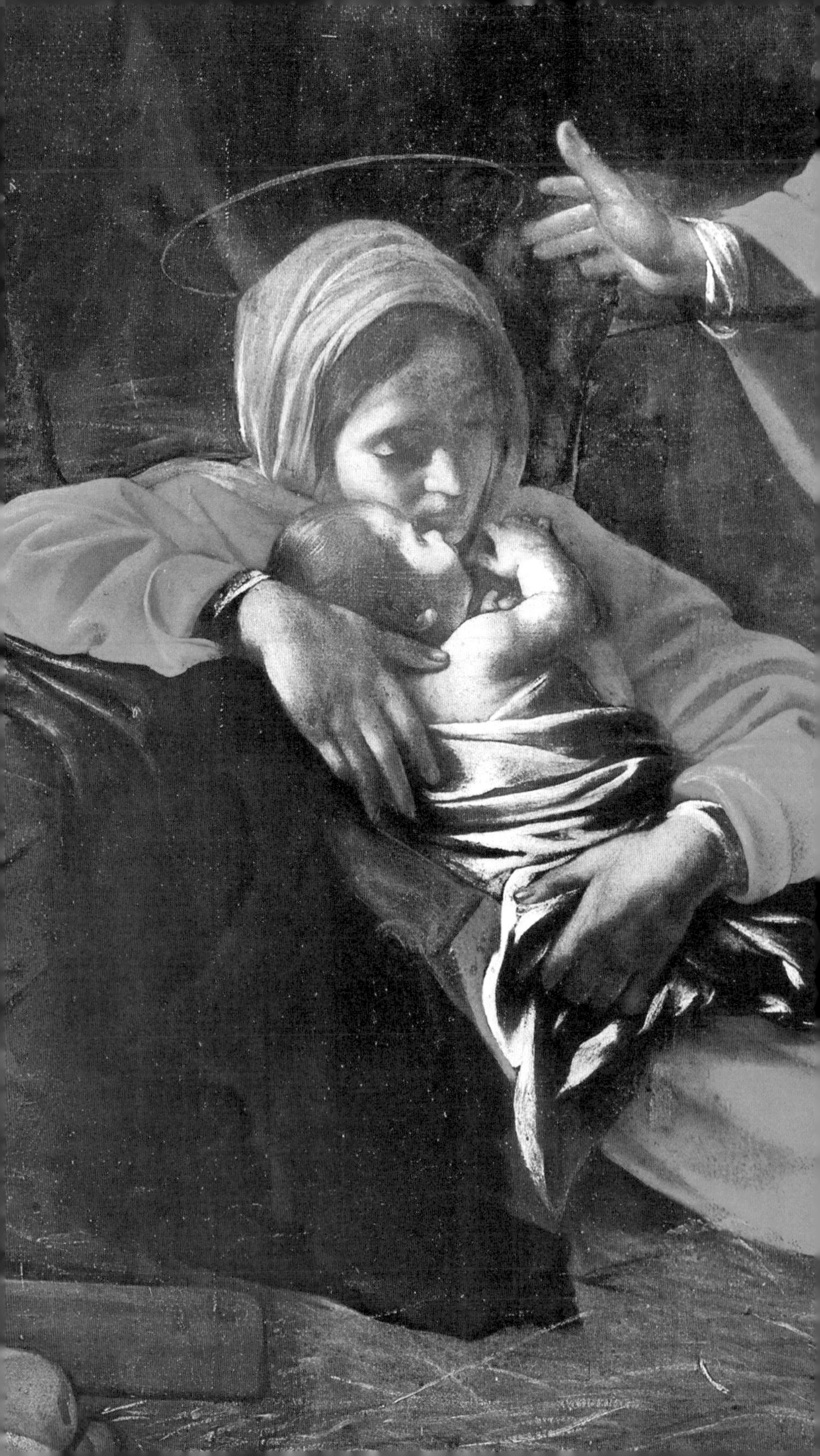

One summer day four centuries ago, a half-crazed, middle-aged man staggered into the little Italian seaside town of Porto Ercole, muttering incoherently in his nasal Lombard accent about a missing boat loaded with paintings. His face, with its scraggly black beard, was a maze of half-healed scars; his sweat-soaked clothing was finely made but worn to rags. He must have been carrying the sword that rarely left his side, but there is no record of it, nor of those who put him to bed in the town's tiny hospital, a place more accustomed to hosting ailing sailors, port workers, and galley slaves. We know only that there on his sickbed, his fever, his wounds, and his desperation carried him off in the heat of July. A terse local record notes: "On July 18 [1610], Michelangelo Merisi da Caravaggio, the painter, died of disease in the hospital of Saint Mary the Helper."[1] We do not know for certain whether that disease was malaria, syphilis, infection, or heartsickness, and it hardly matters; what mattered, then and now, was the work that

Michelangelo Merisi da Caravaggio, *The Adoration of the Shepherds*, 1609, detail. Museo Regionale Interdisciplinare, Messina, Italy. Artefact/Alamy Stock Photo.

this sad, desperate painter had left behind, including the boatload of paintings he had been madly chasing along the coast; those canvases landed in Naples, where one, a *John the Baptist*, was snapped up by portly, powerful Cardinal Scipione Borghese to grace his growing gallery of art.

Four hundred years after the painter's lonely death, the crowds that flock to any show bearing his name prove that Caravaggio speaks to our time as clearly as he did to his own, despite the fact that we like to think of our globalized, technological, democratic age as an entirely different world from the violent Italy of feudalism and religious repression that forged his inimitable way of painting. Epochal differences may divide his reality from ours, but there are also similarities so deep between our cultures that the man who was once called "Rome's outstanding painter" can still lay plausible claim to his title.[2]

There is the matter, for instance, of Caravaggio's radiance; the painter who became a master of darkness began his career in a blaze of light, with a simple basket of fruit (its yellow background was added later). The basket itself teeters cleverly on the painting's lower edge, threatening to tumble into real space, but the immediacy of the optical illusion is not really what rivets viewers to this little still life; rather, it is Caravaggio's positive exultation in the forces of life itself, the juice that ripens fruit, the spiky vigor of leaves and branches, the suggestive contrast between different textures of decay: soft spots in the centers of pears or papery dryness along the edge of a leaf. The quickening he captures is evanescent, but the veins of the crumpling leaves, the skin of the rotting fruits, and the weave of the unassuming basket are positively luminous.

Another early painting of a boy with fruit, now in the Borghese collection, shows how carefully Caravaggio, just arrived in Rome, must have been looking at the velvet textures of Federico Barocci, and particularly at Barocci's mastery of grays and browns, muted tones that the elder painter brought to life in his rendering of flesh and drapery by bathing them in flushes of hot pink. Caravaggio has tried a similar technique on the boy's exposed shoulder, and he would continue to study how the blush created by blood surging through capillaries makes even painted skin seem to come alive. At this point in the painter's career, the fruit is more convincing than the boy, who is more a type than a personality; it would have been hard to predict that the older Caravaggio would become so penetrating a painter of character.

Other early Caravaggio paintings show Barocci's influence as well: the large-eyed, watchful donkey in Caravaggio's brightly colored *Rest on the Flight into Egypt* in the Doria Pamphilj Gallery recalls the irresistibly soft fur of Barocci's animals, which Caravaggio would have known—at the very least—from two paintings (a *Visitation* and a *Presentation of the Virgin*) in the Roman church of Santa Maria in Vallicella, and we can see the younger man's experimentation with shades of beige in the background of his *Penitent Magdalene* in the same Doria Pamphilj collection, a background that is an experiment in pure, muted color and soft texture, testing the capacities of slick oil on rough canvas to awaken, as Barocci does, the whole range of our sense of touch.

Barocci, born in Raphael's home city of Urbino and active in Rome in the 1560s, is not usually a painter we associate with Caravaggio; his bright palette, soft textures, gentle subjects, and intimate moods seem far removed from the stark lighting and high drama that became the younger artist's specialties. Yet it is Barocci who gets at the heart of a quality that may explain Caravaggio's continued draw, for Barocci is a compassionate, even sentimental painter, and Caravaggio confronts the harsh realities of his time with his own piercing compassion, though that compassion has often turned into outrage.

Caravaggio's career in Rome is filled with outbursts of anger, recorded in police dockets from three different Roman jails, but it is hard to know now whether he came to Rome angry or lost his temper when a tender spirit met the experience of the city's mean streets—or its dark, corrupt alcoves. His tousle-haired *Boy with a Basket of Fruit*, probably painted as a show of skill, retains an air of innocence despite his bare shoulder and proffered present, but the louche characters that Caravaggio painted for his first important patron, Cardinal Francesco Maria Del Monte, must have parted company with innocence long before. The devilish little imp who personifies *Love Victorious* has all the hallmarks of a real boy: long nose, small teeth, premature wrinkles, genitals off-kilter—but it is love as pure carnality, and love as wickedness.

The late Franca Trinchieri Camiz has shown convincingly that another series of paintings—Caravaggio's *The Lute Player* in its various versions and a multiple image, *The Musicians*—probably portrayed Pietro Montoya, a Spanish castrato who lived in Cardinal Del Monte's house.[3] These youths' open rosebud mouths imply that their range of skills went beyond music, and their air of boredom hints at a whole greenhouse stocked with such Venus flytraps.

Perhaps it is time to recognize these boys for what they are, to realize that the message in their troubled eyes is not "Come hither" but rather "Help me!"—that is, if the light in their young faces has not been extinguished altogether, as it seems to have been in the used-up redhead who cringes in the rear guard of *The Musicians*. Look long enough, and carefully enough, at *Love Victorious*, and the impish grin freezes on the child's face: How much longer does he need to maintain it, and the rest of his overused body, underneath the weight of his fake cherub wings? His eyes convey fear, perhaps hatred, and, most of all, unspeakable sadness.

The same profile, the same baby-soft hair and crooked genitalia, appear on the enigmatic little creature known as *John the Baptist*, wriggling on a furry pelt as he clutches a ram close. The ram's eyes are as kindly as an old dog's, the little boy's are frightened, and Caravaggio has portrayed the two of them together as if they are fellow sacrificial victims, the gentle ram destined for the butcher's knife, the boy for another kind of violent assault—he recoils visibly from Caravaggio's scrutiny, as if the painter were an accomplice rather than a compassionate witness to some great ongoing injustice.

In and of themselves, the paintings suggest that it may have been Caravaggio's experience with Cardinal Del Monte that turned both his palette and his soul into a battleground between light and darkness. It is hard to see these strange, etiolated boys without thinking about their part in the play of dominance and submission that made up the essence of all courtly life, including the life of the Curia. It was a play of dominance and submission that also, necessarily, involved Caravaggio, the cardinal's painter.

Cardinal Del Monte was a proud Florentine who served in Rome as ambassador for the grand duke of Tuscany, as well as a prince of the Church; he was, therefore, in close touch with his native city's intellectual forefront, the same environment that had only recently produced the young Galileo Galilei, a professor since 1592 at the University of Padua. Del Monte was also an alchemist who performed experiments with distillation in his suburban villa, or casino, a building that still survives amid the hotels and night-clubs clustered around the Via Veneto. There, in 1597, Caravaggio painted a ceiling for the cardinal showing the three divine brothers Jupiter, Neptune, and Pluto, seen from below in what was usually called "heroic nudity"—although this trio's nudity, like that of their little nephew, Cupid, looks more clinical than heroic, and Caravaggio achieved it by standing on a mirror and painting his naked self. The crystal spheres of the heavens spin between the three gods, the largest of them traversed by the transparent belt of the Zodiac. Caravaggio executed this ceiling in the oil he knew (his canvas has been tacked up onto the ceiling) rather than experimenting with fresco, provoking criticism from his rivals in Rome—but he would have been criticized in any case as his reputation grew.

His experience with Cardinal Del Monte must have lent a natural-philosophic impetus to his ongoing experiments with dark and light. Contemporary natural philosophers had been focusing intense attention on optics, lenses, and mirrors (Giovanni Battista della Porta) and on a more abstract consideration of shadows (Giordano Bruno). Caravaggio himself is recorded in one notarial document as having owned only fourteen books, but in Cardinal Del Monte's house he would have had access to a vast library and to erudite conversation; what he made of either we will never know for certain, but it is tantalizing to guess.

Clearly he absorbed his patron's ideas along with his habits, and clearly his later paintings suggest strong reactions to this heated combination of learning and decadence. What did it mean for the cardinal to walk beneath the image of a triply naked Caravaggio every time he entered his laboratory? What did pursuit of the philosopher's stone have to do with young castrati, or with the Church? As Caravaggio pondered life and alchemy, standing above his mirror in a studio near Piazza Navona in Rome to paint the elemental gods of antiquity, that great writer on shadows, Giordano Bruno, languished for a fourth year in the prisons of the Roman Inquisition, accused of heresy but not yet convicted.

Yet Cardinal Del Monte also recommended Caravaggio for his first significant religious commission, *The Calling and Martyrdom of Saint Matthew*, for a chapel in the French national church in Rome, San Luigi dei Francesi (Saint Louis de France), executed between 1599 and 1600, followed by a commission for the chapel's altarpiece in 1602. *The Calling of Saint Matthew* revealed Caravaggio as an extraordinary painter of psychological states; within a dark room, a group of tax collectors gathers around a table as Jesus and Saint Peter enter from the street. Jesus has just delivered his order, "Follow me," and Caravaggio shows us how the words have struck each person within this den of publicans. One young man with bright silken sleeves bows his head as if to duck the summons, a stricken look on his face; two very young men in plumed hats look on as if they have not quite heard. An elderly clerk fixes his myopic gaze on the pile of coins they have amassed, as bearded, balding Matthew, dapper in his white hose and cockaded velvet hat, points at his own chest as if to say, "Who, me?"

In fact Jesus, young and earnest, points his hand in no particular direction, while the apostle at his side aims his own pointing finger at one of the young peacocks in a plumed hat who stares without reacting; Caravaggio makes us realize that the Lord's command has been aimed at them all (and at us, too, for that matter), but only Matthew has had the wit to receive it. The chapel's opposite wall shows the terrible price that Matthew will pay for having followed the summons: a young executioner strikes him down in his priestly robes, as the tax collector turned evangelist prepares to baptize new converts, who scatter in the confusion. In the painting's background, behind the executioner's pale, muscular shoulder, we see Caravaggio himself bearing witness to the cruel murder, but not, perhaps, to Matthew's celestial vision, a daringly contorted cherub who confers the palm of victory, victory over death, to the dying saint. The artist's grief implores us not simply to look, but to ponder the mysteries of martyrdom.

From this moment onward, most of Caravaggio's commissions would involve religious subjects, and it is as a religious painter that he would make his greatest impact on the course of contemporary art in Italy. His paintings provide boldly independent readings of the Bible and the lives of the saints, readings that emphasize both the human tragedies and the human hopes distilled into these old, old stories. His implicit readings may feel fresh and independent, but they nonetheless adhere to a strictly orthodox idea of Catholic Christianity. Caravaggio does not upset the Bible; an apostle in his own right, he makes the Bible upset us.

Caravaggio rejected his first version of the *Conversion of Saint Paul* when he finally installed it in its intended setting, a chapel in the venerable Roman church of Santa Maria del Popolo. For all its exotic beauty, this *Conversion*, with its dramatic dawn landscape (one of Caravaggio's only paintings of the sky), proved too crowded with figures to make much impact in its cramped setting. The artist replaced it with the simpler, more rustic panel that has hung ever since in the Cerasi Chapel of Santa Maria del Popolo, with a magnificent horse gingerly removing its foreleg from the vicinity of the stricken Paul, who writhes on the ground, knocked flat on his back by his sudden change of heart.

But religion, however deeply he felt it, could not heal Caravaggio's spirit. As he grew more famous, he also seems to have grown ever more angry; his name appears repeatedly in police records from Rome's amazingly complete, centuries-old State Archive: records from the tribunals where Caravaggio stood trial for his violent acts, transfers of real estate, notarized contracts, payment slips, and tantalizing mention of painters named Michelangelo who worked around the year 1600 that lack enough corroborating information to confirm that this Michelangelo can only be the painter from Caravaggio.

Not one of Caravaggio's jails survives today; dreadful places, they were razed in a series of campaigns for prison reform in the mid-seventeenth century. One, the Corte dei Savelli, has been engulfed by the Venerable English College in Rome. Once a baronial palazzo, the dilapidated structure is where, after conspiring to murder her violent, abusive father, the young Roman aristocrat Beatrice Cenci and her relatives were imprisoned and tortured in 1599; upholding the patriarch's authority was more urgent in the Rome of Pope Clement VIII than the suffering, physical, sexual, and psychic, of his tormented family. Caravaggio may well have witnessed her execution, just as he was formulating his ideas for *The Martyrdom of Saint Matthew*. He may also have seen Giordano Bruno burn at the stake a few months later by order of the same pope, and he certainly saw the inside of the same prison where Bruno spent his final week: Tor di Nona, built around an ancient Roman guard tower along the bank of the flood-prone Tiber River, demolished and transformed into a theater half a century after Caravaggio and Bruno crossed its slimy threshold.

The crime that drove Caravaggio from Rome was murder, for killing the local gangster Ranuccio Tomassoni over a game of tennis—the street where it happened is still called Via di Pallacorda—Tennis Street. He would spend the rest of his life rushing from one place to the next: Naples, then Malta, then Sicily, Naples again, and finally the malarial coast of Tuscany and the neat little bay of Porto Ercole. With every stop, his painting grew thinner on the canvas and more monumental in its composition.

The paintings from his brief sojourn in Sicily reflect his straitened circumstances: an *Adoration of the Shepherds* from Messina and a ruined *Annunciation* that has long hung in Nancy. These large canvases, like Caravaggio's *Burial of Saint Lucy* in Syracuse and his *Beheading of John the Baptist* in Valletta, Malta, are anchored by bold perspective constructions that spring into their full three-dimensional relief only when they are seen from a considerable distance, and then they are stunning.

John the Baptist appears again and again in Caravaggio's work, as a young man in the wilderness, but his most moving portrayal of the saint is the *Beheading* in Malta, where the Hebrew prophet appears as the adult victim of a thoroughly urban crime, a slit throat in a back alley that looks for all the world like Strait Street, the notorious "gut" of Valletta. The painter trains his eye on a pitiless world, but his eye itself is the essence of pity—one of his greatest paintings, in Naples, celebrates the *Seven Acts of Mercy* that were to guide the conduct of any sincere Christian's life. Bravely, he faced the disturbed eyes of Cardinal Del Monte's troubled boys and, as soon as he could, turned his talents away from the gaudy silks of the papal court to the shabby throngs of the poor, with their big rough hands, broken fingernails, grimy skin, and spotless faith.

He reserved evident admiration, too, for the hardy Knights of Malta, whose ranks he nearly joined until another summer brawl cut that career short on the eve of his investiture. He painted old women as fully developed souls, not as specimens of ravaged skin or addled vanity. If Judith winces as she severs the Assyrian general's head in *Judith Beheading Holofernes*, her maidservant looks on with unflinching resolve. In the second, subdued version of *Supper at Emmaus* it is the old innkeeper's wife who alone of all the company has recognized the resurrected Jesus as he breaks bread with his disciples, bowing her head in quiet acknowledgment. The disciples are still too excited by their conversation to reflect on what is happening to them—"Did not our hearts burn within us?" they will remember. But the old woman already knows, and Jesus actually turns, ever so subtly, in her direction. Caravaggio has set up yet another line of pure energy that connects distant figures within his paintings, and those paintings with us.

After all he had seen and done, after all his explosions of rage, the slashings, verbal and physical (he was arrested once for the scurrilous verses he directed against his rival, Giovanni Baglione),[4] the fugitive Caravaggio painted a *Burial of Saint Lucy* in Syracuse, Sicily, as breathtaking as the Maltese *Beheading of John the Baptist*, tragic portrayals of senseless violence that also chronicle great acts of God. The bishop's hand extended to bless Saint Lucy's corpse throbs with the literal power to raise the dead, but we can feel the electric connection between hand and saint only when the painting's perspective snaps all its pieces into place within a deep vortex of space. An *Adoration of the Shepherds* painted in Messina on his arrival in Sicily shows the Virgin Mary pressing her face close against her baby's, shielding him from the bleakness of their surroundings: for she is sitting on the dirt floor of a stable in her red robe and ultramarine mantle, leaning against a manger amid a farmer's tools, with animals and ragged shepherds looking on. With a dramatic diagonal beam of light, the painter connects them all: the two close-pressed faces of mother and child (and the bond they express) cast their glow on the faces of the shepherds, and the dingy stable turns, through Caravaggio's masterful management of perspective, into a mighty cathedral.

However tormented he may have been in body and soul, Caravaggio continued to see the world with the same clarity that glows from his golden basket of fruit: optical light and its geometric projection, and, perhaps still more intensely, the light of divinity as it glows in the works of nature, and in the compassion of the human soul.

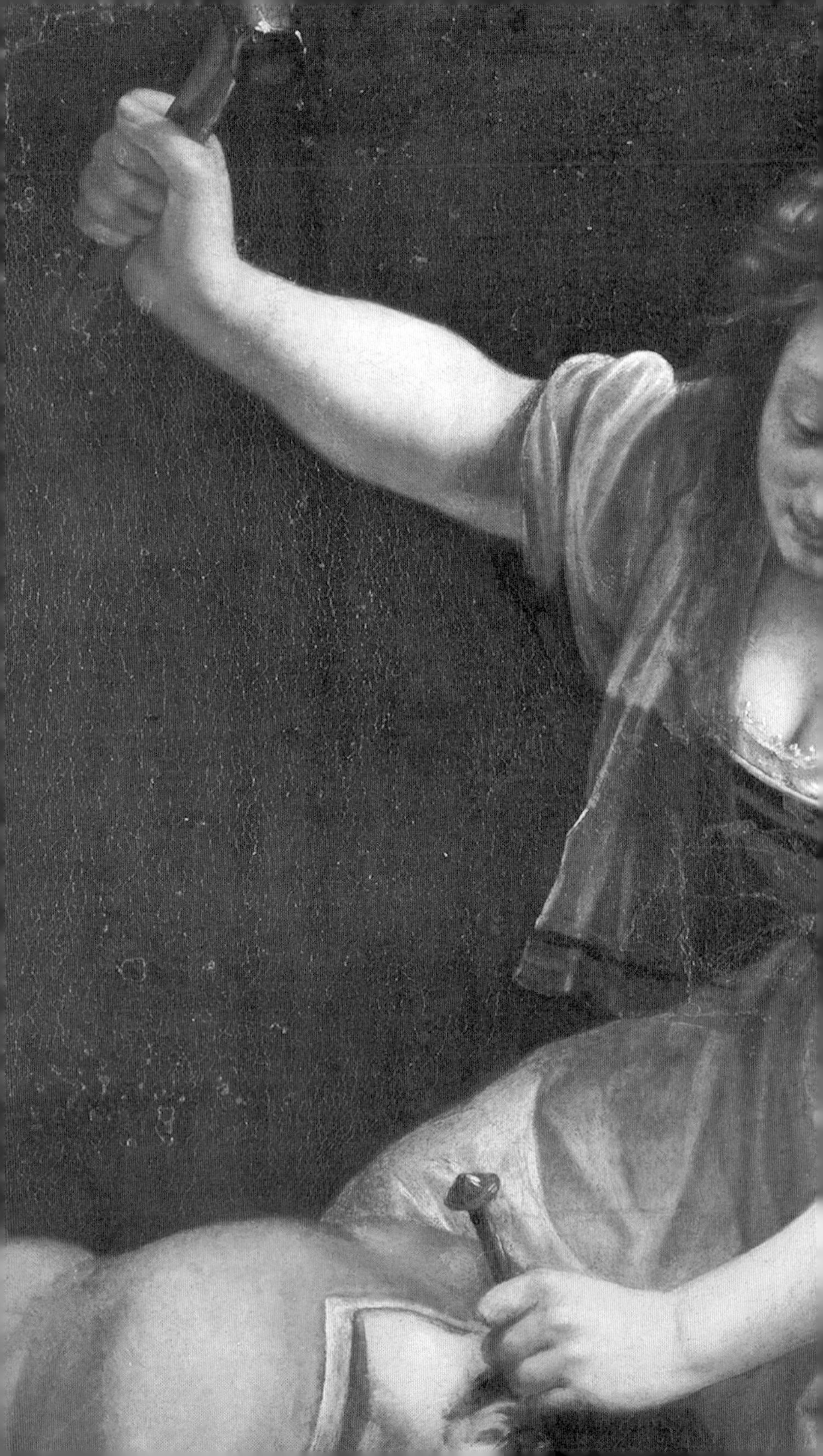

11 *Women Artists and the Boundaries of Art*

In 1971, Linda Nochlin, then an assistant professor of art history at Vassar, published an essay asking "Why Have There Been No Great Women Artists?"[1] The title was meant to provoke, and it did. The punch of her rhetorical question lay not in its apparent dismissal of women's artistic achievements, but rather in the clever way it set the adjective "great" in a position of such slippery subjectivity. Six years later, together with another art historian, Ann Sutherland Harris, she mounted an exhibition in several US venues featuring women artists from the Renaissance to the present.

The undisputed revelation of "Women Artists, 1550–1950" was a seventeenth-century Italian painter named Artemisia Gentileschi, whose imposing—but until then little-known—*Susanna and the Elders* (1610), painted before she had turned twenty, showed outstanding skill. More pointedly, however, this painting of a terrified young woman, surprised at her bath by two old lechers, evoked

Artemisia Gentileschi, *Jael Killing Sisera*, 1620, detail. Museum of Fine Arts (Szépművészeti Múzeum), Budapest, Hungary. Photo © Fine Art Images/Bridgeman Images.

the dramatic start of the artist's own professional life. The show of 1977 also included female Old Masters of established reputation: Renaissance painters like the Cremonese aristocrat Sophonisba Anguissola and the Bolognese Lavinia Fontana; eighteenth-century professionals like the pastel portraitist Rosalba Carriera, whose Venetian studio was once as essential a stop on the Grand Tour as that of her male colleague Pompeo Batoni in Rome, and the Swiss-born Angelika Kauffmann, represented by a self-portrait that showed the dark-haired, porcelain-skinned beauty making a definitive choice between painting and music. Kauffmann's specialty would be the manly preserve of classical history painting.

Beauty also probably played a certain part in establishing the reputations of the enigmatic Russian flapper Tamara de Lempicka (not included in "Women Artists") and Argentine-born Leonor Fini (whose admirers included the great literary critic Edmund Wilson). Although "Women Artists" may have been more of a grab bag than an encyclopedic retrospective, the exhibition still achieved its fundamental aim: to present women artists as fully competent, then and now, even in the restrictive sense of "artist" as synonymous with "easel painter in the modern Western tradition."

The virtuosity of the Old Masters was shaped by a system that took them in as children and sustained them ever afterward in a collective endeavor—such notorious misanthropes as Michelangelo and Caravaggio still spent their lives in the constant company of assistants. Girls were largely excluded from this world—Artemisia Gentileschi's experience suggests why—but this does not mean that girls lacked artistic talent, or, necessarily, that this talent was inevitably destined to be utterly thwarted by an accident of birth.

Painting may have been a largely male preserve, but it was never exclusively so. Like Orazio Gentileschi, Tintoretto taught his daughter Marietta how to paint alongside his sons; so did Lavinia Fontana's successful father, Prospero, and Fede Galizia's father, the miniaturist Nunzio. Sophonisba Anguissola was only the most talented among six painting sisters. And when Artemisia Gentileschi, the most ambitious of them all, established her own independent workshops in Florence, Rome, and Naples, she used her father's studio as her model; the architectural painter Viviano Codazzi collaborated with her much as Agostino Tassi had done with Orazio.

There is a fundamental problem, however, with restricting artistry to painting, either in the Renaissance or now. In the first place, Renaissance artists were also goldsmiths, sculptors, architects, military engineers, city planners, and designers of the sugar sculptures called "triumphs"—*trionfi.* Secondly, there were (and are) other preserves of wit and invention that have belonged predominantly to women, with their own traditions of apprenticeship and proficiency. These traditions have been relegated for several centuries to the status of craft rather than art, and the objects they have produced often wear out more quickly than painting, sculpture, and architecture. In their own way, however, they have been just as essential, as artistic, as art itself.

A fully equipped baroque altar, for example, only began with the arts as we usually define them—its architecture, its sculptural decoration, and its painted altarpiece. In full glory, it was also lit by lamps of silver or bronze, by candles in ornate metallic or enamel candlesticks. The stone surface of its table would be covered by satin or velvet, intricately embroidered in silk or metallic thread, topped by cloths of white linen lined in lace, tatted, crocheted, or elaborately interwoven. Along the tops and bases of the pilasters in most baroque churches, there are still rows of small studs where embroidered hangings can be fastened on festival days, and these fittings are by no means gone: the Chiesa Nuova in Rome is resplendent in red and white every March 16, Santa Maria Maggiore in Florence has a gorgeous set of blue-and-white appliquéd festival hangings, and Palermo provides a veritable treasury of liturgical textiles.

This needlework and lace, meticulous in its perfection and complex in its design, is largely the work of women, and it requires the same coordination of hand and eye that Raphael needed to make a painting. Indeed, every woman who could was expected to sew, and few girls or women were ever seen with idle hands. Mary Queen of Scots whiled away her imprisonment with her "needyll," and the calm, gradual rhythm of creation was surely the best sedative available to her. If we have no Leonardos and Michelangelos from this embroidered world, it is partly because so many towels and handkerchiefs have worn to rags, and partly because we have not been looking for greatness in their humble beauty. In the meantime, we do have that remarkable document, the Bayeux Tapestry, a historical chronicle embroidered by Norman noblewomen.

In the years since Linda Nochlin wrote an article that really asked "Why are there no 'great' women painters in the modern European workshop tradition?," what were once known as the "minor" arts have changed status to become the "decorative arts." This shift is no small matter, for many of these items originally cost more than the works of what has been considered "high" art. In many ways the most interesting answers to Nochlin's question about women artists are those that emerge from setting the work of women painters and sculptors within a broader range of women's—or human—handiwork.

In effect, this broader interpretation of the artistic impulse is now put forward routinely in exhibitions, not only in contemporary shows where "Fiber Arts" have garnered recognition in their own right, but also in historical exhibitions where objects such as Iranian carpets, Turkish damask, and Italian embroidery can keep company with Murano glass, Bellini paintings, and Ottoman weaponry as equal clues into the essence of Renaissance Venice. Women's hands were no less involved than men's in creating the aesthetic environment in which people lived.

Clearly, moreover, women's handiwork had immense importance in earlier societies. Archaeologists now generally assume that the first potters, like the first farmers, may well have been women. In ancient Greece, where a single word, *techne*, described every kind of handwork from painting to weaving to blacksmithing, a goddess, Athena, ran the show, except for the smithy where the gods ordered up their armor (and perhaps the shoes for Pegasus and Apollo's horses of the sun): that dark, dirty realm belonged to lame Hephaistos. The earliest architectural remnants in Italy, of Iron Age houses (2,600 years ago), show that the single most important article of furniture, the central idea behind the plan of these dwellings, was a great standing loom, the pride of the *materfamilias*, the mother of the family. Its rows of threads, in Latin the *ordo*, constituted the original meaning of the word "order"; thanks to increasingly sophisticated methods of archaeological investigation and conservation, we are able now to see just what those ancient fabrics looked like, and they are amazing.

It no longer sounds implausible when ancient Greeks write about the intricate textiles made by legendary weavers like Penelope and Arachne, or about historical weavers, like the women of Athens who created a new dress, or *peplos*, for the statue of Athena Polias on the Acropolis. The rows and registers of figures on these fabrics were, in their own way, as carefully composed and worked out as a play by Sophocles or a frieze by Phidias. In a domestic setting, a mother's loom was also as likely to produce a complex interwoven design as it was a rough bolt of homespun. The proverbial Roman woman's epitaph, *Domi mansit, lanam fecit* ("She stayed at home and made wool"), praises a creator with the same verb, *facere*, that artists used.

In the rest of the world, the legendary artistry of Penelope and the archaeologically attested ingenuity of Iron Age matrons still flourishes in artful craft traditions, as the Norwegian artist and entrepreneur Annemor Sundbø discovered when in 1983 she bought an old factory in Oslo that reduced castoff woolen knits to "shoddy," the combed fiber that more frugal generations used as stuffing for mattresses and comforters. The shoddy factory came complete with its own rag pile, but rather than simply feed the rags to her shredding machine, Sundbø first performed her own archaeological investigation, eventually saving some fifteen hundred pieces as something between a museum and a knitted archive.

The oldest knitwork Sundbø discovered in her late twentieth-century rag pile was a pair of seventeenth-century mittens, discarded alongside heavily patched longjohns, black-and-white fishermen's sweaters, and decades of stylish pullovers and jackets adapted, often with clever variations, from patterns published in women's magazines that ranged from the late nineteenth to the mid-twentieth century.

Rather than simply catalog her repertory, Sundbø has written several books describing how these knitted garments reflect four hundred years of changing Norwegian society.

At the same time, in order to understand how these various pieces were made, she has recreated many of her castoffs: a remarkable combination of historical and sociological research undertaken with genuine respect for all the "loving hands at home" who preserved the people of Norway from the elements with resource-fulness and style. Meanwhile her factory, Torridal Tweed, continues to recycle its piles of wool shoddy as if Norway were still a land of frugal fishermen rather than one of the wealthiest nations in the world.

At about the same time that Annemor Sundbø took possession of her rag pile, at the opposite extreme of Europe, Consiglia Azzopardi had begun to take a similarly pointed interest in the lacemakers of Malta.

Here the story has a definite and surprisingly recent beginning: in 1846, a parish priest on the Maltese island of Gozo handed a narrow ribbon of Genoese bobbin lace to two local sisters, who learned its complicated technique and passed the skill on to their friends.

Within two decades, Maltese lace had become an important cottage industry, with its own identifying motifs, international distribution (including to Queen Victoria's court), and a transforming role in the lives of the women who were able to turn this newly acquired skill into a source of income. While writing about lace as a key to recent Maltese social history, Azzopardi has actively promoted the tradition's survival by teaching its techniques, combining, like Annemor Sundbø, ingenious research with perpetuation of a manual skill having plausible claims to the status of art. (One can now take a degree in Lace Studies at the University of Malta.)

American quilting provides a similarly complex social picture, in its fabrics, its designs, its historical connections with particular groups, from enslaved Africans to Pennsylvania Dutch, and now with its lively presence, as with so many handicrafts, on the Internet, a medium that blithely levels any distinction between high and low, major and minor arts, amateurs and professionals. The Internet reveals, as plainly as any other source, that the question about the place of women in art is really a question about the place of women in the artistic marketplace.

Yet here, too, in the world of art narrowly conceived, women have consistently stood in the avant-garde, beginning with the small number of women who were part of the avant-garde movement that first resolved to distinguish art from handicraft, the maestri of the Italian Renaissance. Giorgio Vasari's *Lives of the Most Excellent Painters, Sculptors, and Architects* did much to single out these three pursuits as more intellectually challenging than all the other forms of handicraft, and their practitioners as divinely inspired geniuses rather than humble manual workers. Michelangelo, with his heroic struggles and his foul temper (not to mention his Tuscan origins), stood as Vasari's paragon, with results that are still with us today: there are many more books written on the agonies and the ecstasies of Michelangelo, Caravaggio, and Leonardo than on their more equable colleagues Raphael, Titian, Bernini, and Rubens.

Yet despite the preconceptions and the practical obstacles that the Italian workshop system posed for women artists, they do appear among Vasari's biographies of the "most excellent," grouped into the chapter he devotes to Properzia de' Rossi. She is the single artist to whom he gives an honorific title: "Madonna Properzia de' Rossi"; but then her temper seems to have rivaled Michelangelo's. Among her specialties were miniature sculptures for the Medici court: a hundred faces carved into a cherry pit, a proper employment, Vasari notes, for her delicate feminine hands (one wonders what he would have made of the late nineteenth- and early twentieth-century American expatriate Edmonia Lewis, part African-American, part Native American, hewing marble in Rome with her hammer and chisel).

The work of some women painters of early modern Italy reflects their direct involvement with handicrafts. Sophonisba Anguissola and Lavinia Fontana pay knowing and meticulous attention to all the other ways in which women plied their hands, painting all the intricate knots in lace collars, ribbons, cuffs, embroidered tablecloths—textures that Titian or Velázquez will evoke instead with an abstract pattern of brushstrokes. Yet some male painters take the same pains to record knots and stitches; as Vasari noted, the fifteenth-century Florentine artist Antonio del Pollaiuolo, best known now as a painter and sculptor, also designed embroidery. In seventeenth-century Haarlem, Frans Hals knew his prosperous neighbors too well to omit a single detail of their intricate, expensive collars, cuffs, coifs, hats, sashes, dresses, and jerkins. No less than his portraits, those remarkable texiles proclaimed good money wisely spent.

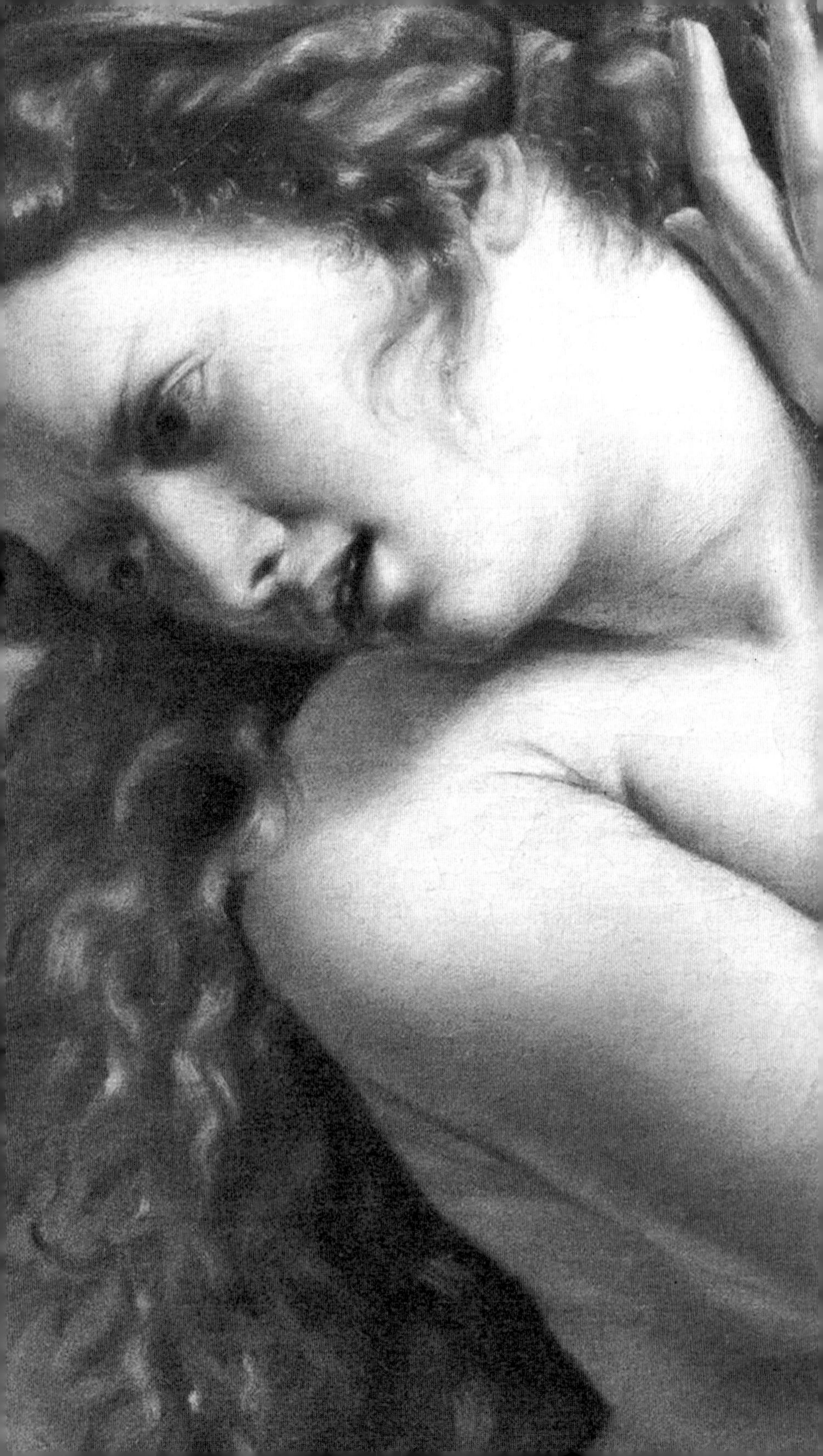

12 *Brutality and Brilliance (Artemisia Gentileschi)*

Roman to the core, Artemisia Lomi Gentileschi described herself as "the spirit of Caesar in the soul of a woman," and it is precisely her epic sensibility that makes her stand out among successful women artists of the past.[1] Unlike the stately neoclassical histories of Angelica Kauffmann or the elegant pastel portraiture of Rosalba Carriera, Artemisia Gentileschi's paintings throb with drama: the young matron Susanna cringes naked under the leering scrutiny of two scheming elders; a buxom, bejeweled Judith saws a broadsword through the neck of the Assyrian general Holofernes, heedless of his spattering blood; the dying Cleopatra writhes under the deadly effects of snakebite. Artemisia's art, like her life, was seldom for the faint of heart.

Her father Orazio was also a painter, who combined conspicuous success in the profession with a chaotic personal life. The elder Lomi Gentileschi was arrested once in Rome for brawling alongside Caravaggio, and the two of them were charged on another

Artemisia Gentileschi, *Susanna and the Elders*, 1610, detail. Schloß Weißenstein, Pommersfelden, Germany. Artexplorer/Alamy Stock Photo.

occasion with writing nasty poems about a rival painter, Giovanni Baglione, whose art and person exuded an unctuous piety that throve all too evidently in papal Rome. Their attacks induced Baglione to sue them for libel:

> Giovanni Baggage you're not worth an "ah"
> Your pictures are sissy pictures
> I want to make sure that with them
> You never earn a cent
> Because with that much canvas
> You could make a pair of breeches
> That wouldn't even cover your shit factory.[2]

Artistically, however, Orazio Gentileschi (the surname he normally used) never fell completely under the sway of his talented friend. He was too much of a colorist ever to adopt Caravaggio's increasingly limited palette, reveling instead in the shimmering greens, luminous yellows, and lacquered surfaces that were the particular glory of seventeenth-century oil painting. An artist of unending versatility, Gentileschi piled up billows of blue-tinged cloud and rosily dimpled flesh with much the same eager appreciation as his contemporary Rubens. And unlike Caravaggio, who eventually stripped away such baroque staples as background, architecture, landscape, and color from his painting to concentrate with riveting intensity on human drama, the adaptable Orazio experimented with every kind of spectacular visual effect, often in collaboration with other artists.

Among these collaborators, one of the most congenial was a short, chubby Tuscan named Agostino Tassi, who made a specialty of dizzyingly convincing architectural perspectives. These Gentileschi populated with figures, so that together they could transform a cardinal's ceiling into a portico on Mount Olympus, or a vault of the Colosseum in the days of ancient Rome. Like many of Orazio Gentileschi's friends, Agostino Tassi led a life of brawls, insolvency, and casual sex. Seventeenth-century Roman police blotters track his frequent movements from one walk-up to the next, shifting between the workers' quarter of Santo Spirito near the Vatican to the artists' quarter near the Piazza del Popolo. Yet despite his unremarkable physical appearance and his seedy reputation, Tassi attracted women, some of whom (such as his sister-in-law) loved him loyally for decades. He was thirty-six when, in 1611, he began to pursue Artemisia Gentileschi behind the back of her father and her three brothers (her mother had died years earlier). She was eighteen.

If Orazio Gentileschi had tried to seclude his daughter from the roughhouse atmosphere of his studio, he was nonetheless eager to teach her his craft. She had already earned a reputation for talent as well as beauty when Tassi bribed her duenna, entered her rooms, and raped her. With promises of marriage, as she later testified, he "induced me afterward to consent affectionately to his desires many times," a relationship cemented by drawing lessons in which Orazio must have hoped she might learn Tassi's skill at perspective.

But Tassi, as all three of them were horrified to learn, already had a wife: the assassins he had paid to kill her before he left Tuscany for Rome turned out to have pocketed their fee without doing the job. Father and daughter sued Tassi for rape and breach of promise: it was the best way, under the circumstances, to salvage Artemisia's reputation. But vindication did not come cheap. To validate her testimony at the trial, in March 1612, Artemisia was subjected both to a medical examination and to a torture called the *sibille*: strings progressively tightened around her fingers (which were expected to yield a truth as infallible as the Sibylline oracle). For a painter of her evident promise, the *sibille* posed a fearsome risk, and they were probably not applied for long; the trial records, preserved in the State Archive in Rome, indicate that the judges of the Governor's Criminal Court found her case believable and ruled swiftly in her favor.

Her testimony makes terrifying reading. In simple, direct language she describes how Tassi had stalked her for weeks before he finally made his move, how her greedy duenna let him into the house, how the first rape became the pretext for more and more forced intimacy. Tassi's slanderous attempts at self-defense, on the other hand, seem to have made no impression on the court. He was given a choice of banishment or five years of slavery as a rower in the papal galleys (although the sentence was never enforced).

Soon afterward Artemisia married a well-born but debt-ridden young Florentine painter named Pierantonio Stiattesi and moved to Florence.

Like Caravaggio's brushes with murder and gutter life, Artemisia Gentileschi's rape and subsequent trial seem to be nearly impossible to separate from her work, which—again like Caravaggio's—is striking both for its violence and for its merciless concentration. Her first large-scale painting is signed and dated 1610, when Tassi may already have been stalking her. Its subject is a tale from the Greek version of the Hebrew Bible (book of Daniel, chapter 13): Susanna, a respectable young married woman, was bathing in her garden when two village elders slipped through her gate and tried to convince her to sleep with them. When Susanna resisted, the conniving elders accused her of adultery, a capital offense. As she was led off to execution, the heroic young Jew, Daniel (the same Daniel thrown into the lions' den), cried out in protest, and forced the villagers into a retrial, in which he demolished the elders' conflicting testimony and ensured that they, not Susanna, were the ones who were put to death. The story was popular in seventeenth-century Italy because it afforded artists an opportunity to portray a female nude who was neither pagan nor disreputable. Artemisia Gentileschi's *Susanna and the Elders* was a remarkable feat for an artist of seventeen; her father may have helped her with it, but the psychological penetration is all hers, and both the play of shadow on Susanna's body and its graceful classical proportions reveal a painter of exceptional promise. She has stripped away the scene's usual garden setting, leaving only the fountain where Susanna sits uncomfortably on a step, cringing as the two elders whisper behind her, crouching over a low marble parapet as their hands and arms creep into the space she must have occupied a moment earlier, before she curled up in horror; the younger man's wandering, insinuating index finger almost touches Susanna's hair. With his jet-black hair and beard, this conspicuously youthful elder has been identified by some art historians as a portrait of Agostino Tassi.

Shortly after the trial, Artemisia painted another popular Biblical story, *Judith and Holofernes*. Normally Judith was shown with Holofernes' severed head in hand, but a decade earlier Caravaggio decided to show the decapitation itself. His canvas was meant to shock, with its gush of scarlet blood spurting from Holofernes' severed jugular and Judith's concentrated scowl, but Gentileschi's version of 1612 or 1613 is even more violently physical. She has compressed the composition, so that the dying general is splayed on his back, his right hand seizing the bodice of Judith's maid in a brutal grip. The young woman calmly continues to press him down as Judith saws a broadsword through his neck, standing well clear of the dark stream of gore cascading down the white sheets of his bed. The model for the Assyrian general has been identified as Agostino Tassi, and there is no mistaking the fact that Judith has the same cleft chin, dark brown hair, and rounded face as Artemisia herself.

This intense focus on individual personality immediately distinguishes the younger Gentileschi's painting from that of her father, despite his dazzling range and the consistency of his technical skill. If Orazio's painting style is as colorfully changeable as a chameleon, the daughter at her best musters the ferocity of Caravaggio.

Revealed beyond doubt as an important new painter, Artemisia rushed off to Florence with her new husband in 1612, leaving her father behind in Rome, where he soon resumed his collaboration with Agostino Tassi. And despite the trauma of her rape, trial, and vindication, there is every reason to believe that some of the later events in her life exerted as significant an effect on her work as those first, terrible experiences in Rome. In Florence, she learned for the first time to read and write. She bore four children and buried three of them. In 1616, at the age of twenty-two, she was elected to the prestigious Florentine artists' guild, the Accademia del Disegno—the first woman to be so honored. She befriended some of the most significant intellectuals in Florentine society, including Galileo, to whom she addressed a surviving letter. For Michelangelo Buonarroti the Younger, she painted an allegory of "Inclinazione," roughly, "Intention," a nude woman seated on a heavenly cloud with a star above her head and a large compass in her hands (decades later, a more prudish descendant had the figure swathed in painted drapes). It was 1616, the year of her admission into the Accademia del Disegno, and Buonarroti paid her handsomely. Once again, as with *Judith and Holofernes*, the figure bears an idealized resemblance to the artist herself at a moment of immense hope and promise. She would continue to act as her own model, posing as a musician, a martyr, and above all as a painter; formally dressed or engrossed in her work, but always, insistently, as a strong artist welded inseparably to the soul and body of a strong woman.

Heroic women would become her specialty, much as Titian was called upon to produce legions of pentitent Magdalenes and reclining Venuses. Her first Susanna was followed by others. She also painted repeated images of Judith and Holofernes in a spray of blood, tangled bedclothes, and stifled screams, and an intense image from 1620 of Jael, "most blessed of tent-dwelling women," hamering a tent peg through the skull of the Canaanite general Sisera (book of Judges, chapters 4–5), curled into a fetal position that would be all innocence if not for the hand that has crept suggestively under Jael's skirts. Next to Jael's hammer, a chiseled inscription identifies the painter (as Artemisia Lomi). Her signatures are often set in fictive stone.

In fact, however, this Caesar-like soul also earned her living by still life painting and portraiture. In 1620, she returned to Rome, where she stayed for the next decade, and began to reveal a versatility as broad as her father's. Her stately portrait of the Roman noblewoman Maria Savelli is as hieratic as a Holbein in its careful cataloguing of every bejeweled, embroidered surface; if there are any similarities to her violent biblical scenes, they lie in her brilliant colors and expert brushwork.

Artemisia's signature appears, with several variations, on nineteen paintings. In an era when artists often left their work unsigned (Caravaggio, for example, wrote his name on only one), scholars, curators, and art lovers are still trying to decide exactly what Artemisia Gentileschi did and did not paint. Sometimes the identifications are easy, like the allegories that are also self-portraits, with her distinctive face and unruly hair recorded without apology. Much of her work is still unknown—either it is lost altogether or we are looking at it without realizing it. Surviving documents such as contracts, letters, or catalogues of collections record paintings that no longer exist or have not yet been identified, artists who have slipped into total oblivion, and patrons and critics who mistake the subject of the painting they are describing. At the same time, legions of unidentified seventeenth-century paintings wait for recognition, some still brightly compelling, some darkened with age, some crusted with grime, some repainted by well-meaning but incompetent restorers, some stripped of their surface by harsh cleaning agents. The temptation to put illustrious names to these orphan canvases can be irresistible, and often no one will be the wiser until two works are put side by side. Moreover, although Artemisia signed at least nineteen of her paintings, signatures can be faked or wiped out, and even the signature on *Susanna and the Elders* has been called into question because its date indicates such incredible artistic precocity—and because at the time she was still classified as illiterate by the Roman courts.

Many of the artist's known later works have lost their angry edge to the press of deadlines, or to the satisfactions of success, or to the sheer fatigue that accompanied every artisan who worked in order to live in the days before retirement plans and health insurance, increasingly so in the last phase of her life from 1630 to 1656, which she spent mostly in Naples, dreaming about a return to Rome. There she must have witnessed the eruption of Vesuvius in 1631 after centuries of dormancy. She certainly answered the call when the bishop of nearby Pozzuoli ordered a series of altarpieces in 1632 for the cathedral of San Gennaro (Saint Januarius), the early Christian bishop martyred in that city's arena. The blood of San Gennaro, preserved in two vials in the cathedral of Naples, brought out in procession during the eruption of 1631, was widely believed to have been the force that finally stopped the volcano, propelling him from a minor saint to the chief protector of Naples and its surroundings. For the cathedral of Pozzuoli, she collaborated with a Roman artist, Viviano Codazzi, who, like Agostino Tassi, specialized in depicting buildings in perspective. Their *San Gennaro in the Arena* takes every opportunity to thrill the baroque eye: a majestic arena packed with spectators (its ruins are still visible in Pozzuoli today), pious Christians facing martyrdom, lions (clearly modeled on Neapolitan mastiffs) who have become suddenly kittenish (or, more accurately, puppyish) in the magisterial presence of the holy man.

Artemisia's San Gennaro is no kindly Saint Nicholas. He is a gaunt ascetic on whom his brocaded robes hang awkwardly, his forehead creased with premature wrinkles. His power is palpably the power of austere prayer rather than cheery goodwill. As with many of her Neapolitan paintings, the surface of this one has worn almost to transparency; she seems to have applied her (expensive) colors ever more thinly—as did Caravaggio in the later stages of his career. And like the late sacred paintings of Caravaggio, it is a splendid work, although many of Gentileschi's admirers do not like it much; it is too conventionally religious, and it is a thoroughly collaborative work, as emphatically Codazzi's as hers. But *San Gennaro in the Arena* brings out several important aspects of Artemisia Gentileschi's artistic personality: her focus on psychology, her adaptability—here in her evident absorption of Neapolitan color schemes of red and black—the versatility required of all baroque designers.

From the beginning of her career to its end, Artemisia, like her father before her, worked in close partnership with other artists. However traumatic her interactions with Agostino Tassi and her father became at one point in her life, she clearly fit comfortably and effectively into the social and commercial structures of a profoundly social and predominantly male profession, hiring apprentices of her own and establishing arrangements with painters such as Codazzi who could complement her own talents—including with another female artist, Giovanna Garzoni, a specialist in still life.

At the very end of his career, Orazio Gentileschi finally called on his distinguished daughter to work with him in partnership. In 1638, Queen Henrietta Maria of England engaged the seventy-four-year-old Orazio to decorate the great hall of her pleasure palace, the Queen's House at Greenwich. The commission called for an *Allegory of Peace and the Arts under the English Crown*, including images of the nine Muses, a subject that Orazio had tackled in Rome together with Agostino Tassi at the very moment when the latter undertook his pursuit of Artemisia. For one reason or another—fatigue, curiosity, a sense of impending mortality, a recognition of his own limitations, a last-ditch hope of reconciliation, or perhaps at the command of Henrietta Maria herself—Orazio

Gentileschi sent for his illustrious daughter from the chill land of the Anglican infidels, and she came.

On her return to Naples from England Artemisia Gentileschi seems to have run out of energy, both physical and creative. Later letters complain about her health, while commissions continued to pour in for the subjects in which she had excelled for decades: Susanna, Judith, and veritable legions of Bathshebas, set against backgrounds by Codazzi.

Declining energy, of course, is hardly rare among achievers, whether they be novelists, scientists, or well-known painters. The fact that Artemisia followed this trajectory only proves how genuinely she succeeded, by every convention of her era and ours. As a painter, she may always have to concede in the end to the ugly swashbuckler Michelangelo Merisi da Caravaggio, whose heroic fury was as great as hers and whose bold innovations shaped the subsequent history of his calling. But in an age that had seen the steady erosion over centuries of women's legal rights, she managed to live out the Italian feminist motto of the 1970s with utter consistency: "Io sono mia." I belong to me.

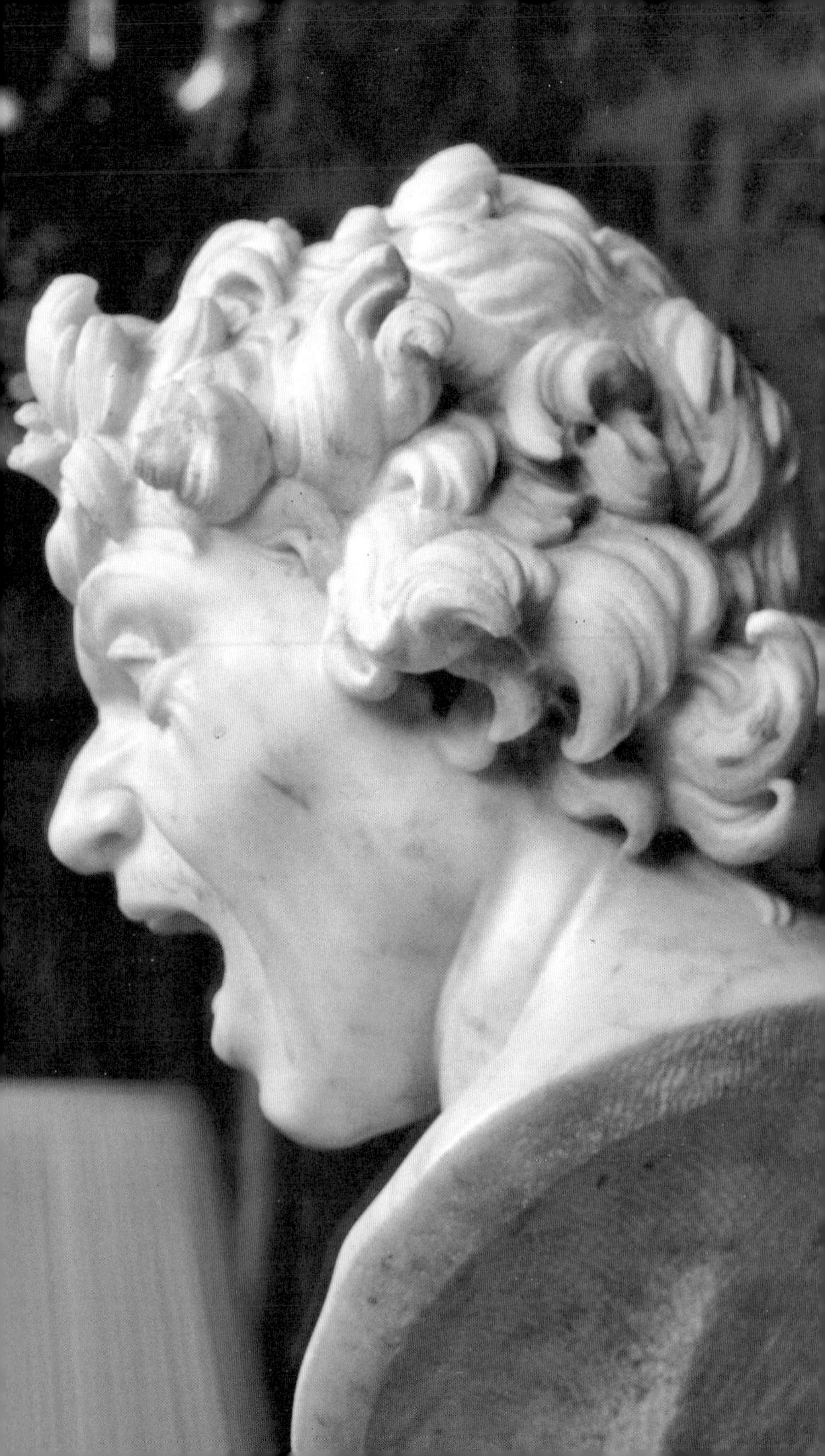

13   *He Had the Touch (Gian Lorenzo Bernini)*

In 1619, at the ripe age of twenty, Gian Lorenzo Bernini set himself the seemingly impossible challenge of carving the human soul in marble. Two souls, in fact: a blessed soul bound for Heaven and a wicked soul newly damned to Hell, the most insubstantial of beings portrayed in solid stone from the neck up.

The *Blessed Soul* is female, with a classical profile and a classical coiffure, crowned with a garland of roses frozen forever. Between her parted lips we can just detect a row of perfect teeth, a feat of detailing that the ancient Greeks and Romans regarded as proof of a consummate sculptor—and Bernini had no intention of lagging behind the ancients, or anyone else. The blessed soul's eyes are carved with irises and pupils upturned toward her heavenly reward, like the pearly-skinned damsels that the painter Guido Reni was churning out at the same moment. In her perfection, the *Blessed Soul* lacks every trace of personality, but perhaps this is the point; she has been purified of every fault.

Gian Lorenzo Bernini, *Anima dannata (Condemned Soul)*, 1619, detail. Spanish Embassy, Rome, Italy/Bridgeman Images.

The *Condemned Soul* by contrast, is male, and unmistakably individual, from his definite features—heavy brow, corrugated forehead, a wisp of mustache—to his wild expression and his crazy flamelike hair, bristling with horror at what he sees before him. He is a self-portrait of Bernini, making faces in a mirror as he envisions the torments of Hell, and we can see not only his full set of rather sharp teeth but also his tongue, so highly polished that it seems realistically wet. To suggest the infernal flames reflected in the *Condemned Soul's* dark, intent eyes, Bernini has hollowed out their irises, leaving a pinpoint of white marble in the center of each to capture a fiery gleam.

In making his imaginative leap into the Inferno, the young artist may have used the *Spiritual Exercises* of Ignatius Loyola, where Hell appeared on the fifth day of the first week of a monthlong discipline. Loyola sounded the depths of perdition by appealing to the five earthly senses, and so does Bernini's marble head. Loyola writes:

First Point. The first Point will be to see with the sight of the imagination the great fires, and the souls as in bodies of fire.

Second Point. The second, to hear with the ears wailings, howlings, cries, blasphemies against Christ our Lord and against all His Saints.

Third Point. The third, to smell with the smell smoke, sulphur, dregs and putrid things.

Fourth Point. The fourth, to taste with the taste bitter things, like tears, sadness and the worm of conscience.

Fifth Point. The fifth, to touch with the touch; that is to say, how the fires touch and burn the souls.[1]

The stench of sulfur and smoke visibly wrinkles the *Condemned Soul's* nose, making those mephitic vapors easier to imagine than the scent of the *Blessed Soul's* crown of roses. Bernini seems to have no doubt about where he and his viewers will end their days.

The artist often served as his own model, especially in the early phases of his career. Some two years before carving these souls for the Spanish monsignor Pedro de Foix Montoya, he created a life-sized statue of Saint Lawrence (1617), his name-saint, who was put to death by roasting on a gridiron. To give the martyred deacon's face a plausible sense of agony, the eighteen-year-old Gian Lorenzo reportedly thrust his own thigh into the fire while watching his face in a mirror. A large-as-life statue of *David* (1623–1624), loading the slingshot that will bring down Goliath, bites his lip with fierce concentration, as Bernini himself must have done so often when he picked up hammer and chisel, or sank his hands into a slab of clay. Like Saint Lawrence, David must have acted as a kind of alter ego for the young sculptor, a small, fierce man of singular charm who had a burning urge to create, and a colossal libido to match.

Like David, marksman, king, and poet, Gian Lorenzo Bernini was precocious, authoritative, and versatile: he had the touch no matter what he put his hand to. He could make limp swags of drapery swirl and throb as if some sort of lifeblood ran through them, like the corkscrew gyres of the cloak that twist around Apollo's loins as he reaches for the nymph Daphne (*Apollo and Daphne*, 1622–1624) and feels her skin turn to bark under his fingertips. Sculpted twenty-five years apart, Bernini's two life-size images of saintly women in ecstasy, Saint Teresa of Avila (*Ecstasy of Saint Teresa*, 1645–1652) and *Blessed Ludovica Albertoni* (1671–1674), convey their passionate spiritual state by the agitation of their heavy clothing as well as the expressive, elusive hints of faces, hands, and feet.

Bernini's tomb of Pope Alexander VII in St. Peter's Basilica (1671–1678) shows a gilt bronze skeleton struggling to emerge from a dense shroud of mottled red marble: a human soul is struggling to break free of its carnal clothing, the flesh rendered as a literal curtain of meat. As simple an object as the black-and-yellow marble drape that clings improbably to a Gothic pillar in the Roman church of Santa Maria sopra Minerva, the tomb monument of a pious widow named Sister Maria Raggi (1647), still flutters after all these centuries in a secret celestial breeze.

For so small a man (the fingerprints preserved on his terracotta models are surprisingly tiny), Bernini exerted a titanic influence on the arts and the cityscape of seventeenth-century Rome, where he spent nearly the whole of his long life. His father, Pietro, was a Florentine sculptor who worked in Naples before settling in Rome with his growing family when Gian Lorenzo was eight. The elder Bernini modeled his own carving technique on imperial

Roman sculpture, with its copious drill work and high polish, but the son departed quickly from his father's distinctive style, using rasp and chisel where Pietro drilled and polished. Already executing sculptural commissions as a teenager, Gian Lorenzo quickly branched out from sculpture into painting, architecture, theater, urban planning, and the vast universe of the decorative arts. Fiery and driven, he became all the greater as an artist because he was forced to compete for attention with stupendous rivals: Pietro da Cortona in painting and architecture, Alessandro Algardi in sculpture, and Francesco Borromini, the greatest—and most demanding—architect of them all.

The magnet that attracted all these talented souls was papal Rome. By the seventeenth century, thanks to the Protestant Reformation and the rise of Spain and France as nation-states, the city had lost political and religious significance. The papacy compensated for those losses by reinforcing Roman, and Catholic, dominion over the arts. For more than six decades, that dominion depended on the versatile hands and ruthless charm of Gian Lorenzo Bernini, whose skills, already from an early age, included the ability to run a large artistic workshop along with an impressive series of building sites, beginning with the perpetual work-in-progress of St. Peter's Basilica. He was notoriously thrifty when it came to paying his subordinates, and several struck out on their own, none more loudly than Borromini, shocked to discover that he was earning one twentieth of the master's salary.

Rome proclaimed its status as a cultural capital in the middle years of the seventeenth century through treasures great and small: musical instruments like the famous Barberini Harp (the pride of Rome's underused, underfunded, glorious Museum of Musical Instruments), Borromini's flawlessly precise drawings, Bernini's *Fountain of the Four Rivers*. A marvelous little bronze Bernini lion on a miniature porphyry crag provides a tabletop version, for the king of Spain, of the most beloved figure from the sculptor's great work of public art.

Bernini may have hated making portraits of other people, but he did it supremely well. We can look right into the blandly impervious face of his great patron, Pope Urban VIII, newly elected and delighted at the prospect of his papacy (in a 1631 engraved portrait by Claude Mellan from a drawing by Bernini), and then we can see the haggard image of Urban ten years later, after his two tragic mistakes, the condemnation of his onetime friend Galileo Galilei for heresy (1633), and his futile war against the feudal stronghold of Castro (1641–1643), have blighted the final years of his reign. The sculptor lavished particular attention on a larger-than-life terracotta bust of Pope Alexander VII, a diplomat with a poet's soul who counted as a true friend, and on the ardently intimate marble portrait bust of his mistress, *Costanza Piccolomini*, about a year before he ordered the slashing of her face.

The tousled hair and open blouse of Bernini's lover are sexy, to be sure, but they are more a sign of the sitter's aristocratic *sprezzatura* than her easy virtue: the equivalent of the haphazardly buttoned cassock we can see in Bernini's portrait of Cardinal Scipione Borghese, a papal nephew, or the wispy, unkempt beard of Pope Innocent X. These casual touches serve as signs that these sitters were once alive, in motion, irregular—as changeable and individual as marble itself under the master's hand. Bernini presents Costanza as a vibrant presence rather than an elaborate doll, the antithesis to Giovanni Lazzoni's bizarrely stylized portrait bust of the papal niece Olimpia Aldobrandini (a work of 1660 now in the Doria Pamphilj Gallery, Rome). Indeed, Bernini's portrait of Costanza Piccolomini would transform the portrayal of women in baroque Rome, inspiring Alessandro Algardi, for example, to sculpt the fearsome dowager Donna Olimpia Maidalchini, Pope Innocent's sister-in-law, with her widow's weeds billowing behind her. If Costanza looks as if she is just about to speak, Donna Olimpia's ominously pursed lips warn us that she has already said her piece.

Bernini's painted self-portraits (and his sculpted image as David) suggest he had the same kind of searing stare as Picasso (and Leonardo, and Titian), and we know what effect Picasso's ardent eyes had on women. Gian Lorenzo Bernini may have been irresistible in similar ways. When he finally married, he sired eleven children—it seems safe to conclude that he liked sex at least as much as he liked carving marble.

But his charisma had its limits. On a March day in 1638, about a year after immortalizing Costanza in marble, Gian Lorenzo, spying from a carriage, caught another man emerging from her house behind St. Peter's: his twenty-five-year-old brother Luigi, whose brilliance by all accounts came close to that of his eldest brother, without Gian Lorenzo's driving ego and middle-aged physique. In a sequence worthy of a baroque action film, for the next hour or so the great artist went berserk. He chased Luigi into the basilica, beat him with an iron rod, cracking two of Luigi's ribs, and then, rapier in hand, stabbing wildly, he began a headlong pursuit across the breadth of baroque Rome. From the Vatican Gian Lorenzo harried the injured Luigi across the Tiber, past the banking district, past the Capitol, up the slopes of the Esquiline Hill to the basilica of Santa Maria Maggiore, the ancient church that rose across the street from the Bernini family home and where the family lies buried by the main altar.

Luigi knew that he was running for his life. He drew far enough ahead of Gian Lorenzo to slip into the basilica and pull its heavy doors behind him. Meanwhile, his frenzied brother, sword in hand, burst into their house as Mamma Bernini looked on in horror—but no Luigi. Then, in his mother's words, Gian Lorenzo, "with disdain for God, the Church, and its Masters," crossed the street to Santa Maria Maggiore, kicking and pounding at the doors, trying desperately to beat them down. Only when his mother appeared on the scene did the fratricidal battle break up; she would later lament to the papal police that her eldest son acted "as if he were master of the world."[2]

Then, fury chilled to icy rationality, Gian Lorenzo turned his attentions to Costanza. Two hours after Luigi had left her house, one of the elder Bernini's servants pulled up with two flasks of the white wine called *greco*; as she reached for the gift, the swift stroke of a razor slashed her face. This ritual disfigurement, called the *sfregio*, was normally reserved for wayward prostitutes, and in the days before antiseptics or antibiotics infection often introduced dreadful complications. The mark of even the most surgically inflicted *sfregio* lasted, of course, for the rest of the victim's life, and there was no mistaking its meaning.

Costanza Piccolomini was twenty-five when her aristocratic face was marked as the face of a fallen woman. Had she taken up with the Bernini brothers for love, or money—at this point she and her husband had little enough of that—or boredom? All told, we know maddeningly little about this strange love quadrangle, three sculptors and a woman of twenty-five, except that it all ended in violence and tears. The wound to her face took weeks to heal; it must have been deep, possibly infected, a blow to her soul as much as to her countenance, but again, we know only the bare outline of the story. A doctor was still caring for her a month after the attack.

Furthermore, because she had been caught in flagrant adultery, albeit by yet another adulterous partner who was not her husband, Costanza was as liable to criminal charges as Gian Lorenzo Bernini, and here the record is ample. The penalties for their respective crimes, assault and adultery, were surprisingly similar in their harshness, but Bernini, at least, had the protection of a pope. His servant was condemned to exile as the material perpetrator of the crime, and Bernini was fined three thousand scudi, a penalty commuted by Urban VIII.

Costanza spent several months in a convent for penitent prostitutes before returning to her husband, who took her back and made a decent life with her; in his will he would call her "my beloved wife." In later years, she became one of Rome's most successful art dealers, working out of her house on what is now called the Vicolo Scanderbeg, just beneath the Quirinal Palace where the president of Italy resides. In her mid-thirties, she bore a daughter, probably fathered by a high-placed prelate, whom she brought up and who married well. Art historian Sarah McPhee, who first brought Costanza's full story to light, has tentatively identified two later painted portraits of her, a dignified widow with her facial scar tactfully omitted.

In baroque Rome, evidently, art, as a matter of honor and reputation, could easily become a matter of life and death. Seventeenth-century Roman police records are filled with the names of painters, sculptors, and architects accused of slander, assault, rape, and, often enough, murder. Caravaggio famously skewered a local thug (Ranuccio Tommasoni, the forerunner of a mafioso) on a Roman tennis court, but the police also booked the painter for writing scurrilous verse, throwing artichokes, and ogling schoolchildren. When Francesco Borromini discovered that one of his workmen was vandalizing marble for the restoration of the Lateran basilica, he ordered his foreman to beat the culprit; when the man died, Borromini was charged with murder. Both Caravaggio and Borromini were actually sent into exile, Borromini for a year, Caravaggio for life, though a pardon seems to have been on its way when the wayward painter collapsed and died along Tuscany's sultry mosquito coast.

Bernini, on the other hand, because of his charm and his position in the Roman art world, escaped punishment. For similar reasons, after about a year, Gian Lorenzo was compelled to forgive his randy brother because he depended so completely on Luigi's skills as an engineer and business manager. Their falling out had at least two lasting consequences for Bernini's life: the following year, by order of the pope and his own mother, he married a twenty-one-year-old girl of good family and blameless reputation, and for the rest of his life he was racked by spiritual struggles with the ideas of Christian guilt and atonement. Saint Lawrence roasting on the grill and the *Condemned Soul* were only the starting points of Gian Lorenzo Bernini's spiritual journey through Heaven and Hell.

Among the visions of Heaven that Bernini supplied to the churchgoers of baroque Rome, none is more impressive than his work inside St. Peter's: from the Baldacchino, the bronze canopy that stands beneath the basilica's gigantic dome, to the monumental reliquary for the Cathedra Petri, the Throne of Saint Peter, an extravaganza that stands somewhere between sculpture and architecture. High on the wall of the basilica's massive apse, clouds of gilded bronze, pierced by a golden-glazed window and populated by legions of the winged babies called *spiritelli*, "little spirits," wait for the rays of the setting sun to set them ablaze with light. Floating beneath the billowing display, the relics of the Throne of Saint Peter, clad in black bronze, are held aloft by four Doctors of the Church, Saints Augustine, Ambrose, John Chrysostom, and Athanasius, the saints' black bronze skin contrasting with their golden robes.

To keep his own volcanic soul out of Hell, the elderly Gian Lorenzo became devoted to a particular means of redemption from sin: contemplation of the blood of Christ. By way of assisting his meditations, he created a peculiar little painting of an airborne crucifix dripping torrents of liquid from wounded hands and feet into a vermilion sea, as a levitating Virgin Mary collects the blood and lymph gushing from her son's side in two chalices. It is a disconcerting image, painted in the aftermath of a decades-long conflict between Catholics and Protestants in Europe (known as the Thirty Years' War of 1618–1648, but a war that had really begun fifty years earlier) and focused obsessively on the physical immediacy of that blood-red sea.

The world into which Gian Lorenzo Bernini brought his glorious visions was a harsh, violent world—to whose violence he had made his own contribution—but the effect of his work has been to bring people together, not only in his own time and place but also in ours, in the Rome of Pope Francis, whose native Argentina is commemorated on yet another of Bernini's creations, the Fountain of the Four Rivers in Rome's Piazza Navona, where the figure representing the Rio de la Plata, symbolizing the Americas, shrinks back in awe at a golden bolt of sunlight that has pierced the mountain on which he perches (the metal of the bolt is long gone, but the carved traces of its trajectory survive). Roman legend says that the personified river is really recoiling in horror at Borromini's facade for the church in front of him, Sant'Agnese in Agone.

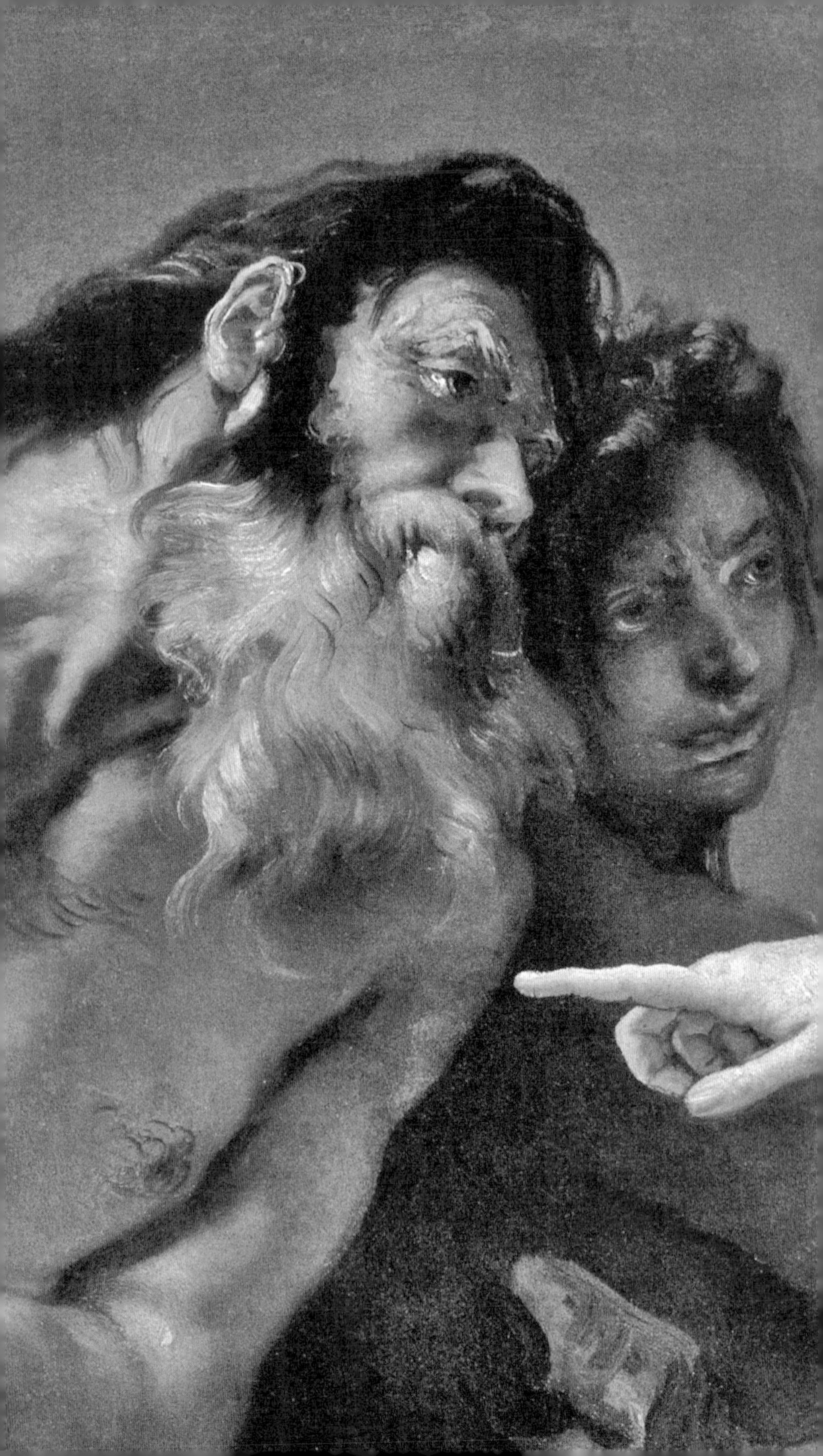

14   *Eros, Mystery, Menace (Giambattista Tiepolo)*

Like Plato's Athens, eighteenth-century Venice no longer played much of a part on any political stage, but that fact had virtually no effect on the vibrancy of the city's cultural life. The merchant-aristocrats who had once ruled the Mediterranean might be lords now of little more than their farms on the neighboring mainland, but their reduced circumstances hardly seemed to matter; the world still came calling. Indeed, the world may well have had more to learn from this older, more humble Venice than from Venice in its arrogant heyday, when the Most Serene Republic held sway over Constantinople, Crete, and the Adriatic Sea.

There is no compelling reason to think that temporal power and insight bear any relationship with one another, nor that loss of power necessarily leads to decadence rather than wisdom, in people or states. Though Thucydides famously had Pericles tell the Athenians "We are the school of Hellas," it was another Athens altogether that would become a school to the world: an Athens

Giovanni Battista Tiepolo, *Neptune Offering Gifts to Venice*, before 1758, detail. Palazzo Ducale, Venice, Italy. © Francesco Turio Bohm. All rights reserved 2023/Bridgeman Images.

chastened by ruinous military defeat, the Athens of Plato, Aristotle, and then of the philosophical schools, a city of enduring, radiant, and no longer overbearing beauty. Thucydides himself began as an ambitious Athenian general, but he wrote his history in exile after a failed campaign—really a failed colonial adventure—that immeasurably deepened his thinking about strategy, resources, and power. The fact that eighteenth-century Venetians had long since deferred to the Ottoman Turks in the Mediterranean and to Britain in the Ocean Sea meant that they could spend their time in other pursuits, not all of them necessarily frivolous. And certainly, the eighteenth-century city was no less beautiful than its more potent, militant predecessor; it may have been more beautiful still.

That eighteenth-century phenomenon we know as the Enlightenment seems to have come to Venice in a literal burst of light, refracted as the picture-perfect perspectives of Canaletto, Bernardo Bellotto, and Francesco Guardi, the soft pastels of Rosalba Carriera, and the brilliant billowing clouds of Giovanni Battista (or Giambattista) Tiepolo's ceiling frescoes. Not since Giovanni Bellini and Antonello da Messina in the late fifteenth century had painters reveled so happily in the brilliance of Venetian light on a sunny day, when sky, water, and city glitter off one another; instead, at the beginning of the sixteenth century, Giorgione's *Tempest* seems to have brought on a spate of stormy artistic weather: Titian, Tintoretto, and Veronese, working especially in oil on canvas, all built their paintings up from a dark brown ground that encouraged the creation of deep contrasts between light and shadow, in clouds, in figures, in architecture. The works of these supreme masters are monumental, majestic, and, in their incessant play of light against darkness, suggestively enigmatic. Altogether, they evoke a Venice of tremendous power and authority—Tintoretto's *Paradiso* for the great hall of the Doges' Palace (1588–1590) is the largest oil painting in the world, a beatific vision that links the city and its government explicitly to the triumphant design of Heaven. In the right light, we can still see the places where bolts of painted canvas have been stitched together to create the gigantic image of Jesus Christ as the Doge of Doges.

Tiepolo, on the other hand, painted most of his ceilings in fresco, that is, by applying pigment to wet, fresh plaster (potentially a risky technique in the damp, salty sea air). This luminous matte ground means that his figures, like his clouds, bask under a light so blindingly intense that it all but banishes shadow. Tiepolo's clouds and figures belong, at the very least, to a different Venice from their predecessors, and perhaps they belong to a different universe, one that runs on principles of Newtonian mechanics rather than the caprice of the ancient gods. It is tempting to trace Tiepolo and his lustrous colors back to the pure beam of Enlightenment reason, but this is a temptation that the late Roberto Calasso urges us to resist:

> Tiepolo: the last breath of happiness in Europe. And like all true happiness, it was as full of dark sides destined not to fade away, but to get the upper hand.[1]

This dark side is what allows us to defend Tiepolo to our own world, given contemporary obsessions with sincerity on one hand and Freudian depths on the other. Not since the Spanish court of Philip ii has there been such an obsession with black as there is in our own day and age—not to mention its French cousin, *noir* (though it is worth pointing out that changes in dyeing technology have perceptibly lightened the most recent blacks in our own visual field). Tiepolo, on the other hand, maintains such an air of detachment, of sophisticated urbanity under his unrelenting flutters of satin tissues and billows of cloud, that many recent critics, from Roberto Longhi in the mid-1950s to Jed Perl in the early twenty-first century, experience his work as repellently chilly. Certainly no Tiepolo character ever touches the emotional extremes of a Caravaggio; no crazed hatred or anguished penitence ever troubles the Venetian painter's bright, populous realm; neither does unbounded love pour forth to oppose such miseries with works of mercy. No matter how elaborately they twine about one another, most of Tiepolo's people are entirely, disconcertingly on their own.

Insistently, the Venetian painter focuses on the pairing of a weathered old man and a young woman with a flawless body, flawless posture, and a superior expression; these are the two members of his painted company of players who can always be trusted to look knowingly down upon the events around them, observing attentively, yes, but too involved in one another to care actively about what happens outside their charmed, hermetic circle. With Caravaggio, strikingly, it is the young men and the elderly ladies who truly understand what is happening before them; they, and sad, stoic Jesus. Caravaggio's characters respond to what they see, passionately, by smirking, laughing, weeping, or bowing their heads in reverence. Tiepolo fixes his focus on the world above and beyond toiling humanity, where this eminently pagan bonded pair of youth and age, male and female, governs his reality; whether they represent—for the moment—Truth and Time, Venus and Vulcan, Hades and Persephone, Venus and Time, deep down they are all one and the same, the eternal wedding of opposites.

People may argue about the relative temperature of Tiepolo's muse, but there is no doubt that he aims for, and achieves, a triumph of eros. His old men are still powerfully muscular, and his milk-white women have the strength of body and will to match their venerable consorts. In *Neptune Offering Gifts to Venice*, Venice, clad in an ermine cape with a pearl-studded golden crown on her head, a republic dressed as a queen, points an imperious finger at the old man of the sea, who, naked as pure water, upends a cornucopia at her feet. Her left hand, grasping a scepter, rests on the sleepy head of Saint Mark's winged lion, the city's heraldic symbol. Despite their languid postures, they are ready to pounce in an instant. The god has been warned.

In a similar vain, Tiepolo returned repeatedly to painting the contrast between a besotted Marc Antony and a majestic, disdainful Cleopatra, acting out the eternal strife of War and Love, Mars and Venus. Venetian velvets, silks, and filigree are the perfect complement to the famous banquet in which Cleopatra dissolved a precious pearl in a goblet of vinegar and drank it down (just as an Italian woman confessed to the *Corriere della Sera* many years ago that when her astronaut lover gave her a moon rock as a gift, the only thing she could think to do was swallow it on the spot).

We might see Proust's "Tiepolo pink" as the eighteenth century's alternative to deep, sleek Titian red, a shade seen at its most intense in the satin drape that flutters across the ceiling of Palazzo Clerici in Milan and lines the collar of the page who accompanies Pharaoh's daughter in *The Finding of Moses* from the National

Gallery of Scotland (an epicene page so sumptuously dressed that he could be the damsel's brother).

The Italian word for pink is *rosa*; thus both Italians and Anglo-Saxons associate the hue almost by definition with the evanescence of flowers, whereas Titian red is the color of heavy auburn hair and deep-pile velvet. And indeed, Tiepolo's pink is a tone of astonishing delicacy, nothing like the forceful, glossy pastels of his French contemporary François Boucher (1703–1770), as hard as a china doll. Tiepolo layers paint so lightly that we can often see the exquisite underdrawing beneath, and are meant to. For all his skill with color, he is as much a graphic artist as a painter, and a great one at that.

The artist produced thirty-three etchings over his career. He called them *Capricci*, "caprices," and *Scherzi di fantasia*, "plays of imagination," mustering the same troupe of traveling players, assembling and reassembling them to tell myths, legends, histories: tales of Troy or the *Chanson de Roland*, allegories to warn against the tricks of Time, and fabrications to exalt the ancestry of any family willing to pay for the privilege, whether it be a Venetian magnate, a Franconian prince-bishopric from Würzburg, or His Most Catholic Majesty, the king of Spain (Tiepolo, like the Tuscan-born composer Luigi Boccherini, died as a courtier in Madrid).

This theatricality was partly a matter of the artist's surroundings: by the eighteenth century, many Venetians virtually lived in costume for months on end. Carnival season began the first Sunday in October, gathered momentum after Epiphany, the twelfth day of Christmas, and culminated in the week before Lent. Masks, and the chador-like dominoes with their three-cornered hats, were permissible on Saint Stephen's Day (the day after Christmas), Ascension Day, and sometimes into June. A wash drawing called *A Stroll in the Rain* by his son Giandomenico (who is as likely to cast an acute eye on contemporary life as he is on the gods of Olympus) catches a group of Venetians from behind as they walk along what may be either the edge of a canal or the strand of the Lido: they include two gentlemen, a well-dressed woman, a child, a dog, and the *commedia dell'arte* character Pulcinella (Punch of Punch and Judy), with his long pointed nose and his long pointed hat.

It is hard to know whether these strollers are based on real people or people imagined, whether this is the theatricality of

Venice as we might have seen it, too, or a theatricality that has been further refined in its passage from the artist's eye to brain to hand. Put another way, did either Tiepolo, father or son, ever create a figure that did not tell a story?

The father's etchings—at least here we are on firm ground—are openly fanciful. The ground slips from beneath us as soon as we try to pin a date on them, but basically they were done when Giambattista was in his forties and early fifties; they are works of his maturity but not his old age. Both the ten *Capricci* and the twenty-three *Scherzi di fantasia* combine and recombine a carefully restricted set of elements—people, bits of scenery—to create mysteriously expansive results, like that impossibly restrictive (and hence revelatory) poetic form, the sestina. What the *Scherzi* really mean is anyone's guess but Giambattista Tiepolo's—and yet there is a particular elusive beauty to insoluble puzzles that lies in part in our own freedom to interpret them just as we wish, no matter what the artist himself may have had in mind.

The people of Giambattista's etchings are anything but reassuring. There are elders, dressed variously as ancient Romans, eighteenth-century Venetians, or Ottoman Turks who might as easily be ancient Jews, Persians, or Egyptians as modern visitors from the Sublime Porte. There are warriors, a mangy dog, a tombstone or tombstones, a pyramid, ancient urns, a barren branch, a writhing snake wrapped around a rod (an emblem signifying the passage between life and death), owls, satyrs, nymphs, skulls, an axe, young men and women. With their air of mystery and menace, the etchings stand somewhere between Nicolas Poussin's painting *Et in Arcadia Ego*, where death intrudes as quietly as a tombstone on a scene of sylvan beauty (a picture so serene, so colorful in soothing blues and greens, that we can almost resign ourselves to our own part in the cycle of the seasons), and Goya's *Caprichos*, very much like Tiepolo's, but where the scene is undeniably a nightmare. Tiepolo's light, as ever, is piercingly bright, but it shines as relentlessly in these alleged caprices and plays of imagination as an interrogation lamp.

Tiepolo, of course, was not the only Venetian for whom antiquity had taken on an aura of menace; however distinctly his infinitely light touch with the burin may divide his engraving style from that of Piranesi, there is a similar sense in their engraved work that the ancient world hovers over the modern like a gathering storm. Ruins are beautiful spurs to the imagination, but they also tell terrible histories of corruption, violence, calamity, destruction, and they give us the measure of our own lives with pitiless precision. Tiepolo, so far as we know, never stood under the shattered vaults of the Basilica of Maxentius or saw the coins that melted when the Visigoths sacked Rome, but he could see enough in Venice itself to suggest that he and everyone he knew were creatures of a day. The shiver of Gothic terror that thrilled the romantics was the dark side of the Enlightenment; there is, after all, no more riveting ghost story than Mozart's *Don Giovanni*. No less than William Blake's Tyger, the Age of Reason burned bright precisely because of, not in spite of, the forests of the night.

Piranesi is not Tiepolo's only kindred soul when it comes to "plays of fantasy." It is clear that the *Capricci* and the *Scherzi di fantasia* grew from the same fertile soil as the rites and symbols of Freemasonry; both the Masons and the artist engage on an abstract level in the age-old struggle of light with darkness, but also enact that struggle on a concrete level by manipulating significant objects. All told, we know remarkably little about Tiepolo's life, and many of its most significant events occurred as a succession of tiny repetitive actions with a brush and paints, or a pen and ink, or a burin and a copper plate, on scaffolding or in his studio. Our only real clues to the other things that might have gone on in his capricious *fantasia* are images, and when the images are as dark and deep as those that trouble his etchings, it would be wrong to see his more conventional mythological works as mere triumphs of surface virtuosity. What was lurking down those canals at night, or on those winter days when the fog hovered over shrouded figures? When epidemics struck? What was it like to take a headful of harlequin players off to the green mountains of Bavaria, or the arid heights of Madrid?

Perhaps Giambattista Tiepolo is not so much an Enlightenment painter as Enlightenment itself. For one of the most striking qualities about Tiepolo (1696–1770) and contemporaries like Georg Friedrich Handel (1685–1759) is the extent to which they still inhabited a world pervaded, perhaps driven outright, by myth.

Isaac Newton, after all, was an alchemist and an Anglican as well as the writer of the *Principia*, and he did not seem to have found these worlds inconsistent. Cotton Mather introduced vaccination to the Americas, but believed just as famously in witches and angels. Even today, the world of myth has never died out entirely—as the Alexandrian poet C. P. Cavafy wrote a century ago, "Just because we smashed their statues, just because we drove them from their temples / The gods did not die because of *that* / Not at all."[2]

For tale-telling is in itself a perpetual act of creation. Myths, in the very old days, were as endlessly flexible as gossip, and gossip is how, in essence, they began: gossip about the gods and heroes, beings as universally famous as celebrities, but gifted, unlike most celebrities, with a true, all-prevailing immortality. And unlike the light passions of celebrities, their wrath was implacable (in Greece, divine wrath even had a special word reserved for it, *mênis*, to distinguish it from the fickle tide of mere human rage). The sixth-century BCE poet Stesichorus famously berated Helen for going off to Troy and was struck blind by that divine lady for his insolence; he retracted his narrative in a second poem that concluded, "You never went to Troy," and she restored his sight. Did Helen really go to Troy, or was the woman Homer portrays on the ramparts of Ilium sighing "O dog-faced me" simply, as Stesichorus asserted, her ghost? In the end, it is you who must always decide, every single time the tale is told.

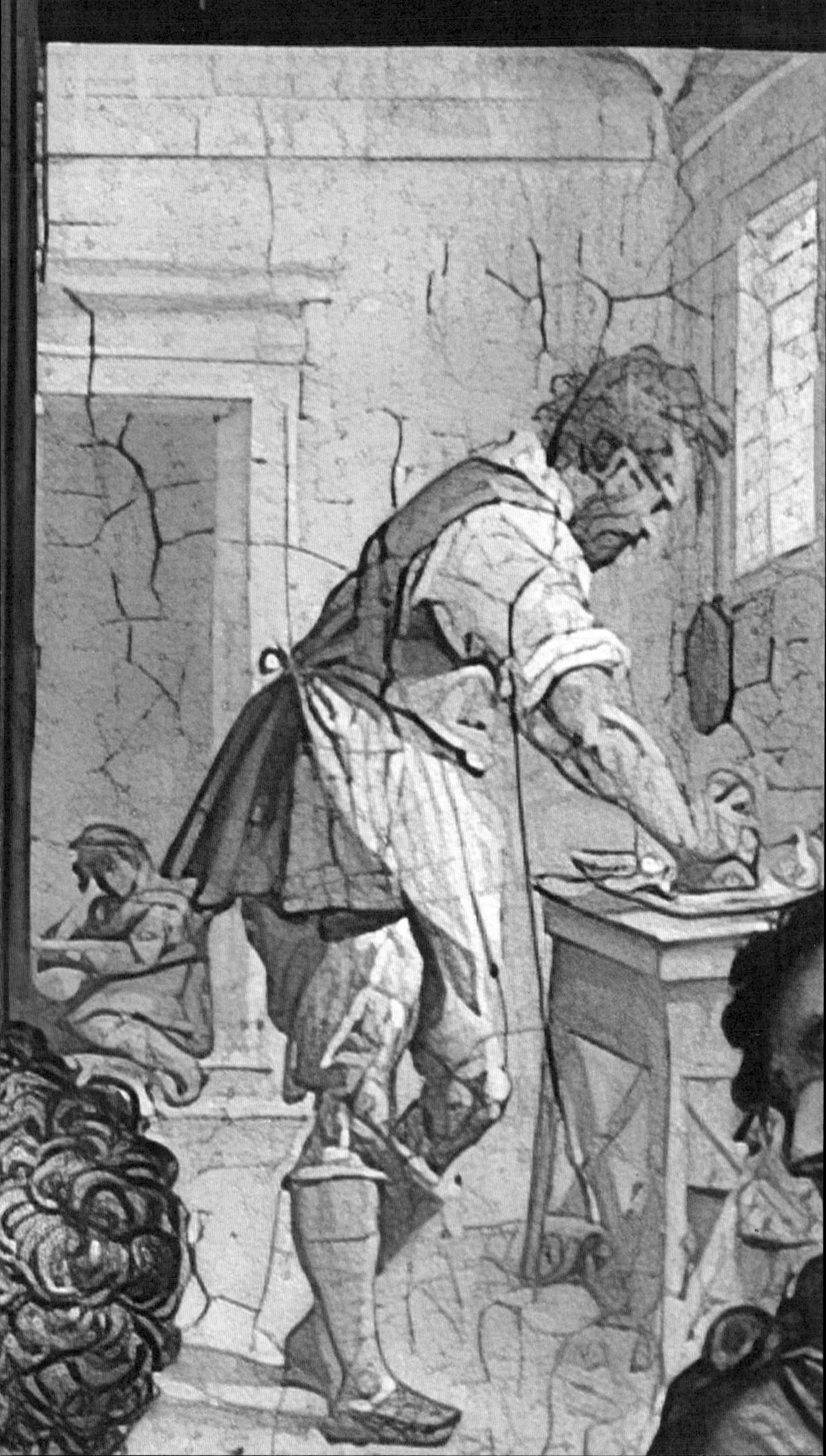

15 *Giorgio Vasari's Passionate Gamble*

Con istudio, diligenza, et amorevole fatica
With study, diligence, and loving labor[1]

One of the most influential books ever written, Giorgio Vasari's *Lives of the Most Excellent Painters, Sculptors, and Architects* first appeared in Florentine bookshops in 1550. The two-volume, three-part work represented a high-stakes gamble both for the thirty-nine-year-old author and for the fifty-one-year-old publisher, the Brabant-born ducal printer Laurens van den Bleeck, long since renamed Lorenzo Torrentino: what interest could the lives of working artists possibly hold for people wealthy enough to afford a book? Fifteen centuries earlier, the ancient Roman admiral Pliny the Elder had included some juicy anecdotes about famous artists in his *Natural History*, but the famous men and women who inspired medieval and early modern biographers were usually exceptional figures whose lives provided readers with models for behavior, good or bad: saints, heroes and heroines of antiquity, heads of state.

Vasari's readers soon discovered, however, that the lives of his "most excellent" artists provided their own opportunities for

Giorgio Vasari, *Saint Luke Painting the Virgin*, after 1565, detail. Saint Luke Chapel, Santissima Annunziata, Florence, Italy. Artefact/Alamy Stock Photo.

moral instruction (indeed, the saintly painter Fra Angelico has since been beatified by the Catholic Church), but also a wealth of more down-to-earth entertainment: Filippo Brunelleschi showing the Florentine city council his scheme for the dome of Florence Cathedral by slamming an egg down on a table; Rosso Fiorentino's mischievous pet monkey, trained to steal grapes from the convent next door; the bishop's monkey who interfered with Buonamico Buffalmacco's half-completed fresco, prompting Buffalmacco, a notorious prankster, to comment, "Your Excellency, you have one idea of how to paint this fresco but your monkey has another."[2]

More importantly, Vasari's *Lives* spelled out a systematic way to look at and evaluate works of art. As the author well knew, people who could afford to buy books could also afford to hire artists, and his carefully calibrated accounts provided a method for distinguishing worthwhile investments from embarrassments or wastes of money. He explained how things were made, and of what; he unlocked pictorial riddles; he told prospective patrons what they could reasonably expect from a worker in a day, a week, or a month, and he described it all with an enthusiasm infectious enough to reverberate down the ages. At the same time, he presented a passionate case to his literate audience for the dignity of artists as outstanding members of civil society, focusing on his mentor Michelangelo as a consummate genius. Thanks to Vasari's skill as artist, theoretician, and storyteller, his *Lives* acquired an instant authority.

The author of this triumphant risk was born into a risky world. The Vasari family came from Arezzo, an ancient Etruscan city that fell under the sway of Rome in the age of Augustus and under Florence in 1384, yet continued to plot rebellion against its overlords at every opportunity. As their name shows (*vasaro* meant "potter") and Giorgio himself confirms, they had been potters and painters for generations, but Giorgio's father Antonio took a significant upward step socially by becoming a cloth merchant. To secure the family's status, the young Vasari, born in 1511, received the scholarly education of a gentleman, in Latin and arithmetic, but Tuscan gentlemen were also taught to draw, and Giorgio became an inveterate scribbler. He was eight years old when his distant uncle Luca Signorelli came to stay with the family in Arezzo, a distinguished painter of eighty who had become a wealthy, well-dressed bon vivant. Luca's young nephew recalled him vividly:

> I remember that when that good old man, impeccably graceful, learned from my tutor that I did nothing in school but doodle, he turned to my father Antonio and said, "Antonio, if you want to keep Giorgino in line, by all means have him learn *disegno*, because even if he becomes a scholar, *disegno*, as for every gentleman, can only bring him utility, honor, and benefit." Then, turning to me as I stood right in front of him, he said, "Learn, little nephew." He said a number of other things about me that I will not reveal, because I know how little I have lived up to the opinion that good old man had of me.[3]

Signorelli also gave young Giorgio a jasper stone to cure his nosebleeds.

The story, from Vasari's *Life* of Signorelli, provides a surprisingly gentle glimpse of a man best known for his terrifying frescoes of the Apocalypse (1504) in the cathedral of Orvieto. It also tells us a good deal about Giorgio himself: exceptionally bright, bursting with energy, and high-strung (nosebleeds can be caused by stress). That early lesson on *disegno* shaped the whole of Vasari's subsequent life: the word meant "design" as well as "drawing"; *disegno* expressed every form of order from God's plan for the universe to the works of human ingenuity, which contemporaries regarded as divinely inspired. The adult Giorgio Vasari would become one of the first people to collect artists' drawings, convinced that these preparatory works most clearly revealed the magical moment when inspiration became concrete idea. He knew from his own experience.

Following Signorelli's advice, the young Giorgio, in addition to his scholarly studies, also began to work as an apprentice to Guillaume Marcillat, a French-born designer famous for his stained-glass windows. The year would have been 1519.

In 1522, the eleven-year-old Vasari's skill in Latin caught the eye of another illustrious relative passing through Arezzo: Cardinal Silvio Passerini, the tutor of the Medici cousins Alessandro, twelve, and Ippolito, eleven, who already understood that one of the two, and only one, would become the eventual head of the Florentine dynasty. Childhood companions, they were turning quickly into bitter rivals. In his hard-working young relative, Cardinal Passerini saw a potential buffer between his two intractable charges. He invited Giorgio to come to Florence to serve as the cousins' companion and study partner, knowing that the difficult position would also provide the young provincial from Arezzo a unique entrée into Florentine society. For the next few years Giorgio lived with an uncle next to the Ponte Vecchio, shared Latin lessons with the Medici cousins, and spent the rest of his time in artists' studios, learning *disegno* from the painter Andrea del Sarto and Baccio Bandinelli, an exquisite draftsman whose statues never quite lived up to the promise of his preparatory drawings. It was all a young man's wildest dream: full immersion in the heart of Florence, mixing with the Medici and Michelangelo and all the artists drawn to their magnetic center; and like a dream it ended abruptly: in 1527, when Giorgio was sixteen, his father died, leaving him as the sole male survivor. He returned to Arezzo to arrange his father's affairs and provide for his mother and sisters, with no available source of added income except his own skill at painting. A series of local commissions in Arezzo were enough to stabilize the family and to buy a modest house that became his real home base in a life of perpetual wandering, but the young painter's reputation began to spread rapidly, thanks in part to his connection with the Medici and in part to his ability to meet a deadline. For the next ten years Giorgio would take commissions in Bologna, Florence, and Rome, making his way through chaos and war in every part of Italy. In 1529, Pope Clement VII, the head of the Medici clan, resolved the competition between Ippolito and Alessandro by appointing Ippolito cardinal of Avignon, sending his furious nephew abroad to remove him from Florence. Alessandro (who may well have been the pope's son) took office as duke of Florence in 1530. Vasari maintained his old friendship with both parties. In 1531, he made his first visit to Rome on Cardinal Ippolito's invitation, then moved to Florence in 1532 to paint Duke Alessandro's portrait several times and decorate a suite of rooms in Palazzo Vecchio, the Florentine city hall. Both cousins died by assassination: Ippolito in 1535, poisoned by Alessandro; Alessandro in 1537, ambushed by yet another Medici heir apparent, Lorenzaccio, who destroyed his own chances of succession by running away from the gory scene rather than standing his ground.

The turmoil took an understandable toll on Vasari, who suffered a breakdown in 1537, cured by a prolonged stay in the wooded monastery of Camaldoli, where he made another important friend, the Rome-based Florentine banker Bindo Altoviti, who offered him hospitality and commissions in Rome while plotting to overthrow the Medici once and for all.

The Florentines, however, had put their fate into the unlikely hands of nineteen-year-old Cosimo de' Medici, a grandson of Lorenzo the Magnificent from a distant branch of the family who turned out, against all expectations, to be an extremely competent ruler. Invested as duke of Florence in 1538, Cosimo quickly began to display an exceptional sensitivity to the persuasive powers of culture: art, literature, architecture, music, pageantry, collecting, all turned to creating a distinct identity for Florence as a great European capital. An outsider himself, the young duke forged an enduring friendship with the little artist from Arezzo, awarding him some of the city's choicest commissions.

But Vasari's heart, in many ways, gravitated to Rome. The city had been kind to him ever since his first trip in 1531 to join his friend Francesco Salviati and his idol, Michelangelo, and in 1545, after years of perpetual movement, he decided to settle in the Eternal City. There he joined the circle of scholars around Alessandro Farnese, the cardinal nephew, or chief administrator, for Pope Paul III (though Alessandro was in fact the pontiff's grandson). Not long afterward, he took part in a remarkable conversation that included the humanist Paolo Giovio, a man of many interests that included biography. As Giorgio himself would later write (with a certain amount of authorial license):

In those days I often went after the day's work to watch the Most Illustrious Cardinal Farnese eat dinner. There were always people around to entertain him with wonderful, refined conversation. . . . One evening . . . passing from one topic to another, as one does in conversation, Monsignor

Giovio said that he had always cherished, and still did, a
great desire to [write] a treatise that discussed men who
were famous in the art of *disegno*, from the time of Cimabue
up to our own. When Giovio had finished this discourse,
the cardinal said, turning to me, "What do you say, Giorgio?
Wouldn't this be a wonderful project?" "Wonderful," I
replied, "Most Illustrious Monsignor, if Giovio will accept
help from someone in the field who can sort things out
and describe them as they really are . . ." "So," added the
cardinal . . . , "you could give him a summary, and an orderly
account of all those artists and their works in order of time,
and that way you could also give them the benefit of your
expertise." . . . And so I sat down to search through my own
memories and my own writings about art and artists. I put
together everything that seemed relevant to the project
and took it to Giovio, who, after he had lavished praise on
my efforts, said to me, "My Giorgio, I want you to take over
the task of setting down the whole text in the way you have
done so well here, because I don't have the heart for it. I
don't know the artistic styles, and I don't know all the details
that you will know; if I were to do the writing, it would turn
out to be a little treatise like Pliny's. Do what I say, Vasari,
because I can tell it will turn out beautifully."[4]

And so it did. By 1547, Giorgio had completed a draft of the
book in Arezzo and turned his boundless energies to a torrid affair
with Maddalena Bacci, the daughter of one of Arezzo's most prominent families, fathering two children in rapid succession. To save
the family's reputation, Maddalena was married off to a captain
in the Florentine militia. Giorgio, meanwhile, contracted a marriage with her eleven-year-old sister, Niccolosa, although the girl
continued to live with her parents for the next two years. In 1550,
with his wife and children firmly installed in the house in Arezzo,
Giorgio decided to seek his fortune again in Florence, and offered
the manuscript of the *Lives* to a Florentine printer with a dedication to Duke Cosimo. It was a brilliant move.

"My aim," the author wrote in his final chapter, an open letter
addressed "to craftsmen," "has been to do good, and at the same

time to delight."[5] Typically, however, he had begun to revise his biographies almost as soon as they saw the light. In 1568, Cosimo, now Italy's one and only grand duke rather than a mere duke, underwrote a second, greatly enlarged edition of the *Lives*. Five years earlier, in 1563, the grand duke had approved the foundation of a state-sponsored art school, the still-thriving Accademia delle Arti del Disegno, with Giorgio Vasari and his scholarly friend Vincenzo Borghini among the founders.

Importantly, then, Vasari saw learning, like technical expertise, as something to be shared rather than hoarded, especially when it involved telling a good story. His work as a painter was technically competent, imaginative in a learned way more appreciated in his day than ours, and—an important consideration for his patrons—delivered on time. Vasari's architectural commissions include one of the most inspired buildings of the Italian Renaissance, the Uffizi in Florence. But he is best known for the written work that spread as widely as print could take it. He did not write it all himself; as with his artistic projects, he employed a vast array of assistants, and the cleric Vincenzo Borghini, one of his closest friends, may have had a significant role in the writing, but the book's organization bears Vasari's unmistakable imprint. The high-strung little artist from Arezzo has exerted a lasting influence on Italian society: as a collector and interpreter of art, especially of drawing, he shaped not only contemporary taste but also the artistic choices of later centuries. Through his writings and as a founder of the state-sponsored Florentine art academy, the Accademia delle Arti del Disegno, he strove to create a systematic theory of art, improving the general competence of artists while battling to elevate their social status. He bears significant responsibility for the cult of genius that still surrounds some of his own artistic heroes, such as Leonardo da Vinci and Michelangelo. To an enormous extent, we continue to see Italian art through his eyes.

He even invented a new kind of literature, the artistic biography, using strong characters and unforgettable anecdotes to ensure, in his own words, that the great artists of the past will never be forgotten. How can anyone forget Buonamico Buffalmacco attaching candles to the backs of cockroaches to scare his master into thinking that a swarm of devils has invaded the studio? Or short, homely, brilliant Giotto, asked why his painted figures are so beautiful and his children so ugly, replying "Because I paint by day and 'sculpt' by night." Or eccentric Piero di Cosimo painting his primeval fantasies on a diet of hard-boiled eggs. Or Morto da Feltre, so enthralled by the buried ruins of ancient Rome that his friends call him "dead man."

Most guidebooks to Rome still retell Vasari's tall tale about how Raphael's infatuation with a Roman baker's daughter kept him from painting frescoes for the wealthy banker Agostino Chigi—at least until Chigi confined the two of them to his palazzo and Raphael managed to finish the commission. Nineteenth-century fantasies continued to elaborate Vasari's invention until we have all been led to believe—as the website of Rome's National Gallery of Art at Palazzo Barberini still attests—that the portrait of a young woman wearing little more than a turban, an armband, and a saucy smile is none other than a portrait of that very *fornarina*, the baker's daughter from Trastevere, rather than, as seems more likely, an ambitious Roman courtesan (Vasari reports that Raphael did a great business in painting portraits of these prominent figures in Roman society).

But Vasari had much more in mind than compiling a random collection of artistic anecdotes to save his colleagues from oblivion. He was certainly an inveterate collector, of drawings, of friends, of biographies, of curious information, and of artistic commissions, but he was also a supremely gifted organizer of time, people, and information. Unlike Leonardo and Michelangelo, whose reputations for untrammeled genius he did much to foster, he finished his commissions promptly, no matter the price to his own health and well-being; indeed, overwork was one of the reasons for his nervous breakdown in 1537. His *Lives of the Most Excellent Painters, Sculptors, and Architects* presented a lucid case, backed by mountains of compelling evidence, for why artists should be regarded as thinkers and philosophers rather than mere manual workers, and at the same time he taught readers how to appreciate the dignity and mastery that even manual workers brought to their labors. He showed literary people how to look at works of art, again by copious example, and by example he also showed artists how to think in literary terms.

In many ways, Vasari's literary project resembles that of the ancient Roman architect Vitruvius, whose *Ten Books on Architecture* he knew both from printed editions and from Raphael's unpublished studies of the ancient author. Vitruvius broke new ground in the age of Augustus by presenting architecture as a liberal art that demanded a broad range of expertise and a deep education at least as much as manual skill—and elevated the practitioners of that art to a higher level of polite society. To the critical analysis of architecture, Vitruvius applied a vocabulary borrowed from ancient rhetoric, and repeatedly claimed to have structured his discussion in the same way that orators structured their speeches: "as order demands" (*uti ordo postulat*). It was customary for sixteenth-century writers on art and architecture to refer to Vitruvius as a grand authority, but there are many reasons to think that Vasari's tribute to the ancient author reflects penetrating study of that challenging text.

A proud Tuscan himself, Vasari regarded Tuscany as the cradle of the arts, and presented Michelangelo as the perfect expression of Tuscan—but also simply human—achievement in painting, sculpture, architecture, and poetry. The idolatry has never ended. The Vatican Museums still funnel visitors relentlessly toward the Sistine Chapel as if Raphael's frescoes were merely a way station on the road to ultimate perfection, an itinerary first charted by Giorgio Vasari.

Progress is essential to Vasari's design, upward progress to higher ranks of society, and artistic progress to higher degrees of complexity, erudition, and sophistication, stretching from Cimabue in the thirteenth century to his own contemporaries, culminating, by careful design, in the life of the author's mentor and hero, Michelangelo Buonarroti. It is no coincidence that the word Vasari uses to describe the overarching literary plan of the *Lives*, *disegno*, is the same word he places at the center of artistic activity of every kind, from God, the first sculptor, shaping Adam from a lump of clay, to Properzia de' Rossi carving a multitude of tiny figures into a cherry pit, to Filippo Brunelleschi revealing the secrets of perspective or laying out the great dome of Florence Cathedral. *Disegno*, our author writes in his preface to the biographies,

the father of our three arts, architecture, sculpture, and painting, proceeds from the intellect and extracts from

many things a universal opinion, similar to a form or
idea, for all the phenomena of nature, that is surpassingly
excellent in its equilibrium [*misura*].[6]

Vasari is an unusually difficult author to translate: it is not
entirely clear in this passage, for example, whether the "surpassingly excellent equilibrium" belongs to *disegno*, to the universal opinion "extract[ed] from many things," or to nature, even
though the basic point is clear enough: from a multitude of data,
disegno learns to extract the essence, and that essence is measured,
balanced, and harmonious. Rhetorically, it was important for a
sixteenth-century Italian preface to exhibit the ancient quality
of *copia*, abundance, to come dressed, that is, in every possible
kind of finery, including long, convoluted sentences—a sure sign
of gravitas—and lofty concepts. This sentence about *disegno*, for
example, already too complicated to allow for clear interpretation,
has hardly begun its journey. My translation of what follows in
Vasari's text has been broken up into separate units to improve
comprehension, but in fact this entire quotation is simply a further
extension of the same sentence as before:

Thus not only in the bodies of human beings and animals,
but also in plants, and in buildings and sculptures and
paintings, it recognizes the proportions that the whole has
with its parts, and that the parts have among themselves
and with the whole, and because recognition gives rise to a
certain concept and opinion, which takes shape in the mind,
that certain thing, which is then expressed with the hands, is
called *disegno*.

We can conclude, then, that this *disegno* is nothing other
than an apparent expression and declaration of the concept
held in the spirit, and of what has been imagined in the
mind and created as an idea.[7]

Once again, there is no way to know definitely what Vasari
means by "it" in "it recognizes proportions": "it" could be nature,
idea, or the mind. Again, however, we do not need absolute precision to catch the general drift of what our author means. Vasari

has clearly been reading Plato, or someone inspired by Plato—that is, almost any writer in fifteenth-century Florence or Rome—and his concept of *disegno* works, like Plato's reality, on two levels: an ideal or mental construct, and a physical object, and of the two the mental construct is the more noble and the more real.

Disegno to Vasari, in short, is both an idea in the mind and that idea's physical expression. In the same way he believed, as did Michelangelo, that the universe had existed in the mind of God as a *disegno* long before the Almighty ever unfurled that grand *disegno* in the act of Creation, and creation, because it proceeded according to divine *disegno*, necessarily exhibited, and continues to exhibit, all the original ideal design's transcendent qualities of measure and proportion. Creation, in turn, once created, began to play out the great moving *disegno* called history. Paradoxically, therefore, Vasari's scheme uses the imagery of serene proportion to describe a world moved by irrepressibly dynamic forces.

The biographer's ideas about measure and proportion, like his criteria for good art and good literature, may have been forged in the crucible of fifteenth-century Florence, but he applied those terms to radically different visual and literary effect. We need only compare the broad planes of one of those scenographic fifteenth-century ideal cityscapes with the vertiginous cleft that splits Vasari's Uffizi, or compare Leonardo's Vitruvian man to a figure by Michelangelo, or Lorenzo Ghiberti's *Commentaries*, with the first artistic autobiography, to the grand design of the *Lives of the Artists*.

For Vasari, *disegno* is intimately connected with the fertile, irrepressible change he calls *invenzione*. Like Vitruvius, he is searching, as an artist, architect, and writer, for secure guidelines to govern that process of invention. As he tells his readers:

In this enterprise, as I have said elsewhere, the writings of Lorenzo Ghiberti, Domenico Ghirlandaio and Raphael of Urbino have been no small help, and although I have put my trust in them, I have nonetheless wanted to compare what they say with examination of their works, because, as you know, long experience teaches sharp-witted painters how to recognize the styles of artists in the same way that a learned and practical executive distinguishes the diverse and various writings of his colleagues, and the individual character of all his closest collaborators, friends, and relatives.[8]

We can do the same with Vasari. In his lifetime, he may have felt like a hardworking wanderer, and a perpetual outsider except in Arezzo, but in nearly sixty-three years of life (he died in 1574) he garnered remarkable success as a painter and architect. His paintings adorn some of the most prestigious interiors in Florence, both sacred and secular: the vast Salone dei Cinquecento in Palazzo Vecchio, the seat of Florentine government, the private apartments of the duke of Tuscany, and the interior of Filippo Brunelleschi's cathedral dome. He designed the government offices known as the Uffizi, and took special pride in the imposing foundation that protects the building from the shifting level and slippery banks of the River Arno. The palazzo he created to house the University of Pisa has served its purpose for four centuries, now as the main building of the illustrious Scuola Normale. In his native Arezzo he transformed the medieval feel of the city's main square, Piazza Grande, by crowning the steeply slanted area with a graceful classical portico, and called for an aqueduct to ensure a steady water supply for the hilltop site. In Rome, he frescoed the walls of the Sala Regia, the ornate reception hall that connects the Sistine Chapel to the pope's private Pauline Chapel. In only a hundred days, he and his assistants completed the frescoes for a large hall in the papal chancery, the Cancelleria. For the Roman palazzo of Bindo Altoviti, the wealthy Florentine banker and inveterate political agitator, he designed a frescoed loggia alongside the Tiber. In Naples, the classical design of his frescoes for the sacristy of the church of Monteoliveto somehow manages to harmonize perfectly with the room's graceful Gothic arches. We can forgive him for painting himself late in life as Saint Luke, the patron saint of artists, whose devotion was rewarded by an epiphany of the Virgin Mary when he set out to paint her portrait. Like the evangelist, Vasari regarded his profession as divinely inspired, and did his best to transmit that inspiration to everyone around him.

By his own admission, Giorgio was neither tall nor handsome; he trusted instead in hard work and diplomacy. Aside from the temporary chaos of his love life as he approached the age of forty, he used his distinctive talents wisely. Education broadened the range of his friendships and his interests, enabling him to create artistic works of great allegorical, mythological, and historical complexity.

But we remember him now with the greatest affection for his *Lives*, for the delicate regard with which he addresses a reading public of artisans as well as scholars, working professionals as well as aristocrats. As he declares in his final chapter:

> But to come at last to the end of such a long discussion, I have written as a painter, and in the order and fashion that I know best, and as for the language in which I speak, Florentine or Tuscan as it may be, I leave the long, ornate sentences, the choice of words and other flourishes of learned speaking and writing, to those who, unlike me, find a pen in their hand rather than a paintbrush, and have a head better suited to writing than to *disegno*. And if I have littered this work with many words that are particular to our art, rather than using the brighter and greater lights of our language, I have done so because I could not do otherwise to be understood by you artists, for whom, as I have said, I have chiefly set myself this task. As for the rest, having done what I could, please accept it willingly, and don't ask me for what I don't know and can't do, taking satisfaction in my good intentions, which have been, and ever shall be, to help and please others.[9]

We know, of course, that he wrote as much more than a simple painter, and that the learned Vincenzo Borghini had more than a casual hand in Vasari's prose. But as my father used to say, "Once you've mastered false modesty, you've mastered everything."

Acknowledgments

Infinite thanks to Thomas Weaver, who broached the idea of this book, supplied the best half of its title, and has seen it through with genteel patience. Lisa Pon, Andrew Butterfield, and Victor Plahte Tschudi read the manuscript, correcting errors and above all affording inspiration by example. Leon Wieseltier, Bruce Falconer, and Sudip Bose have provided essential sustenance over the years as wellsprings of ideas and sage editorial advice. Noah Charney opened my eyes to Giorgio Vasari. For the perceptive eyes of Michael Shae, Dana Prescott, Ingrid Edlund-Berry, Nancy Winter, Giovanna Lenzi, Livio Pestilli, Jed Perl, Deborah Rosenthal, Terence Ward, Idanna Pucci, Caroline Howard, and Eugenio Lo Sardo, *grazie infinite*.

This book is dedicated to the memory of Robert Silvers, who, on an intuition of Grace Dudley, made it all possible.

Rome, November 2023

Notes

Introduction

1. Hesiod, *Theogony*, 1.26–28. Author's translation.

2. The ancient geographer Strabo seems to infer that this is Aristotle's comment: he quotes the aphorism (which may have been well known) without an attribution in his *Geographica* 2.3.6 but identifies the speaker as Aristotle in *Geographica* 13.1.36.

3. "Quella parola, valent'huomo, appresso di me vuol dire che sappi far bene, cioè sappi far bene dell'arte sua, così un pittore valent'huomo, che sappi depinger bene et imitar bene le cose naturali." Transcripts of the documents of the 1603 trial are available online from the Archivio di Stato di Roma in connection with the exhibition *Caravaggio a Roma: una vita dal vero*, "Il processo del 1603," https://archiviodista toroma.beniculturali.it/it /237/il-processo-del-1603.

Chapter 1

1. "Bertoldo suo creato": Giorgio Vasari, "Vita di Donato scultore fiorentino," in *Vite de' più eccellenti pittori, scultori e architettori* (Florence: Giunti, 1568), vol. 3, 226.

2. "Molto bella": Vasari, "Vita di Donato scultore fiorentino," 223.

Chapter 2

1. Mia Cinotti, "Caravaggio, gli enigmi, l'Ecce Homo 'Massimi'," in Maurizio Calvesi, ed., *L'ultimo Caravaggio e la cultura artistica a Napoli e in Sicilia e in Malta* (Siracusa: Ediprint, 1987), 43–58.

2. Giorgio Vasari, "Vita di Antonello da Messina," in *Vite de' più eccellenti pittori, scultori ed architettori* (Florence: Giunti, 1568), vol. 3, 306.

3. Vasari, "Vita di Antonello da Messina," 306.

4. Vasari, "Vita di Antonello da Messina," 306.

5. Giovanni Carlo Federico Villa, *Antonello da Messina. Dentro la pittura* (Milan: Skira, 2019), paraphrasing Roberto Longhi, "Breve ma veridica storia della pittura" (written 1914, first published in Roberto Longhi, *Scritti giovanili, 1912–1922* [Florence: Sansoni, 1961]).

6. Leonardo Sciascia, *L'ordine delle somiglianze* (Milan: Classici d'Arte Rizzoli, 1967), https://www.bartolomeo dimonaco.it/pittura-anton ello-da-messina-lordine -delle-somiglianze/.

7. "Ma se il volto è quello che ha dipinto Antonello—il volto della sofferenza e degli ultimi—è lui che amiamo e vogliamo amare": Giorgio Montefoschi, "Gesù, il volto degli ultimi ritratti da Antonello da Messina," *Corriere della Sera*, February 17, 2019.

Chapter 3

1. Giorgio Vasari, "Vita di Raffaello da Urbino pittore e architetto," in *Vite de' più eccellenti pittori, scultori ed architettori* (Florence: Giunti, 1568), vol. 4, 212.

2. Letter of Sebastiano del Piombo to Michelangelo, July 2, 1518, Florence, Archivio Buonarroti, IX, no. 468; published in Paola Barocchi and Renzo Ristori, *Il carteggio di Michelangelo*, vol. 2 (Florence: Sansoni 1967), 32, https:// www.memofonte.it/home /ricerca/singolo_23.php?id =304&daAnno=&aAnno =&Mittente=Del%20Piombo %20Sebastiano&Destinatario =Buonarroti%20Michelan gelo&Luogo_Mittente =&Luogo_Destinatario =&Trascrizione=&Colloca zione=&Bibliografia=&cerca =cerca&.

3. Vasari, "Vita di Raffaello da Urbino pittore e architetto," 187.

Chapter 4

1. Fabio Chigi (Pope Alexander VII), *Chisiae familiae commentarii*, Vatican Library, MS Chigi a.I.1, transcribed by Giuseppe Cugnoni, *Agostino Chigi il Magnifico* (Rome: R. Società Romana di Storia Patria, 1878), 65.

2. Letter of Sebastiano del Piombo to Michelangelo, January 28, 1520, Florence, Archivio Buonarroti, IX, no. 470; published in Paola Barocchi and Renzo Ristori, *Il carteggio di Michelangelo*, vol. 2 (Florence: Sansoni, 1967), 212–213, https://www.memo fonte.it/home/ricerca /singolo_23.php?id=452 &daAnno=&aAnno =&Mittente=Del%20 Piombo%20Sebastiano &Destinatario=Buonarroti %20Michelangelo&Luogo _Mittente=&Luogo_Destin atario=&Trascrizione =&Collocazione=&Biblio grafia=&cerca=cerca&.

3. "Me ha decto che io l'ò contentato più di quello lui dessiderava": letter of Sebastiano del Piombo to

Michelangelo, December 29, 151[9]; British Museum, Add. MS 23744, c. 1r; published in Barocchi and Ristori, *Il carteggio di Michelangelo*, vol. 2, 206–207, https://www.memo fonte.it/home/ricerca/sin golo_23.php?id=447&da Anno=&aAnno=&Mittente =Del%20Piombo%20Seb astiano&Destinatario =Buonarroti%20Michelan gelo&Luogo_Mittente =&Luogo_Destinatario =&Trascrizione=&Colloca zione=&Bibliografia=&cerca =cerca&.

4. Sebastiano del Piombo, letter to Michelangelo, February 2, 1531, Florence, Archivio Buonarroti, IX, n. 48; published in Barocchi and Ristori, *Il carteggio di Michelangelo*, vol. 3 (Florence: Sansoni, 1973), 299–300, https://www .memofonte.it/home/ricerca /singolo_23.php?id=807 &page=1&daAnno=&a Anno=&Mittente=Del%20 Piombo%20Sebastiano& Destinatario=Buonarroti %20Michelangelo&Luogo _Mittente=&Luogo_Destina tario=&Trascrizione=&Collo cazione=&Bibliografia =&cerca=cerca.

5. Vittore Soranzo, letter to Pietro Bembo, June 8, 1530; published in Francesco Sansovino, ed., *Delle lettere da diversi Re et Principi et Cardinali et altri huomini dotti a Mons. Pietro Bembo* (Venice: Francesco Sansovino, 1560), vol. 1, 110[v].

6. Giorgio Vasari, "Vita di Sebastian Veneziano frate del Piombo e pittore," in *Vite de' più eccellenti pittori, scultori e architettori* (Florence: Giunti, 1568), vol. 5, 345.

7. "Infingardo e negligentissimo": Vasari, "Vita di Sebastian Veneziano frate del Piombo e pittore," 96.

8. Vasari, "Vita di Sebastian Veneziano frate del Piombo e pittore," 101.

Chapter 5

1. Giorgio Vasari, "Vita di Andrea del Sarto fiorentino pittore," in *Vite de' più eccellenti pittori, scultori e architettori* (Florence: Giunti, 1568), vol. 4, 341–342.

2. Giorgio Vasari, "Vita di Andrea del Sarto fiorentino pittore," in *Vite de' più eccellenti pittori, scultori e architettori* (Florence: Lorenzo Torrentino [Laurens van den Bleeck], 1550), vol. 4, 342.

3. Vasari, "Vita di Andrea del Sarto fiorentino pittore" (1550), 356–357.

4. "Disegna, Antonio, disegna Antonio, disegna e non perder tempo." Note by Michelangelo on a sheet of pen and ink and red chalk drawings by his pupil Antonio Mini, British Library 1859, 0514.818.

Chapter 6

1. Giorgio Vasari, "Vita di Michelagnolo Buonarroti fiorentino pittore, scultore, architetto," in *Vite de' più eccellenti pittori, scultori e architettori* (Florence: Giunti, 1568), vol. 6, 3: "la vana infinità di tante fatiche, gli ardentissimi studii senza alcun frutto e la opinione prosuntuosa degli uomini, assai più lontana dal vero che le tenebre dalla lucc."

2. Vasari, "Vita di Michelagnolo Buonarroti fiorentino

pittore, scultore, architetto," 3–4.

3. "'L papa per la vecchiezza non mi mancassi": letter of Michelangelo Buonarroti to Leonardo Buonarroti, February 16, 1550, Florence, Archivio Buonarroti, IV, no. 92; published in Giovanni Poggi, Paola Barocchi, and Renzo Ristori, *Il carteggio di Michelangelo*, vol. 4 (Florence: Sansoni, 1979), 341, https://www.memo fonte.it/home/ricerca /singolo_23.php?id=1139 &daAnno=1550&aAnno=1550 &Mittente=Buonarroti%20 Michelangelo&Destinatario =Buonarroti%20Leonardo &Luogo_Mittente=&Luogo _Destinatario=&Trascrizione =&Collocazione=&Biblio grafia=&cerca=cerca&.

4. Ascanio Condivi, *Vita di Michelangelo Buonarroti* (Rome: Antonio Blado, 1553), 2r.

5. The French cryptographer Blaise de Vignère, quoted in William C. Wallace, *Michelangelo, God's Architect* (Princeton: Princeton University Press, 2019), 133.

6. As he wrote his nephew Leonardo in 1557: "I have always taken these pains and continue to, because many believe, and I do myself, that I have been put here by God." ("E questa diligentia ò sempre usata e uso, perché, come molti credono e io ancora, esservi stato messo da Dio.") Letter of Michelangelo Buonarroti to Leonardo Buonarroti, July 1, 1557, Arezzo, Archivio Vasari 12, cc. 22 ff.; published in Giovanni Poggi, Paola Barocchi, and Renzo Ristori, *Il carteggio di*

Michelangelo, vol. 5 (Florence: Sansoni, 1983), 110–111, https://www.memofonte
.it/home/ricerca/singolo_23
.php?id=1258&daAnno=1557
&aAnno=1557&Mittente
=BuonarrotiMichelangelo
&Destinatario=Buonarroti
%20Leonardo&Luogo
_Mittente=&Luogo_Destina
tario=&Trascrizione=&Collo
cazione=&Bibliografia
=&cerca=cerca&.

7. Letter of Michelangelo Buonarroti to Giorgio Vasari, 22 June 1555, Arezzo, Archivio Vasari, 12, c. 14; published in Poggi, Barocchi, and Ristori, *Il carteggio di Michelangelo*, vol. 5, 35–36, https://www.memo
fonte.it/home/ricerca/sin
golo_23.php?id=1207&page
=6&daAnno=&aAnno
=&Mittente=&Destinatario
=&Luogo_Mittente=&Luogo
_Destinatario=&Trascrizione
=amor%20di%20Dio&Collo
cazione=&Bibliografia
=&cerca=cerca&.

Chapter 7
1. Giorgio Vasari, "Descrizione dell' opere di Tizian di Cador pittore," in *Vite de' più eccellenti pittori, scultori e architettori* (Florence: Giunti, 1568), vol. 6, 155.

2. Laurentino García y García, "Garibaldi 1860. La visita di un 'mito' a Pompei," in Luciana Jacobelli, ed., *Pompei: la costruzione di un mito: arte, letteratura, aneddotica d'un icona turistica* (Rome: Bardi, 2008), 73–84.

3. C. P. Cavafy, "Ο καθρέπτης στὴν εἴσοδο," 1930, https://cavafy.onassis.org
/object/xbs3-gt2r-tye9/.

Chapter 8
1. "Il più terribile cervello che mai habbia avuto la pittura": Giorgio Vasari, "Descrizione dell' opere di Tizian di Cador pittore," in *Vite de' più eccellenti pittori, scultori e architettori* (Florence: Giunti, 1568), vol. 6, 468.

2. Vasari, "Descrizione dell' opere di Tizian di Cador pittore," vol. 6, 468.

3. Carlo Ridolfi, *Vita di Giacopo Robusti detto il Tintoretto, celebre pittore cittadino venetiano* (Venice: Guglielmo Oddoni, 1642), 5.

4. Letter of Pietro Aretino to Jacopo Tintoretto, April 1548, in Pietro Aretino, *Lettere*, ed. Paolo Procaccioli (Rome: Salerno Editrice, 2000), vol. 4, 266, no. 429.

Chapter 9
1. Antonio Asciscio Palomino de Castro y Velasco, *El museo pictorico y escala optica: El Parnaso español pintoresco y laureado* (Madrid: Lucas Antonio Bedmar, 1724), vol. 3, 286, s.v. "Dominico Greco escultor, pintor, y arquitecto": "Pero èl viendo, que sus Pinturas se equivocaban con las de Ticiano, tratò de mudar de manera, con tal extravagancia, que llegò à hazer despreciable, y ridicula su Pintura, assi en lo descoyuntado del dibujo, como en lo desabrido del color."

2. Italian Renaissance poets took the ancient poets' use of the verb "sing" for the performance of poetry quite literally, but most of those instrumental settings are lost. There are several tunes associated with *Erotokritos*,

but whether Kornaros composed them is unclear. See Ingrid Rowland, "The Cultural Context of the *Erotokritos* of Vitzentzos Kornaros," *Studi Umanistici Piceni* 33 (2013), 227–237.

Chapter 10
1. Porto Ercole, Archivio parrocchiale, Libro dei Capitoli della Collegiata di Sant'Erasmo, entry of July 18, 1609 [1610]; image published in Rossella Vodret, *Caravaggio 1571–1610* (Rome: Silvana Editoriale, 2021), 75.

2. The contract with Tiberio Cerasi for the Cerasi chapel in Santa Maria del Popolo calls Caravaggio "Eximius pictor in Urbe": Stefania Macioce, *Michelangelo Merisi da Caravaggio. Documenti, fonti e inventari, 1513–1875* (Rome: Ugo Bozzi, 2010), doc. 502.

3. Franca Trinchieri Camiz, "Music and Painting in Cardinal Del Monte's Household," *Metropolitan Museum Journal* 26 (1991), 213–226.

4. See chapter 12.

Chapter 11
1. Linda Nochlin, "Why Have There Been No Great Women Artists?," *ARTNews* 69, no. 9 (January 1971), 22–37, 67–71.

Chapter 12
1. "Uno animo di Cesare nell'anima duna donna": letter of Artemisia Gentileschi to Don Antonio Ruffo, November 13, 1649, in Eva Menzio, *Artemisia Gentileschi, lettere precedute dagli atti*

del processo per stupro (Milan: Abscondita, 2004), 128.

2. "Gioan Bagaglia tu non sai un ah / le tue pitture sono pituresse / volo vedere con esse / che non guadagnarai / mai una patacca / che di cotanto panno / da farti un paro di bragesse / che ad ognun mostrarai / quel che fa la cacca . . ." Reprinted in *Caravaggio a Roma: una vita dal vero*, "Il processo del 1603," https://archiviodistatoroma.beniculturali.it/it/237/il-processo-del-1603.

Chapter 13

1. Ignatius of Loyola, *The Spiritual Exercises of St. Ignatius of Loyola*, trans. P. Elder Mullan, S.J. (New York: P. J. Kennedy and Sons, 1914), Week 1, Day 5, 44–46.

2. Letter of Angelica Bernini to Cardinal Francesco Barberini, published in translation in Franco Mormando, *Bernini: His Life and His Rome* (Chicago: University of Chicago Press, 2011), 101–102.

Chapter 14

1. Roberto Calasso, *Tiepolo Pink*, translated from the Italian by Alastair McEwen (Milan: Adelphi, 2006), 3.

2. C. P. Cavafy, "Ἰωνικόν," https://www.onassis.org/el/initiatives/cavafy-archive/the-canon/song-of-ionia.

Chapter 15

1. Giorgio Vasari, "Descrizione dell'opere di Giorgio Vasari pittore e architetto aretino," in *Vite de' più eccellenti pittori, scultori e architettori* (Florence: Giunti, 1568), vol. 6, 369.

2. Giorgio Vasari, "Vita di Buonamico Buffalmacco pittor fiorentino," in *Vite de' più eccellenti pittori, scultori e architettori*, vol. 2, 169.

3. Giorgio Vasari, "Vita di Luca Signorelli da Cortona pittore," in *Vite de' più eccellenti pittori, scultori e architettori*, vol. 3, 639.

4. Vasari, "Descrizione dell'opere di Giorgio Vasari pittore e architetto aretino," 389.

5. Giorgio Vasari, "L'autore agli artefici del disegno," in *Vite de' più eccellenti pittori, scultori e architettori*, vol. 6, 411.

6. Giorgio Vasari, "Della pittura, Capitolo xv, Che cosa sia disegno," in *Vite de' più eccellenti pittori, scultori e architettori*, vol. 1, 111.

7. Vasari, "Della pittura, Capitolo xv, Che cosa sia disegno," 111.

8. Vasari, "L'autore agli artefici del disegno," 411.

9. Vasari, "L'autore agli artefici del disegno," 412.

Bibliography

Andrea del Sarto: The Renaissance Workshop in Action. Exhibition at the J. Paul Getty Museum, Los Angeles, June 23–September 13, 2015; Frick Collection, New York City, October 7, 2015–January 10, 2016. Catalog of the exhibition by Julian Brooks with Denise Allen and Xavier F. Salomon. Los Angeles: Getty Publications, 2015.

Antonello da Messina. Exhibition at the Galleria Regionale della Sicilia di Palazzo Abatellis, Palermo, December 14, 2018–February 10, 2019. Catalog of the exhibition edited by Giovanni Carlo Federico Villa. Rome: Mondomostre, 2019.

Antonello da Messina. Exhibition at the Palazzo Reale, Milan, February 21–June 2, 2019. Catalog of the exhibition edited by Caterina Cardona and Giovanni Carlo Federico Villa. Milan: Skira, 2019.

Azzopardi, Consiglia. *Gozo Lace: An Introduction to Lace Making in the Maltese Islands.* Gozo, Malta: C. Azzopardi, 1992.

Barocco a Roma: La meraviglia delle arti. Exhibition at the Fondazione Roma Museo, Palazzo Cipolla, Rome, April 1–July 26, 2015. Catalog of the exhibition edited by Maria Grazia Bernardini and Marco Bussagli. Milan: Skira, 2015.

Calasso, Roberto. *Tiepolo Pink.* Trans. Alastair McEwen. Milan: Adelphi, 2006.

Caravaggio. Exhibition at the Scuderie del Quirinale, Rome, February 20–June 13, 2010. Catalog of the exhibition edited by Claudio Strinati. Milan: Skira, 2010.

Dickerson, C. D., III, Anthony Sigel, Ian Wardropper, et al., eds. *Bernini: Sculpting in Clay.* New York: Metropolitan Museum of Art; New Haven: Yale University Press, 2015.

El Griego de Toledo. Exhibition at the Museo de Santa Cruz and other venues, Toledo, Spain, March 14–June 14, 2014. Catalog of the exhibition edited by Fernando Marías. Madrid: El Viso, 2014.

Garrard, Mary C. *Artemisia Gentileschi around 1522: The Shaping and Reshaping of an Artistic Identity.* Berkeley: University of California Press, 2001.

Hale, Sheila. *Titian: His Life.* London: Harper, 2012.

Lavin, Irving. *Bernini at Saint Peter's: The Pilgrimage.* London: Pindar, 2015.

Marías, Fernando. *El Greco: Life and Work—A New History.* Trans. Paul Edson and Sander Berg. London: Thames and Hudson, 2014.

McPhee, Sarah. *Bernini's Beloved: A Portrait of Costanza Piccolomini.* New Haven: Yale University Press, 2015.

Michelangelo and Sebastiano. Exhibition at the National Gallery, London, March 15–June 25, 2017. Catalog of the exhibition edited by Matthias Wivel, Piers Baker-Bates, et al. London: National Gallery, 2017.

Ng, Aimee, ed. *Bertoldo di Giovanni: The Renaissance of Sculpture in Medici Florence*. New York: Frick Collection in association with D. Giles, Limited, London, 2019.

Nochlin, Linda. *Bathers, Bodies, Beauty: The Visceral Eye*. Cambridge: Harvard University Press, 2008.

Portraits of the Soul. Exhibition at the Museo Nacional del Prado, Madrid, November 6, 2014–February 8, 2015. *Bernini: Roma y la monarquía hispánica*, catalog of the Prado exhibition by Delfín Rodríguez Ruiz. Madrid: Museo Nacional del Prado, 2015.

Raphael 1520–1483. Exhibition at the Scuderie del Quirinale, Rome, June 2–August 30, 2020. Catalog of the exhibition edited by Marzia Faietti and Matteo Lafranconi, with Francesco P. Di Teodoro and Vincenzo Farinella. Milan: Skira, 2020.

Sundbø, Annemor. *Invisible Threads in Knitting*. Trans. Carol Huebscher Rhoades. Kristiansand: Torridal Tweed, 2007.

Sundbø, Annemor. *Kvardagsstrik: Kulturskattar frå fillehaugen* [Everyday knitting: treasures from a rag pile]. Oslo: Norske Samlaget, 1994.

Sundbø, Annemor. *Setesdal Sweaters: The History of the Norwegian Lace Pattern*. Trans. Amy Lightfoot. Kristiansand: Torridal Tweed, 2001.

Tintoretto: Artist of Renaissance Venice. Exhibition at Palazzo Ducale, Venice, September 17, 2018–January 6, 2019, and National Gallery of Art, Washington, March 24–July 19, 2019. Catalog edited by Robert Echols and Frederick Ilchman. Washington, DC: National Gallery of Art, 2018.

Tiziano. Exhibition at the Scuderie del Quirinale, Rome, March 5–June 16, 2013. Catalog of the exhibition edited by Giovanni Carlo Federico Villa. Milan: Silvana, 2012.

WACK! Art and the Feminist Revolution. Exhibition at the Museum of Contemporary Art, Los Angeles, March 4–July 16, 2007, and P.S.1 Contemporary Art Center, Long Island City, February 17–May 12, 2008. Catalog of the exhibition edited by Cornelia H. Butler and Lisa Gabrielle Mark. Los Angeles: Museum of Contemporary Art; Cambridge: MIT Press, 2008.

Wallace, William C. *Michelangelo, God's Architect: The Story of His Final Years and Greatest Masterpiece*. Princeton: Princeton University Press, 2019.

The MIT Press
Massachusetts Institute of Technology
77 Massachusetts Avenue, Cambridge, MA 02139
mitpress.mit.edu

The MIT Press would like to thank the peer reviewers who provided comments on drafts of this book. The generous work of academic experts is essential for establishing the authority and quality of our publications.

This book was set in Haultin by Jen Jackowitz. Printed and bound in Canada.

Library of Congress Cataloging-in-Publication Data is available.

ISBN: 978-0-262-54909-7

10   9   8   7   6   5   4   3   2

EU Authorised Representative: Easy Access System Europe,
Mustamae tee 50, 10621 Tallinn, Estonia
Email: gpsr.requests@easproject.com